Components

MITCHELL'S BUILDING SERIES

The volumes in this series of standard text books have been completely re-written and re-illustrated by specialist authors to bring them into line with rapid technical developments in building and the consequent revision of syllabuses. All quantities are expressed in SI units and there are tables giving imperial conversions. Also included are the main CI/SfB classifications with cross references to the relevent volumes and chapters in *Mitchell's Building Series*.

The series will be invaluable to students preparing for the examinations of the RIBA, RiCS, IQS and IOB. It provides an ideal text for the Ordinary and Higher National Certificates, and the City and Guilds of London Institute courses in building. It is also a useful reference for practising architects, surveyors and engineers.

The six related volumes are:

ENVIRONMENT AND SERVICES
Peter Burberry Dip Arch MSc ARIBA

MATERIALS
Alan Everett ARIBA

STRUCTURE AND FABRIC Part 1
Jack Stroud Foster FRIBA

STRUCTURE AND FABRIC Part 2
Jack Stroud Foster FRIBA
Raymond Harington Dip Arch ARIBA, ARIAS

COMPONENTS
Harold King ARIBA
revised by Derek Osbourn Dip Arch (Hons) RIBA

FINISHES
Alan Everett ARIBA

See also
INTRODUCTION TO BUILDING
Derek Osbourn Dip Arch (Hons) RIBA

COMPONENTS

This volume considers the performance requirements for Components for buildings and the effectiveness of typical solutions. It includes 253 drawings, 20 tables and a comprehensive index. References to sources of more detailed information are made throughout the following chapters:

1 Component design
2 Joinery
3 Door
4 Windows
5 Glazing
6 Roof lights
7 Ironmongery
8 Balustrades
9 Demountable partitions
10 Suspended ceilings
11 Industrialized system building

Harold King, the author of the Components chapters of the original Components and Finishes *volume published in 1971, was Lecturer in Building Technology at the School of Architecture, The University of Newcastle upon Tyne.*
Derek Osbourn is Head of School, Department of Environmental Design at the Polytechnic of North London

MITCHELL'S BUILDING SERIES

Components

Harold King *ARIBA*

revised by Derek Osbourn *Dip Arch (Hons) RIBA*

B T Batsford Limited   London

Printed and bound in Great Britain by
Anchor Brendon Limited, Tiptree, Essex
for the publishers
B T Batsford Limited
4 Fitzhardinge Street, London W1H 0AH

Contents

CONTENTS

7

Contents of other volumes

The reader is referred to the five other related volumes in *Mitchell's Building Series* for the following:

Acknowledgment for the 1971 edition of *Components and Finishes*

Figure and page numbers refer to the 1971 edition

The authors and publishers thank the many individuals and firms who have given help and advice in the preparation of this book and those who have given permission to quote from technical literature and other material.

The author of *Components* chapters 1 to 11 and *Roofings* chapter 18 thank the following for the use of drawings on which various figures are based:

Abbey Hanson Rowe and Partners for figure 76
D. Anderson and Son Limited for figures 268, 269 and part of 255
Boulton and Paul (Joinery) Limited for figure 111
The British Woodwork Manufacturers Association (EMJA Certification Trademark) for figures 45, 107, 110 and 119
Cape Universal for corrugated asbestos cement sheet roofing pages 401 to 410
Copper Development Association for copper roofing figures 280 and 281
Crittal Hope Limited for figures 121, 122, 164 and 167
Crosby and Company Limited for figures 10 and 56
Dixon Components (Building) Limited for figure 223
Expamet Contracts Limited for figures 228, 229 and 230
Fulbora Limited for figure 258
Gardiner Architectural Engineering Limited for figures 94, 135, 136 and 138
Grahams (Seacroft) Limited for figure 102
Aldam Coburn Limited for figures 86, 87, 88 and 92
Hill Brothers Glass Company Limited for figure 166
F. Hills and Sons Limited for figure 75
Louvre (Windows) Limited for figure 140
Lead Development Association for figures 120, 305 and 307
The Marley Tile Company Limited for figures 274, 275, 276, 277, 306 and 308
Mandor Engineering Limited for figure 80
The Nuralite Company Limited for page 393
Paramount Asphalte Limited for figure 256

Permanite Limited for figure 255
Robin Architectural Products for figure 169
The Ruberoid Company Limited for figures 261, 263, 264, 265, 266, 267, 271, 272 and 273
Stramit Limited for figure 225
Tenon Contracts Limited for figures 137, 222 and 224
CIP Tentest Limited for figure 233
Venesta International Construction Materials Limited for figure 226
The author is also indebted to the following:
Arnold Ashton for practical advice regarding joinery manufacture and timber jointing
R. Baker of F. and E.V. Linford Limited for advice on joiner's shop production in chapter 2
R.H. Burford of Crosby and Company Limited for advice in chapter 3 on doors
R.E. Hale of Crittal-Hope Limited for help and advice on the metal windows section in chapter 4 and the SCOLA window-walling in chapter 11
Geoffrey Hamlyn Dip Arch FRIBA for making available the material relevant to the SCOLA system of Industrialized Building in chapter 11 and figures 234 to 247 inclusive
Peter Martin ARICS for reading and commenting on Component Design, chapter 1
A. Morris and T. Temple of Boulton and Paul (Joinery) Limited for information on the factory production of joinery components in chapter 2
Tenon Contracts Limited for information and advice on demountable partitions, chapter 9
G.E. Till and H.A. Bolton of The Ruberoid Company Limited for advice on built-up bitumen felt roofing in chapter 18
Mr Turley of MAC Engineering for advice on Ironmongery, chapter 7

Grateful thanks are due, in addition, to Robert Humphreys for his invaluable work in drawing diagrams and to G.W. Dilks for assisting. To E.M. Thomas for ably translating tape to typescript and to Thelma M. Nye for her most helpful and patient editorial advice.

Hexham 1971   H K

Acknowledgment for the 1979 edition of Components

The publisher's desire to bring about this new edition of *Components* (as a separate volume from *Components and Finishes*) coincided with the tragic death of its original author, Harold King. Most of his excellent work remains, but I have made necessary alterations to bring it in line with current practice and attitudes.

I am grateful to the Director General and Clerk of Greater London Council for permission to quote from the London Building Acts 1930-39 and the Constructional By-laws made under these Acts, to the Controller of Her Majesty's Stationery Office for permission to quote from the Building Regulations 1976, and to the Directors of the following organisations for their kind permission for quotations to be made from their publications:

The Building Research Establishment
The British Standards Institution
The Fire Research Station
The Princes Risborough Laboratory
The British Woodworking Federation
Research and Development Associations of the construction industry

My gratitude also goes to those already listed under Harold King's acknowledgment who responded to my request for current information regarding their original contribution, the Velox Company Limited for their window details in figures 177 and 178, Hodkin and Jones (Sheffield Limited) for figure 166, and Timber Research and Development Association for their information on page 132 regarding the work of the Norwegian BRE.

David Clegg of the RIBA Services Limited gave invaluable guidance on the CI/SfB classification codings, and George Dilks proved very tolerant in producing new drawings and altering existing drawings.

I am indebted to my friend and colleague, Alan Everett, who not only redrafted the 'Joinery' chapter, but up-dated the 'Glazing' chapter and also helped me so willingly throughout. Leslie Coburn, senior lecturer in carpentry and joinery at the Polytechnic of North London, also gave valuable guidance during the preparation of the 'Joinery' chapter. Lastly, sincere thanks are given to Thelma M Nye for patience and helpful editorial advice.

London 1979   DO

SI units

Quantities in this volume are given in SI units which have been adopted by the construction industry in the United Kingdom. Twenty-five other countries (not including the USA or Canada) have also adopted the SI system although several of them retain the old metric system as an alternative. There are six SI basic units. Other units derived from these basic units are rationally related to them and to each other. The international adoption of the SI will remove the present necessity for conversions between national systems. The introduction of metric units gives an opportunity for the adoption of modular sizes.

Full details of SI Units and conversion factors are contained in the current edition of the *AJ Metric Handbook.*

British Standards, Codes of Practice and other documents are being progressively re-issued in metric units, although at the time of going to press many of those concerned with Building Construction have yet to be metricated. In addition, it should be noted that new Codes of Practice are now being issued as ordinary BSs and not as formerly BCPSs.

Multiples and sub-multiples of SI units likely to be used in the construction industry are as follows:

Multiplication factor	Prefix		Symbol
1 000 000	10^6	mega	M
1 000	10^3	kilo	k
100	10^2	hecto	h
10	10^1	deca	da
0·1	10^{-1}	deci	d
0·01	10^{-2}	centi	c
0·001	10^{-3}	milli	m
0·000 001	10^{-6}	micro	μ

Further information concerning metrication is contained in BS PD 6031 *A Guide for the use of the Metric System in the Construction Industry,* and BS 5555:1976 *SI units and recommendations for the use of their multiples and of certain other units.*

Quantity	Unit	Symbol	Imperial unit × Conversion factor = SI value		
LENGTH	kilometre	km	1 mile	=	1·609 km
	metre	m	1 yard	=	0·914 m
	millimetre	mm	1 foot	=	0·305 m
			1 inch	=	25·4 mm
AREA	square kilometre	km^2	1 mile^2	=	2·590 km^2
	hectare	ha	1 acre	=	0·405 ha
			1 yard^2	=	0·836 m^2
	square metre	m^2	1 foot^2	=	0·093 m^2
	square millimetre	mm^2	1 inch^2	=	645·16 mm^2
VOLUME	cubic metre	m^3	1 yard^3	=	0·765 m^3
	cubic millimetre	mm^3	1 foot^3	=	0·028 m^3
			1 inch^3	=	1 638·7 mm^3
CAPACITY	litre	l	1 UKgallon =		4·546 litres

continued...

Quantity	Unit	Symbol	Imperial unit × Conversion factor = SI value		
MASS	kilogramme	kg	1 lb	=	0·454 kg
	gramme	g	1 oz	=	28·350 g
			1 lb/ft (run)	=	1·488 kg/m
			1 lb/ft^2	=	4·882 kg/m^2
DENSITY	kilogramme per cubic metre	kg/m^3	1 lb/ft^3	=	16·019 kg/m^3
FORCE	newton	N	1 lbf	=	4·448 N
			1 tonf	=	9 964·02 N
				=	9·964 kN
PRESSURE, STRESS	newton per square metre	N/m^2	1 lbf/in^2	=	6 894·8 N/m^2
	meganewton per square metre	MN/m^2† or N/mm^2	1 tonf/ft^2	=	107·3 kN/m^2
			1 tonf/in^2	=	15·444 MN/m^2
			1 lb/ft run	=	14·593 N/m
			1 lbf/ft^2	=	47·880 N/m^2
			1 ton/ft run	=	32 682 kN/m
	*bar (0·1 MN/m^2)	bar			
	*hectobar (10 MN/m^2)	hbar			
	*millibar (100 MN/m^2)	m bar			
VELOCITY	metre per second	m/s	1 mile/h	=	0·447 m/s
FREQUENCY	cycle per second	Hz	1 cycle/sec	=	1 Hz
ENERGY, HEAT	joule	J	1 Btu	=	1 055·06 J
POWER, HEAT FLOW RATE	watts	W	1 Btu/h	=	0·293 W
	newtons metres per second	Nm/s	1 hp	=	746 W
	joules per second	J/s	1 ft/lbf	=	1·356 J
THERMAL CONDUCTI-VITY (k)	watts per metre degree Celsius	W/m deg C	1 Btu in/ft^{2}h deg F	=	0·144 W/m deg C
THERMAL TRANS-MITTANCE (U)	watts per square metre degree Celsius	W/m^2 deg C	1 Btu/ft^{2}h deg F	=	5·678 W/m^2 deg C
TEMPERATURE	degree Celsius (difference)	deg C	1 deg F		$\frac{5}{9}$ deg C
	degree Celsius (level)	°C	°F	=	$\frac{9}{5}$ °C+32

* Alternative units, allied to the SI, which will be encountered in certain industries

† BSI preferred symbol

A guide to the SI metric system

1 Component design

In order that the form of a component may be properly devised, its function must be carefully defined. Up-to-date manufacturing techniques, user requirements, anthropometric data, and the properties and behaviour of materials, together with appropriate cost analysis data, must be considered in order to reach conclusions which will lead to the design of a satisfactory component. Anthropometric data relates to the measurements of the human form, and this information has a direct influence on design of specific components such as fittings, and doors and windows. The study of anthropometrics is also particularly important when considering design in respect of disabled people, and users of wheel chairs.

Components such as windows, ceiling panels and wall and partition units are commonly used in multiples or in combination with each other, and frequently in long runs, thus requiring interrelated preferred dimensions, based on a universally acceptable system of dimensional co-ordination. Sizes should be determined initially from the results of user requirement studies. Following from this, the controlling factors arising out of the appropriate manufacturing techniques must be determined in consultation with manufacturers at an early stage in the development work. These factors include the degree of dimensional accuracy and standardization which is capable of being attained, the method of assembly, the costs of tooling up, the methods of handling stock and problems associated with site and factory transportation and storage.

Today, the design of most components must suit factory production methods and be easy to fix on the site. The design team will develop the component to give a satisfactory performance against a concise specification, based on research and careful assessment of information received from the client or potential user.

FACTORY PRODUCTION

It is necessary for the designer of a component to understand the discipline of factory production so that collaboration with the manufacturer at design stage will be more useful. Two methods of factory production are appropriate to the manufacture of building components namely, *flow line production* and *batch production.*

Flow line production

Where *flow line production* is in operation, a stream of component parts in various stages of completion travel by conveyor belt through a number of work positions to completion. At each work position, one or more operations are carried out until at the final work position, at the end of the assembly line, the component is complete. The operations are standardized at each work position and careful organization is required so that the necessary materials are always available. Flow line production methods can be highly automated which means a high level capital investment in automatic machinery but using a minimum of labour. With this type of manufacturing process it is not easy for alternative operations to be carried out at a particular work position, but provided that the alternative work can be done in the same space of time as the standard operation, then the system can be modified to this extent. An example would be the fitting of different types of opening light in a standard frame surround. A flow line system is most efficient however when uninterrupted by alternative operations. This presupposes complete standardization, which in its turn requires the development of a co-ordinated system of sizes and dimensions. Flush doors are normally produced by a flow line system, and it is obvious from this example that where a large number of components is involved and the quality of the raw material can be carefully controlled, then factory production and factory applied finishes produce an article of better quality and value, than traditional methods.

Batch production

Batch production, is the setting up of machinery to manufacture a batch of components. An example of this would be the moulding of jambs and rails for a timber window, followed by the manufacture of a batch of sill sections, after the machines have been reset. Batch production is not only adopted for machinery operations but is also used for the assembly of parts where quantities, in mass production terms, are comparatively small, or where there is too much variety to allow the efficient use of flow line techniques. Batch production is also the appropriate method where the cost of processing is low in comparison to the cost of setting up the process. In connection with the production of timber components woodworking machines have a high rate of production in relation to the time taken to set the machine up. The relationship of the cost of production to the cost of setting up can however be made more economical if the variety of sections and mouldings can be reduced, for a particular component. Thus where the same moulded cross section of timber can be used for the various parts of say a glazed window wall, then the cost of one machine setting will be spread over the cost of the total length of the moulded sections for the job.

In practice, combinations of both flow line and batch methods are used, for example, in the factory production of timber components the machining will probably be done by batch production, and the assembly of the timber sections into the completed component will be carried out by flow line techniques. It must always be remembered however, that production techniques are continuously being examined, modified, and improved in an effort to overcome difficulties and disadvantages, and it is essential that consultation at design stage be fully developed to facilitate this process.

A simple production line would be a single and continuous operation with the input of raw materials at one end and with the output of finished goods at the other. At the start of the production line there will be a store of raw materials which will allow certain fluctuations in delivery. Where one operation takes longer to perform than the others the line will have to be split or additional machines or men introduced at this point. Storage will also have to be provided at the end of the production line to absorb fluctuations in demand. The theoretical layout of a production line will almost certainly be inhibited by physical limitations of factory space. The proportion of overheads is not so high with mass production as against short runs of a component produced on a small scale. The percentage of the working year during which the factory is operating to full capacity is also a significant element in the cost per unit of the component. Machinery should be capably of being modified so that improvements in the design of a component can be incorporated without undue capital expenditure. In order to produce components economically there is an optimum output in terms of the number of components produced relative to the nature of the component and the type of plant used. However standardized a production system is, it is inevitable that some components will be required to be non-standard or may be required in such small numbers as to make them uneconomic to produce on the standard production line. The higher the degree of automation the more difficult it is to produce non-standard items, and it must be expected that non-standard products will be more expensive and with an extended delivery period. It follows from this that manufacturing techniques which can produce related components economically over the widest possible range, will be more acceptable in the long term.

To allow a manufacturer greater control over the production and detailing, it is a good system to invite quotations for components on the basis of performance specification which indicates the parameters within which the product must perform. The successful contractor, at this stage, can then be consulted in respect of detail and development work.

The various processes in the factory production of a range of standard timber windows are detailed in chapter 4, pages 61-64.

PERFORMANCE SPECIFICATION

Every component will have to fulfil a number of requirements in respect of a minimum standard of performance which will be expected from the component must first be set down, and from these considerations the performance specification can be devised. A *performance specification* is a description of the required performance and functions of a component. The specification should, wherever possible, be in measurable terms, and include information as to the required life of the component. This type of specification is of course different from the traditional *product specification* which describes the materials, standards of workmanship and method of manufacture of a component. A product specification relies on description in terms of current trade practice and thus the performance of a component is pre-determined by the writer and the manufacturer's advice is not normally sought. A performance specification on the other hand does not specify materials or methods of production but by stating the performance standard required allows the manufacturer to select suitable materials and production methods. Thus the incentive to develop economic methods of production lies with the manufacturer.

The success of the performance specification as a descriptive method depends on an agreed list of terms or headings upon which a description of the performance of a component may be based. This will then form the basis of a common means of communication between the architects, structural engineers, services engineers and quantity surveyors who are concerned with description of components. Reference should be made to *Performance Specification Writing for Building Components* DC 9 published by HMSO, which provides guidance notes on the content of performance specifications.

The performance specification should first des-cribe the component and its use in general terms giving information sufficient to allow an intending manufacturer to decide whether he is able to submit a tender. The CI/SfB Classification Symbol should be used. The manufacturer should be invited to state the type and quality of components already manufactured by him which will, in his opinion, satisfy the specification. Reference should be made to any British Standard Specification or Code of Practice which applies to the component and further reference should be made to the Building Regulations or other Acts which may be relevant. The Specification should state the required maximum and minimum life of the component. Manufacturers should be required to give the planned life of the component and their recommended method of maintenance. Any guarantees required to be provided by the manufacturer and the nature of any insurance cover should be specified.

The following check list based on DC 9 is a summary of the main properties relative to a selected list of components as a guide to the contents of a Performance Specification. It is important to note that the numbering system is based on the Master List of Properties (CIB Report No. 3 1964) published by the International Council for Building Research Studies and Documentation, thus providing a direct link between component and material properties.

This is a check list and it will depend upon particular requirements to be met whether a property should be specified or not. In certain cases the performance specification writer will be unable to set quantified values for the properties but may request the component manufacturer to furnish details in respect of a component offered in response to a performance specification.

Heading	CIB No.	Window	Roof finish	Partition	Internal door set	Ceiling	Floor finish
GENERAL INFORMATION	1.1						
Description of component	1.1.01	×	×	×	×	×	×
Type and quality		×	×	×	×	×	×
Identification of standards,	1.1.02						
quality mark	1.1.03	×	×	×	×	×	×
Purpose and use	1.1.04	×	×	×	×	×	×
Accessories	1.1.05	×	×	×	×	×	×

Table 1 Properties to be considered when preparing performance specifications for typical components and finishes

continued . . .

Heading	CIB No.	Window	Roof finish	Partition	Internal door set	Ceiling	Floor finish
COMPOSITION and MANUFACTURE	1.2						
Composition	1.2.01	×	×	×	×	×	×
Manufacture and assembly	1.2.02	×	×	×	×	×	×
SHAPE, DIMENSION, WEIGHT	1.3						
Shape	1.3.01	×	×	×	×	×	×
Dimension	1.3.02	×	×	×	×	×	×
Geometric properties	1.3.03	×	×	×	×	×	×
Volume	1.3.04	—	—	—	—	—	—
Weight	1.3.05	×	×	×	×	×	×
GENERAL APPEARANCE	1.4						
Character of visible face	1.4.01						
Evenness	1.4.01.1	×	×	×	×	×	×
Appearance	1.4.01.2	×	×	×	×	×	×
Transparency, translucency	1.4.02	×	—	×	×	×	—
PHYSICAL, CHEMICAL AND BIOLOGICAL PROPERTIES	1.5						
Specific weight	1.5.01	×	×	×	—	×	×
Internal structure	1.5.02	×	×	×	×	×	×
Chemical formulation and material specification	1.5.03	×	×	×	×	×	×
Penetration of air and gases	1.5.04	×	×	×	×	×	×
Properties relating to the presence of water	1.5.05						
Moisture content	1.5.05.1	×	×	×	×	×	×
Solubility in water	1.5.05.2	×	×	×	×	×	×
Capillarity	1.5.05.3	×	×	×	×	×	×
Water absorption	1.5.05.4	×	×	×	×	×	×
Water penetration	1.5.05.5	×	×	×	×	×	×
Water vapour penetration	1.5.05.6	×	×	×	×	×	×
Drying and evaporation	1.5.05.7	×	×	×	×	×	×
Moisture movement	1.5.05.8	×	×	×	×	×	×
Thermal properties	1.5.06						
Thermal movement	1.5.06.1	×	×	×	×	×	×
Specific heat	1.5.06.2	—	×	×	—	×	×
Freezing and melting point	1.5.06.3	—	—	—	—	—	—
Radiation coefficient	1.5.06.4	×	×	×	—	×	×
Thermal conductance	1.5.06.5	×	×	×	×	×	×
Warmth to touch	1.5.06.6	—	—	×	×	—	×
High and low temperatures	1.5.06.7	×	×	×	×	×	×
Thermal shock	1.5.06.8	×	×	×	×	—	×

Table 1   continued . . . .

Heading	CIB No.	Window	Roof finish	Partition	Internal door set	Ceiling	Floor finish
Strength properties	1.5.07						
Tension	1.5.07.1	×	×	×	×	×	×
Compression	1.5.07.2	×	×	×	×	×	×
Shear	1.5.07.3	×	×	×	×	×	×
Bending	1.5.07.4	×	×	×	×	×	×
Torsion	1.5.07.5	×	×	×	×	×	×
Impact	1.5.07.6	×	×	×	×	×	×
Hardness	1.5.07.7	×	×	×	×	×	×
Resistance to fatigue	1.5.07.8	×	×	×	×	×	×
Mechanical properties	1.5.08						
Resistance to mechanical wear	1.5.08.1	×	×	×	×	×	×
Resistance to the insertion and extraction of nails and screws	1.5.08.2	×	×	×	×	×	×
Resistance to splitting	1.5.08.3	−	×	×	×	−	×
Resistance to tearing	1.5.08.4	−	−	×	−	−	×
Resistance to bursting	1.5.08.5	−	−	−	−	−	−
Rheological properties (flow and deformation)	1.5.09	×	×	×	×	×	×
Frictional resistance	1.5.10						
Coefficient of friction	1.5.10.1	−	×	−	−	−	×
Degree of slipperiness in use	1.5.10.2	−	×	−	−	−	×
Adhesion	1.5.11	−	×	−	−	−	×
Acoustic properties	1.5.12						
Sound absorption, sound reflection	1.5.12.1	×	−	×	×	×	×
Sound transmission	1.5.12.2	×	−	×	×	×	×
Optical properties	1.5.13						
Light absorption, light reflection	1.5.13.1	×	×	×	×	×	×
Light transmission	1.5.13.2	×	−	×	×	×	−
Light refraction and dispersion	1.5.13.3	×	−	×	×	×	−
Optical distortion	1.5.13.4	×	−	×	×	×	−
Electrical properties	1.5.14						
Electrical conductivity (electrical resistance)	1.5.14.1	×	×	×	×	×	×
Dielectric constant	1.5.14.2	−	−	−	−	−	−
Liability to develop and shed electro-static charges	1.5.14.3	×	×	×	×	×	×
Effect of sunlight	1.5.15	×	×	×	×	×	×
Effect of electro-magnetic and particle radiation	1.5.16	−	−	×	×	×	×
Effect of freezing conditions	1.5.17	×	×	×	×	×	×

Table 1 continued ....

Heading	CIB No.	Window	Roof finish	Partition	Internal door set	Ceiling	Floor finish
Effect of fire	1.5.18						
Combustibility	1.5.18.1	×	×	×	×	×	×
Fire resistance	1.5.18.2	×	×	×	×	×	—
Surface spread of flame	1.5.18.3	×	×	×	×	×	—
Effect of chemicals	1.5.19	×	×	×	×	×	×
Effect of impurities	1.5.20	×	×	×	×	×	×
Effect of fungi, micro-organisms and insects	1.5.21	×	×	×	×	×	×
Effect of other building materials	1.5.22	×	×	×	×	×	×
Changes of behaviour during use	1.5.23	×	×	×	×	×	×
Setting time	1.5.23.1	—	×	—	—	×	×
Heat evolution in preparation and application	1.5.23.2	—	×	—	—	×	×
Change in volume	1.5.23.3	×	×	×	×	×	×
Properties important from the point of view of hygiene	1.5.24						
Toxicity	1.5.24.1	×	×	×	×	×	×
Odour	1.5.24.2	×	×	×	×	×	×
Taintability	1.5.24.3	×	×	×	×	×	×
Tendency to deposit dust	1.5.24.4	—	×	×	—	×	×
Injury to skin	1.5.24.5	×	×	×	×	×	×
Liability to vermin infestation	1.5.24.6	×	×	×	×	×	×
Liability to become dirty, ease of cleaning	1.5.24.7	×	×	×	×	×	×
Safety	1.5.24.8	×	×	×	×	×	×
DURABILITY	1.6						
Durability of the component or assembly	1.6.01	×	×	×	×	×	×
Durability of specified component parts	1.6.02	×	×	×	×	×	×
Guarantee of durability	1.6.03	×	×	×	×	×	×
PROPERTIES OF THE WORKING PARTS, CONTROLS, ETC.	1.7						
Method of operation	1.7.01	×	—	×	×	—	—
Connection data	1.7.02						
Mechanical connection	1.7.02.1	×	—	×	×	—	—
Connection to power supply	1.7.02.2	×	—	×	×	—	—
Performance data	1.7.03						
Mechanical data	1.7.03.1	×	—	×	×	—	—
Capacity	1.7.03.2	—	—	—	—	—	—
Other performance data	1.7.03.3	×	—	×	×	—	—

Table 1   continued

Heading	CIB No.	Window	Roof finish	Partition	Internal door set	Ceiling	Floor finish
Consumption of energy and ancillary materials	1.7.04						
Supplied energy	1.7.04.1	×	−	×	×	−	−
Ancillary materials	1.7.04.2	×	−	×	×	−	−
Efficiency	1.7.05	−	−	−	−	−	−
Manoeuvrability and control	1.7.06	×	−	×	×	−	−
Other technical data	1.7.07						
Mechanical	1.7.07.1	−	−	−	−	−	−
Thermal	1.7.07.2	−	−	−	−	−	−
Electrical	1.7.07.3	−	−	−	−	−	−
Secondary effects and disturbances during operation	1.7.08	×	−	×	×	−	−
WORKING CHARACTERISTICS	1.8						
Ease of handling	1.8.01	×	×	×	×	×	×
Consistence, workability, working time	1.8.02	−	−	−			
Ease of cutting, sawing, bending, etc.	1.8.03	−	×	×	×	×	×
Capability of being jointed to other components	1.8.04	−	×	×	×	×	×
Fixing	1.8.05	×	×	×	×	×	×
Surface treatments	1.8.06	×	×	×	×	×	×
Capability of withstanding rough handling	1.8.07	×	×	×	×	×	×
Capability of withstanding storage	1.8.08	×	×	×	×	×	×

Table 1 *Properties to be considered when preparing performance specifications for typical components and finishes*

DIMENSIONAL CO-ORDINATION

Dimensional co-ordination is a system of arranging the dimensional framework of a building so that components can be used within the framework in an inter-related pattern of sizes. It is necessary to establish a rectangular three-dimensional grid of basic modules into which the component will fit. This principle is illustrated in figure 1. It is very important to remember that the modular grid does not give the size of the component, but allots space for it, and so in order to fit correctly, the component will always be slightly smaller than the space allowed for it as shown in figure 2. The first step in producing a rational system of dimensional co-ordination is to agree on the basic dimensions of the enclosing fabric of the building. This building fabric is also known as the *environmental envelope*. The principle of relating components to a planning grid, in this case a module of 100 mm, is shown in figure 3. There are a number of British Standards which give recommendations for the controlling limits of the dimensions and sizes for the structure and components in building, see page 35. It is thus recognized that the rationalization of the building process and the use of industrialized methods will involve the use of an increasing range of factory produced components and, in order to obtain the maximum economy of production and to avoid the waste involved in cutting on site, it is

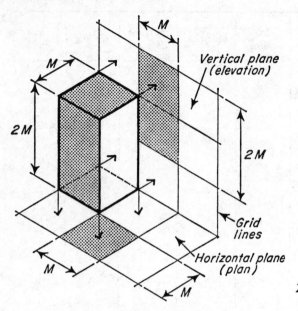

1 Three-dimensional grid of basic modules

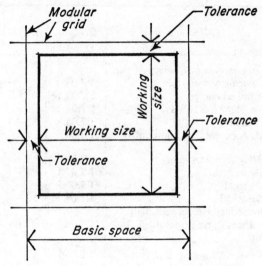

2 Space relationship component to grid

essential that the dimensions of building components are co-ordinated by reference to an agreed range of sizes.

Terms used

An understanding of the various terms used in connection with dimensional co-ordination in building is necessary, since descriptions which previously have been loosely used have now specific meaning.

The following definitions are taken from BS 2900 1970 *Glossary of Terms: Recommendations for the Co-ordination of Dimensions in Building – Metric Units.*

Dimensional co-ordination   The application of a range of related dimensions to the sizing of building components and assemblies and the buildings incorporating them.

Modular co-ordination   Dimension co-ordination using the international basic module (of 100 mm), multimodules, sub-modules and a modular reference system.

The multimodule of 300 mm, the international basic module of 100 mm, and sub-modules of 50 mm and 25 mm are equivalent to the respective units of size recommended in BS 4011 for the derivation of co-ordinating sizes for building components and assemblies, generally subject to a maximum co-ordinating size of 300 mm based on the 50 mm and 25 mm sizes. See page 22.

Multimodules of 300 mm, 600 mm, 1200 mm, 3000 mm, and 6000 mm, are under consideration internationally for certain categories of buildings.

Module   A convenient unit of size which is used as an increment or coefficient in dimensional co-ordination.

Basic space   A space bounded by reference planes, assigned to receive a building component or assembly including, where appropriate, allowance for joints and tolerances.

Modular grid   A reference grid in which the distance between consecutive parallel lines is the international basic module or a multiple thereof.

Building component   Building material formed as a distinct unit.

Modular building component   A building component whose co-ordinating sizes are in accordance with BS 4011.

Assembly   An aggregate of building components used together.

Co-ordinating space   A space bounded by co-ordinating planes, allocated to a building com-

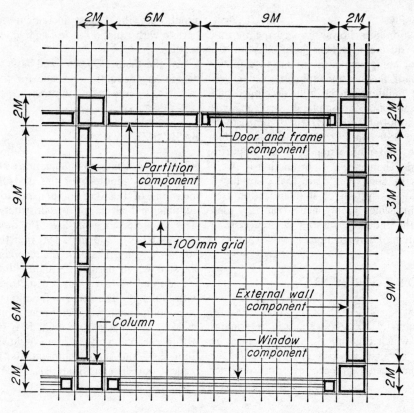

3   Modular co-ordination of components

ponent or assembly, including allowance for joints and tolerances.

Dimensional co-ordination thus relates industrial techniques to the building process by co-ordinating the size of components within a basic framework, establishing a reference system to enable components to be located, and specifying a system of tolerances. The co-ordination of dimensions is closely connected with the overall development of building technology and the evolution of new building processes.

The traditional pattern of trade following trade with materials cut and fitted on site, made it possible for the later trades to make good any inaccuracies in earlier work. With industrialized processes, completed components arrive on site and there is little opportunity for correcting any errors which may have occurred previously, say during the coding of the working drawings with reference to the choice

of a particular component. Thus, industrialized building presupposes a complete and careful appraisal of requirements at planning stage, and decisions cannot be left until the time the building is being erected.

Simplification of constructional detail at the design stage will assist the mechanization of the manufacturing process and, in order to achieve this, it is necessary to reach agreement on the range of sizes to which particular components are made, so that a manufacturer can arrange production in large enough batches to make large scale investment viable.

The present 'closed' systems of building (see page 245) each have their own dimensional disciplines, eg placing of stanchions, range of floor to ceiling heights, and component sizes. Thus, the components are dimensionally co-ordinated within the particular system, but not within the construction

21

industry generally.

Rationalization has, however, occurred in that a number of different systems have adopted the same range of components, as for instance in the use of standard fenestration units. In order that industrialized building can be fully developed and its economic advantages completely realized, it is necessary to adopt an agreed system of dimensional co-ordination, both on a national and an international scale, and metrication gives the opportunity to do this. Dimensional co-ordination is essential if ranges of components are to be developed towards an 'open' system of standardization (see page 245) in which components can be used throughout the industry without reference to a particular system of construction.

PREFERRED MEASUREMENTS

The increment, or pattern of change of dimension, within a system is important since it determines the norm to which a group of components can be produced in a range of sizes appropriate to the particular component. In each case the designer should use the largest increment available, compatible with function in use and economy in manufacture.

All the theoretical sizes and basic sizes are stated before any deduction is made for fixing or manufacturing tolerances and jointing.

BASIC SIZE

BS 4011 makes recommendations as to the basic sizes to be adopted for the co-ordination of dimensions of building components for all types of building and all forms of construction. The basic sizes are selected as follows (in descending order of preference): 300 mm, 100 mm (basic module), 50 mm, 25 mm. These are the recommended dimensions to which designers should adhere, and which are adopted by Government departments concerned with building. The relative functional requirement of a component will determine which preference is taken as a basis for design. It is important that within each category such as windows, wall panels, floor slabs and similar components, which may be made from different materials, the preferred sizes

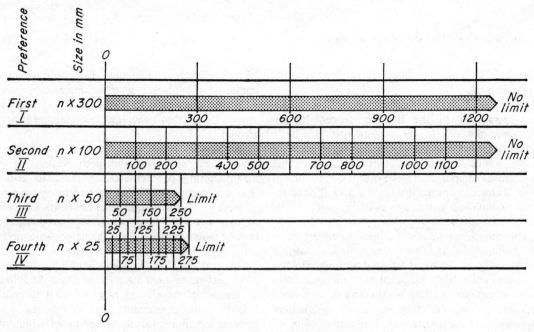

4 *Preferences for sizing building components and assemblies (BS 4011: 1966)*

should be the same whatever material is used for fabrication.

Where a number of small components is necessary to build up an assembly, as in the case of a metal window, the various parts must be made to fit together so that the overall size of assembly will fit the basic opening size. The basic size of a component is the fundamental dimension of the

Figure 6, illustrates the situation of a modular component within the planning grid and shows the manufacturing and jointing tolerances which must be accommodated. It will be seen that the basic space must take into account the difference between the expected maximum and minimum component size, with an allowance for minimum joint thickness against maximum component size,

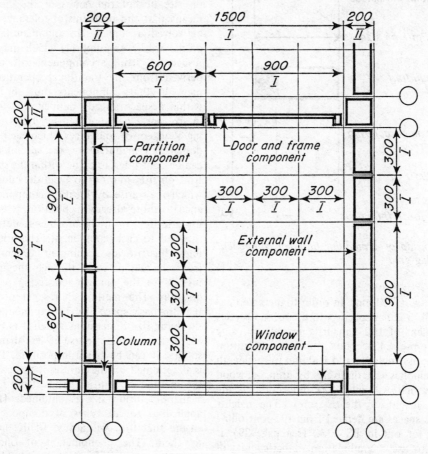

5 *Dimensional co-ordination of components*

component bounded by the plane of a modular grid. The space on the modular grid designed to receive the component, must include an allowance for joints and tolerances. This space, into which the component will fit, is known as the *basic* or *modular space*. The preferred sizes are shown in graphical form in figure 4, and figure 5 gives an example of the dimensional co-ordination of components using the preferences set down in BS 4011.

or alternatively, maximum joint thickness against minimum component size. Figure 7 shows the basic spaces for standard steel windows. See also figure 123, page 148, for the basic spaces for purpose-made steel windows. Increased flexibility in respect of modular spacings can be obtained in several ways. For example, in the case of the basic spaces for standard steel windows, the lengths of the basic spaces conform to BS 4011 first preference

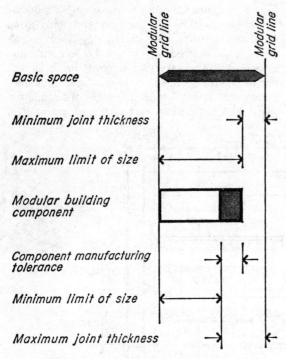

6 *Relationship of a modular building component to a planning grid*

in increments of 300 mm. In order to increase flexibility to fill modular spacings to the second preference increment of 100 mm, it is possible by using one or more pressed steel box mullions, or partition covers in the assembly, to add 100 mm to the length of the assemblies, alternatively by using a wood surround, which will add 100 mm both to the length and height of the assembly. The heights of the basic spaces are derived from the controlling dimensions set out in BS 4330 (see page 29). It is possible to use a combination of basic units of standard frames to fill intermediate heights, and by this means all modular lengths and heights from 900 mm upwards can be achieved in increments of 100 mm.

TOLERANCES

Any system of tolerances is intended to enable components to fit together without, on the one hand, the need for cutting down to size on site, or on the other hand, excessively wide joints or the ubiquitous cover strip to make up undersized units. Thus it is necessary for components to be manufactured so that the maximum and minimum sizes do not fall outside known limits. Assembly of components on site has increased the importance of tolerances and factory manufacture of components has taken the matter of cutting and fitting on site out of the hands of the craftsman. This means that the problems of tolerance and fit must be solved at the design and manufacturing stage of the work. Assumptions which must be made in respect of fitting a component into a building are derived from the traditional operations of craftsmen, in that components must be made to fit within a space already defined, and that variations in size are accommodated by joints. Thus by stating a system of tolerances which can be used during design and manufacture, the size of a component can be controlled to come within the space allocated to it on site. In order to avoid the cumulative errors which may arise by locating components by reference to those already in position, it is necessary to use grid lines or modular planes to define the spaces assigned to each component. The grid or modular lines thus provide a complete system of reference from the design stage through the manufacturing process to the placing and fixing of the item in position. The method in respect of tolerances is that the basic space of the component is the same as the basic size dimensions which it is to occupy. Its actual size must of course be less than its basic size so that it can be fitted in position. The difference is determined by the nature of the component and the method of jointing. Thus, from the actual size a manufacturing size is obtained. This system is applicable to all types of components and will ensure that they will always fit the space allocated to them. The phenomenon of one component infringing on the space which should be occupied by its neighbour, and this effect becoming accumulative, is known as *creep* and is avoided by the use of the grid lines.

Tolerance limits must take into account the general factors of manufacture, the problems of site erection and the disciplines imposed by the design of the joint between components. The characteristics of the materials from which the component is made must be considered in respect of the problems of twisting, warping and bending.

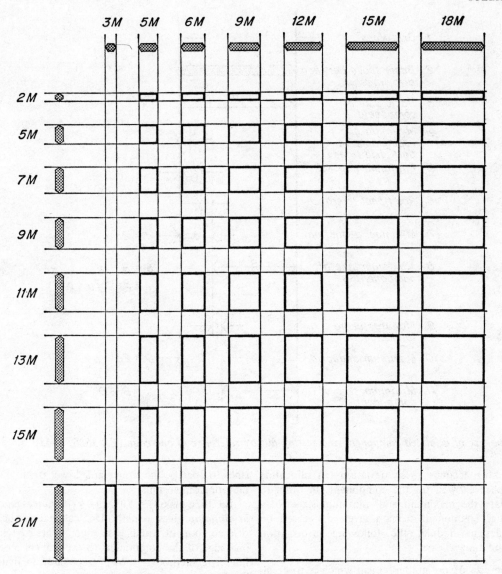

M = 1 module of 100 mm and refers to the size of opening into which. the window fits

7 *Basic spaces for standard steel windows (domestic type) — see also figure 128 for purpose made steel windows*

Tolerance should be expressed as an addition or subtraction from the given 'average' or work size of a component. Thus a component of work size 890 mm with a manufacturing tolerance of 5 mm would be expressed as 890 mm ± 5 mm. The maxi- mum permitted size of this component would be 895 mm and the minimum size 895 mm. The actual measurement of the component delivered to site would be somewhere between the maximum and minimum permitted size. The joint design would

25

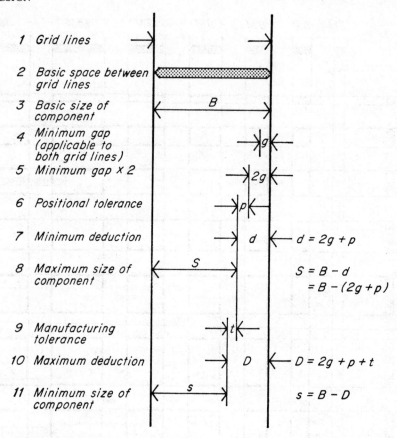

1 Grid lines

2 Basic space between grid lines

3 Basic size of component — B

4 Minimum gap (applicable to both grid lines) — g

5 Minimum gap × 2 — $2g$

6 Positional tolerance — p

7 Minimum deduction — d — $d = 2g + p$

8 Maximum size of component — S — $S = B - d$
   $= B - (2g + p)$

9 Manufacturing tolerance — t

10 Maximum deduction — D — $D = 2g + p + t$

11 Minimum size of component — s — $s = B - D$

8 The size of a jointed component and setting out by reference to one edge (BS 3626: 1963)

take into account these deviations in allocating the space allowed for the component. In order to calculate the maximum and minimum sizes for a modular component from a given size based on the design module, the following information must be known:

1 The size of the minimum gap which is to be allowed between the component and the module line or plane of reference in respect of the jointing technique.
2 An allowance to take into account the inaccuracy in the positioning of a component on site. This position tolerance is determined from a knowledge of site assembly procedures.
3 Information on the tolerance to be expected in manufacture which must be obtained from the makers.

From these three allowed variations it is then pos-

sible to specify the upper and lower of the manufacturing dimensions.

BS 3626 (1963) *A System of Tolerances and Fits in Building* gives a method of calculating the size of a component which is set out on site by relating one edge of the component to the grid (or module) line. The method is shown graphically in figure 8, See footnote, page 32.

The difference between the basic size B and the maximum size S is known as the minimum deduction d, which comprises two quantities. The first is the minimum gap g, or the permissible distance between the component and the grid line (thus the least distance between two components when assembled will be the sum of their respective minimum gaps, and this distance must be related to the least practicable width of joint). The second quantity in the minimum deduction is the positional tolerance p; the degree of accuracy to which the com-

26

ponent is to be assembled. Minimum gap is applied to each side of the component, thus:

$$S=B-d=B-(2g+p).$$

The minimum size s of the component is derived from the maximum size S, taking account of the manufacturing tolerance t, the value of which is determined by practical consideration of, on the one hand, the cost of obtaining any desired degree of accuracy in the fabrication of the component, whether in a factory or on side and, on the other, the maximum permissible width of join, $t=S-s$.

Figure 9, again from the BS, shows the method of calculation of the size of a component where it is to be set out by reference to a centre line. By relating the component to the centre line, the variation in the size of the joint is reduced, since the manufacturing tolerance is distributed on each side of the component.

The acceptance of an agreed standard of tolerances also presupposes the acceptance of a system of factory inspection to guarantee that the manufacturing tolerances are maintained. If the designer demands a greater degree of accuracy than the site circumstances or joint detail warrant, then the cost of production will be unnecessarily high. Thus the tolerances should be as generous as the circumstances permit.

To establish tolerance allowances the following procedure is usual. The nominal dimension of a procedure is usual. The nominal dimension of a component is fixed and this dimension indicates the zone into which the component must at all times fit. This nominal dimension will be measured between the controlling grid lines and should normally be a simple number since it is by this dimension that the component's size will be identified. The component must fit into this nominal zone in such a way that inaccuracies in manufacture or assembly do not cause overlap or creep over the boundary. Thus the actual size of the component will be less than its normal size. The actual size is the dimension specified to the manufacturer and is then subject to manufacturing tolerances. The upper and lower limits of manufacturing tolerances will be determined by consideration of the nature of the materials of the component, the manufacturing processes and the method of control. When the manufacturing tolerances are known, the assembly position must be examined. The tolerance allowed for placing the component in position

should allow enough room for manoeuvre. This will depend upon the detail of the component and particularly in respect of its profile and on the assembly techniques to be adopted. Account must now be taken of the form of joint, the jointing material to be used, the method of application

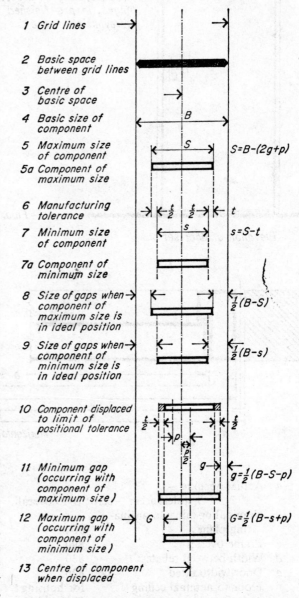

9 The size of a jointed component and setting out by reference to the centre line (BS 3626 : 1963)

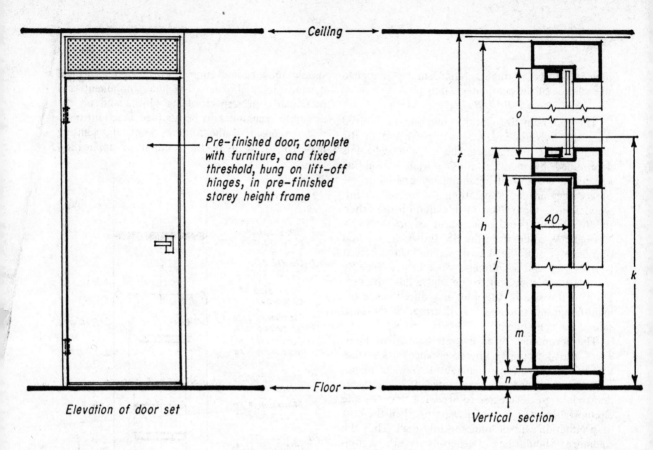

Pre-finished door, complete with furniture, and fixed threshold, hung on lift-off hinges, in pre-finished storey height frame

Ceiling

Floor

Elevation of door set

Vertical section

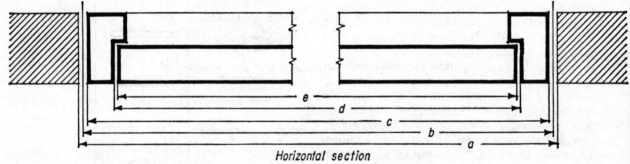

Horizontal section

		mm				mm
a	Actual opening— tolerances: −zero; +10 overall		h	Floor to ceiling set frame overall	$f - 15$	
b	Nominal opening co-ordina- ting plane	900	j	Door height set frame overall	2090	
c	Frame overall	890	k	Door height set opening	2100	
d	Width between rebates	830	l	Door and clearances	2045	
e	Door width fitted	826	m	Door height fitted	2040	
f	Floor to nominal ceiling	for housing: 2300, 2350, 2400	n	Threshold thickness	15	
			o	Over panel rebate	for housing: 177, 227, 277	

Dimension f and b are grid line (or basic space) dimensions

10   *Dimensions for standard door set*

and the necessity of subsequent maintenance. The maximum and minimum joint widths therefore determine the actual limits of positional tolerance. If the maximum gap is too wide for the jointing technique proposed or the minimum gap is too small, then the actual sizes must be adjusted, and it may be necessary to insist on more accurate manufacturing tolerances. Any extra cost involved will have to be set against the advantages of the chosen jointing method. Further information concerning jointing is contained in BS 4643:1970 *Glossary of terms relating to joints and jointing in building.*

In the design of a component, the designer must first select the basic size B or modular space within which the component is to fit. Then the manufacturing tolerance must be agreed t. The designer must then determine the minimum gap g that is practicable between the component and the grid line in respect of the jointing technique to be used. This joint may be a butt joint in the case of built-in furniture components placed next to each other, or it may be a mastic joint between a window and the structural frame. The minimum practical positional tolerance must next be decided p, that is to say the amount of space for manoeuvring into position that can be allowed. Then the three fundamental sizes can be calculated as follows with reference to setting out to one edge:

Minimum size $= s = B - (2g + p + t)$
Maximum size $= S = B - (2g + p)$

Where B = basic size of component
$\quad g$ = minimum gap between component and grid line
$\quad p$ = positional tolerance
$\quad t$ = total manufacturing tolerance.

It follows that if the components are factory made, the manufacturer should state in the catalogue the basic size of the component and the minimum and maximum manufacturing sizes. Where information on these is available, they have been included in the appropriate text in this volume.

Grid lines required for positioning the component should always be shown on the drawing, together with the basic size and minimum gap. The builder should always set out profile on site in accordance with the grid lines, and then set out the component position within this framework.

Figure 10 shows the dimensions of a standard

door set designed to fit a basic space of 900 mm wide x 2300, 2350 or 2400 mm high. These are the BS 4330 floor to nominal ceiling controlling dimensions for housing. The figure illustrates the large number of standard dimensions which follow from the choice of overall controlling dimensions. Because of the complete standardization of these dimensions the door would be manufactured complete on 'lift off' hinges, and both door and frame could be prefinished, and fitted with standard lock, latches and threshold. The door set is standardized also in respect of width of frame to 57 mm, 70 mm and 95 mm width of unit, to take various widths of partitions, and all falling within the 100 mm preferred dimension zone.

CONTROLLING DIMENSIONS

The use of grids for the setting out of spaces to be occupied by components is described in BS 4330. The BS makes the following recommendations in respect of vertical dimensions: 'The selection of sizes between controlling lines is made for floor to ceiling heights, heights of zones and floors and roofs and floor to floor or floor to roof heights'. Also recommendations are made in respect of changes in level. Figure 11 shows the zones 'A', 'B' and 'C' which are relevant to the controlling dimensions.

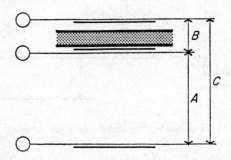

11 Floor to ceiling heights

Vertical controlling dimension

'A' a floor to ceiling height in mm determined by user requirements to be selected from the following range (2100) 2300, (2350) 2400, 2500, 2600, 2700, 2800, 2900, 3000 mm. The 2100 mm increment applies only to domestic garages, multi-storey car

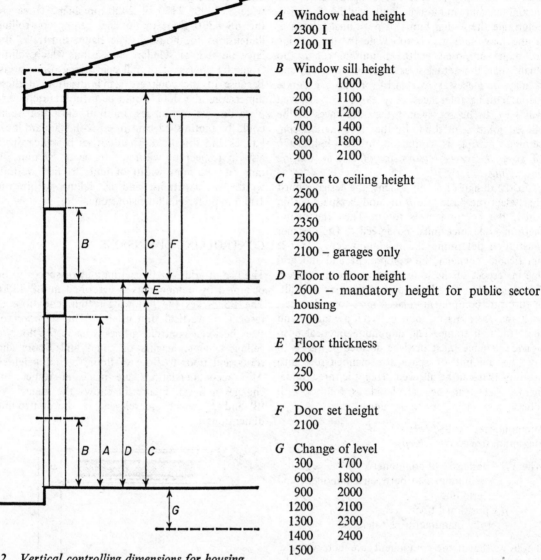

12   Vertical controlling dimensions for housing

A   Window head height
    2300 I
    2100 II

B   Window sill height
    0   1000
    200   1100
    600   1200
    700   1400
    800   1800
    900   2100

C   Floor to ceiling height
    2500
    2400
    2350
    2300
    2100 – garages only

D   Floor to floor height
    2600 – mandatory height for public sector housing
    2700

E   Floor thickness
    200
    250
    300

F   Door set height
    2100

G   Change of level
    300   1700
    600   1800
    900   2000
    1200   2100
    1300   2300
    1400   2400
    1500

parks and farm buildings, and the 2350 mm height is an additional option for housing only.

'B' the space required within the zone in mm for the structure, services and suspended ceilings to be selected from the following range: 100, 200, (250), 300, 400, 500, 600, 900, 1200, 1500, 1800, 2100 mm, with greater heights in multiples of 300. The 250 mm increment applies only to housing.

'C' floor to floor and floor to roof heights given in mm can be selected from the following range: (2600), 2700 mm with greater heights in multiples of 300 mm from 2700 to 8400 mm and thereafter in multiples of 600 mm. The 2600 mm increment applies only to housing. In order to make the best use of dimensions in co-ordinated components the dimensions 'A' and 'B' should add up to the dimension 'C'. As an example, the vertical controlling dimensions for housing are illustrated in figure 12.

Horizontal controlling dimensions

There are two methods of locating controlling lines in relation to load bearing walls and columns as shown in figures 13 and 14;

1 on the axial lines of the load bearing walls or columns (figure 13) or
2 the boundaries of the zones (figure 14).

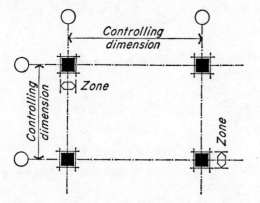

13 Horizontal controlling dimensions: axial lines

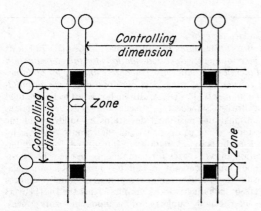

14 Horizontal controlling dimensions: zone boundaries

The controlling dimensions should be selected from the following range in respect of the widths of the zone to be allowed for columns and load bearing walls: 100, 200, 300, 400, 500 and 600 mm. If greater widths are required they should be in multiples of 300 mm at a first preference, or 100 mm as a second preference, in accordance with BS 4011. The choice of controlling dimensions for the spacing of zones (whichever method is used) should be made from the following: 900 mm in multiples of 300 mm, except that 800 mm may be used for housing. In respect of the intermediate controlling dimensions where joints are most likely to occur within the building between components and assemblies, the following points are made: *Window sill heights.* The height of the controlling line for a window sill should be selected from multiples of 300 mm as a first preference, and 100 mm as a second preference. In respect of *window head heights,* the height of the controlling line for the window head should be selected in accordance with a multiple of 300 mm as a first preference, and 100 mm as a second preference.

The controlling dimensions provide the framework within which buildings may be designed and to which building components and assemblies should be related. Intermediate controlling dimensions are subdivisions of the main framework. The controlling line represents the key reference plane and controlling lines for vertical dimensions represent boundaries for zones, floors and roofs. Controlling lines for horizontal dimensions indicate the axes of load bearing walls and columns or alternatively the boundaries of zones, within which the wall or column lies. A controlling line is shown in respect of the British Standard by a chain dotted line or unbroken line with a circle at the end of the line, as in figure 15. A zone is defined

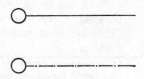

15 Controlling dimension lines

as a space between vertical or horizontal reference planes which is provided for a building component. For instance, zones for floors and roofs contain the structure which will include the finishes, the services, the suspended ceilings and where appropriate allowances for camber and deflection. Zones for load bearing walls contained in the structure will include an allowance for finishes. The British Standard is based on information derived by comparison of building types as follows: Education, health, housing, offices, industrial, hotels, shops and farm buildings. A building designed as part of a local authority building programme, financed by the Department of Education and Science, the Ministry of Health, and the Department of Environment, must be designed in metric units in accordance with the various recommendations put forward by these official bodies. Modular co-ordination in practice is illustrated in the many industrialized systems of building now in use. Although the sizes of components are related within a given system and are dimensionally co-ordinated with each other they are not necessarily co-ordinated with components in other systems. The many closed or separate industrialized building systems now in use may lead to a more open or general form of industrialized building in which factory made components are widely interchangeable.

Further reference

BS 2900: 1970   *Recommendations for the Co-ordination of Dimensions in Building. Glossary of Terms.*

BS 4011: 1966   *Recommendations for the Co-ordination of Dimensions in Building. Basic Sizes for Building Components and Assemblies*

BS 4330: 1968   *Recommendations for the Co-ordination of Dimensions in Building. Controlling Dimensions*

BS 4606: 1970   *Recommendations for the Co-ordination of Dimensions in Building. Co-ordinating sizes for rigid Flat sheet material used in Building*

PD 6432:   *Dimensional Co-ordination in Building. Arrangements of Building Components and Assemblies within functional groups*

    1969   Part 1 *Functional groups 1, 2, 3 and 4*

    1969   Part 2 *Functional group 5*

PD 6444:   *Recommendations for the Co-ordination of Dimensions in Building*

    1969   Part 1 *Basic spaces for structure external envelope and internal division*

    1971   Part 2 *Co-ordination sizes of fixtures furniture and equipment*

PD 6446: 1970   *Recommendations for the Co-ordination of Dimensions in Building. Combinations of sizes*

For further information on modular co-ordination see *Modular Primer* by Eric Corker, ARIBA and A. Diprose, ARIBA, also the *Co-ordination of Dimensions for Building* published by the RIBA, and *the Metric Handbook* published by the Architectural Press.

Reference page 26

The British Standards Institution have issued DD 22 (Draft for Development): *Recommendations for the co-ordination of dimensions in building: Tolerances and fits for building: The calculation of work sizes and joint clearance for building components*. The Draft, although it is not to be regarded as a British Standard, supersedes BS 3626. It describes dimensional and positional deviations in building and the way these affect components and their joints. Statistically based methods of calculation are introduced, for the determination of work sizes for components and for the assessment of joint clearance in building design. Recommendations for the specification of component sizes and tolerances are given; including worked samples. Thus the Draft covers the inter-related subjects of component work, sizes, tolerances and dimensional requirements of joints.

The Recommendations give guidance on the selection of co-ordinating sizes for modular building components in greater detail from the incremental basis specified in BS 4011, through the controlling dimensions of BS 4330 to the spatial requirements for assemblies of components (basic spaces) given in PD 6444, and the guidance in selecting optimum sizes for additive components in PD 6446.

The Recommendations are of a provisional nature since the methods of calculating are as yet untried in practice. Designers are recommended to use the method of calculation set out in the Draft to establish how closely this theory corresponds to the actual behaviour of components before, during and after their assemble on site.

The principal British Standard Specifications relating to components in building construction

BS 455: 1957   *Schedule of Sizes for Lock and Latches for Doors in Building.*

BS 459   *Doors*
- Part 1   *Panelled and Glazed Wood Doors*
- Part 2   *Flush Doors*
- Part 3   *Faced Fire Check Flush Doors, and Wood and Metal Frames [half-hour and one-hour types]*
- Part 4   *Matchboarded Doors*

BS 544: 1969   *Linseed Oil Putty for use in Wooden Frames*

BS 565: 1972   *Glossary of Terms Relating to Timber and Woodwork*

BS 584: 1967   *Wood Trim [softwood]*

BS 644:   *Wood Window*
- Part 1: 1951   *Wood Casement Windows*
- Part 2: 1958   *Wood Double-Hung Sash Windows*
- Part 3: 1951   *Wood Double-Hung Sash and Case Windows (Scottish type)*

BS 990:   *Steel Windows generally for Domestic and Similar Buildings:* Part 2 1972 Metric Units

BS 1202   *Nails*
- Part 1: 1974   *Steel Nails*
- Part 2: 1974   *Copper Nails*
- Part 3: 1974   *Aluminium Nails*

BS 1210: 1963   *Wood Screws*

BS 1227   *Hinges* Part 1(a) 1967 *Hinges for General Building Purposes*

BS 1245: 1975   *Metal Door Frames – Steel*

BS 1285: 1963   *Wood Surrounds for Steel Windows and Doors*

BS 1422: 1956   *Steel Sub-Frames, Sills and Window Boards for Metal Windows*

BS 1567: 1953   *Wood Door Frames and Linings*

BS 4787:   *Internal and external wood door-sets, door leaves and frames*
- Part 1: 1972   *Dimensional requirements*

BS 5277: 1976   *Doors: Measurements of dimensions and defects of general flatness of door leaves*

BS 5278: 1976   *Doors: Measurements of dimensions and defects of squareness of door leaves*

BS 5369: 1976   *Methods of testing doors; behaviour under humidity variations of door leaves placed in successive uniform climates*

BS 1186   *Quality of Timber and Workmanship in Joinery*
- Part 1: 1971   *Quality of Timber*
- Part 2: 1971   *Quality of Workmanship*

BS 3827   *Glossary of Terms relating to Builders' Hardware*
- Part 1: 1964   *Locks*
- Part 2: 1967   *Latches*
- Part 3: 1967   *Catches*
- Part 4: 1967   *Door etc furniture*

BS 4951: 1973   *Builder's hardware: lock and latch furniture [doors]*

BS 2911: 1974   *Letter Plates*

BS 3589: 1963   *Glossary of Terms used in Building*

BS 3621: 1963   *Thief Resistant Locks for Hinged Doors*

British Standard Codes of Practice Relevant to Component Design and Installation

CP 3 chapter 1   Part 1:1964 *Lighting: Daylighting*

CP 145   *Glazing Systems:* Part 1 1969 *Patent Glazing*

CP 151   *Doors and Windows including Frames and Linings:* Part 1 1957 *Wooden Doors*

CP 152: 1972   *Glazing and Fixing of Glass for Buildings*

2 Joinery

General references
The design and practice of joinery, J. Eastwick-Field and J. Stillman, Architectural Press Ltd
Joinery, C.H. Tack, PRL, HMSO.
Handbook of Fixings and Fastenings, Bill Launchbury, Architectural Press Limited
Joinery is generally understood to be the fabrication and fixing of timber components such as windows, doors, stairs, built-in fittings, and of external items such as gates, the surfaces of all of which are planed (ie *wrot*), and usually sanded. The ease of working timber, and its 'warm' and interesting appearance, encourage its use.

The quality of joinery work depends upon design, materials and workmanship. The designer must, therefore, understand the principles of design, specify exactly the type and quality of timber and other materials, and the standard of workmanship required and bear in mind the available facilities for manufacture and fixing.

Internally, unprotected wood soon becomes dirty and dull, so exposed surfaces are often stained and/ or treated with a natural or synthetic resin varnish, or with french or wax polish—clear finishes which considerably enhance the natural appearance of timber. Alternatively, wood is painted. It is important to note that the smoothness of the wood surface determines that of applied finishes.

Externally, all unprotected timbers 'weather' to a uniform grey. Clear finishes can preserve the new appearance of timber, but they require frequent maintenance. See *MBS: Finishes,* Chapter 6.

Timber is often used as a strong and inexpensive core, so that metal faced plywood, and metal drawn on wood sections, are economical means of obtaining the appearance of metals. Timber windows are available with sections encapsulated in pvc sheet.

Increasingly, 'solid' timber is being used in conjunction with plywood, blockboard, chipboard, hardboard, plastics laminates and metal sheets and sections. Although sliced wood veneers, often having exotic grain patterns, continue to be glued to surfaces internally, plastics impregnated paper laminates simulating wood are now commonly used. These can be easily cleaned but they are not resistant to scratching and abrasion and are, therefore, not suitable for counter tops and working surfaces.

Principles of good joinery design can be deduced from knowledge of the properties of the materials to be used and the intended conditions of use, eg light or heavy duty, internally or externally. Designs can invariably be improved by careful observation of the behaviour of prototypes.

The limitations of hand and of machine work must be taken into account. For example, a spindle cutter cannot form a square end to a groove; either a separate machine operation or hand work is required. Although joinery can be remarkably accurate, inaccuracies are inevitable in fixing, and more so in refixing removable sections such as glazing beads, so these should be either recessed or projected in relation to the sashes to which they are attached, see figure 159, page 184 and 111 page 133.

Arrises, (ie corners) are better slightly rounded, since sharp arrises are difficult both to obtain and maintain, and the tendency for paint and clear finishes to 'run away' from such corners is undesirable particularly externally.

The choice of the right timbers requires knowledge of the characteristics and properties of timbers in general, of the available species, and of the conditions to which specific joinery components will be subjected — see page 36. Nomenclature, anatomy and properties of timbers, and causes and means of avoidance of deterioration, are dealt with in chapter 2 of *MBS Materials* by Alan Everett.

Traditional naming of timbers is confusing. It will be noted, for example, that the unqualified description *deal* does not relate to any particular species, and the need to use the names given in BSs 881 and 589: 1974 for hardwoods and softwoods respectively, is emphasised. Similarly, the terms used in BS 565:1972 *Glossary of terms applicable to timber, plywood and joinery,* should always be used.

All timber for building must be dried slowly (ie *seasoned*), if only to avoid too rapid drying and consequent splitting, or to make it receptive to preservatives. Twenty-five per cent maximum moisture content is advised for vacuum/pressure impregnation and twenty two per cent for organic solvent type preservatives. Timber for joinery must be dried to levels as near as possible to the relatively low moisture contents it will assume, which normally necessitates *kiln seasoning*. This minimises shrinkage in service, and sometimes expansion, remembering that timber can be too dry. It also reduces thermal conductivity and vulnerability to fungal attack and makes surfaces suitable for gluing and surface finishes. Seasoning is not irreversible, so that priming of joinery 'at works' and protection from the weather in transit to the site and on the site, are necessary. Ideally, timber would not be installed until buildings are heated and 'dried out' and buildings are maintained at constant relative humidities, but normally joinery must be designed and fixed to permit some moisture movement in service, eg by using narrow widths and tongued and grooved joints, or where widths are glued together, as in 'solid' table tops, by employing fixings which allow the overall widths of tops to change with changes in the moisture content of the wood resulting from variations in the humidity of the surrounding air. Incidentally, paint and clear finishes can only delay such movements.

The extra cost of radially cut timber is justified where the smaller movement in its width, and freedom from the 'cupping' of plain sawn timber are critical — as in drawing boards, and/or where an interesting appearance is desired — as that given by 'silver grain' rays in oak.

The low thermal conductivity and capacity of timber and the low thermal movement in its length favours its choice for various uses. Timber retains its strength at high temperatures, and in appropriate thicknesses which allow for losses due to charring it can provide useful degrees of *fire resistance*, eg even in encasures to protect steel structures. Intumescent strips, which expand in fires, are valuable in sealing gaps around and between fire-resisting doors, and as beads for fire-resisting glazing. The *spread of flame*[1] classification of timbers can be effectively improved by impregnation with, or by surface applications of, fire retardants, although

1 BS 476 terms — see *MBS Materials*

these cannot make timber *non-combustible*[1] and adhesives and surface treatments may not be compatible with them.

As timber changes dimensions to differing extents, tangentially and radially, and longitudinal movement is negligible, some distortion such as cupping, diamonding, and twist of boards having twisted grain, is inevitable with changes in moisture content, but it must be emphasised that conformity with BS 1186: Part 1: *Quality of timber in joinery* will minimise such tendencies. 'L' shapes cut out of solid timber should be avoided and complex shapes are best 'built-in' by gluing together mutually compensating pieces into a balanced laminate. Plywood, which has an uneven number of plies with their grain running in opposed directions, demonstrates these principles.

Although timber tends to expand when it is wetted and to return to its former size when it dries again, it must be remembered that if it is restrained while it absorbs water, when it dries it shrinks from the restrained size and becomes smaller than it would have been had it not been restrained — a phenomenon known as *stress setting*. The effects of this permanent shrinkage are obvious where gaps form between timber flooring after flooding, (and indeed, when wooden tool handles loosen when they dry after having been wet).

Unless timber is an inherently durable heartwood, or has been impregnated with preservative and the effects of wetting and drying are acceptable, joinery should be designed to minimise the likelihood of wetting by rain or other causes. All such timber should be protected by damp proof courses and membranes and flashings, and it should be kept above splash rising from pavings and projecting surfaces. Joinery should be designed to be self-draining with no horizontal surfaces and with devices such as lined channels and weep tubes to remove condensation from glass on the inside of windows. Defective joints, and cracks must be avoided where they would allow water to flow or be blown into, or to enter timber by capillary action.

A common defect has been the rotting of the lower rails of sashes. Condensation from the inner face of glass enters the wood through defective back putties, the wood swells and cracks the outside paint at a joint, and further water enters. Paint is not a preservative, and in this case it only serves to retain water and fungal decay follows, particularly if sapwood which has not been treated with preservative is present – the sapwood of all species is *non-durable* or *perishable*. Because most softwoods contain sapwood it is now considered essential to preserve them where they are used in windows and external doors and frames and cladding, even if these are to be painted.

A Norwegian method for protecting the lower members of windows is described on page 132.

The National House Builders' Registration Council requires timber for claddings, window frames, casements and sashes and external door frames to be treated with preservative, or a preservative and paint system, (NHBRC *Practice Note* No. 1 describes acceptable preservative treatment), unless one of the following *durable* timbers is used:

Afrormosia	Keruing	Sapele
Agba	Makoré	Sweet chestnut
Afzelia	American White oak	Teak
Gurjun	European oak	Utile
Idigbo	Japanese oak	Western red
Iroko	Red meranti	cedar
Kapur	Red seraya	Yang

The Practice note states, however, that the sapwood of these timbers should be treated with preservative.

The Building Regulations 1976: Schedule 5, contain similar requirements for boards forming the weather-resisting parts of external walls. End grain is especially vulnerable and if it is cut on site the NHBRC advises that ends should be immersed in preservative for at least one minute, or if this is not practicable, two brush coats should be applied. It must be noted that preservatives should be applied liberally, unlike paint which is 'brushed out'.

Preservatives may adversely affect putties, mastics, window and door furniture and paints. Generally, forty-eight hours must be allowed before applying a primer on a surface which has been treated with preservative and three-four days may be necessary where copper naphthenate preservatives were used. Internally, even *perishable* woods, such as beech, do not require preservative if they are kept 'dry'.

Although timber has a high strength:weight ratio it must not be forgotten that some joinery members are highly stressed, if only occasionally, and eventualities such as persons standing on tables

must be foreseen. Concentrations of stress at joints as, in those in side hung, double glazed casement windows, determine jointing methods and these in turn may determine the minimum sizes of the members to be joined.

The economical use of the *standard sizes* of sawn timber is dealt with under *Sizes*, pages 39-40.

Choice of timbers for uses

If the properties of available timbers are systematically matched to known performance requirements it is often possible to use a timber which is more suited, and yet less costly, than the conventional choice. For example, members in stronger timbers can be smaller and may cost less, than those in 'cheaper' but weaker timbers.

The botanical descriptions: *hardwood* and *softwood* are rarely helpful. Thus, although most hardwoods are denser and therefore stronger than most softwoods, hardwoods are not necessarily hard and softwoods are not always soft, eg yew. Also, hardwoods include species with heartwood having both the greatest and least resistance to fungal attack, and softwoods include species having both 'small' and 'large' moisture movements.

Timbers vary considerably in their properties and appearance, between species, and even between parts of one tree. Hence, information can relate only to average specimens of any species and this, including reference to properties such as: strength, nailing, gluing and resistance to cutting, blunting effect on tools, drying characteristics durability and resistance to impregnation, and suitability for bending is found in:

MBS: Materials chapter 2
Timber selection by properties, Part 1: Windows, doors, cladding and flooring, PRL, HMSO (Further parts will deal with other uses)
A handbook of hardwoods, PRL, HMSO
A handbook of softwoods, PRL, HMSO
BS 1186: Part 1: 1971 *Quality of timber in joinery*

This BS gives the suitability of thirty-six hardwoods and ten softwoods which are available in this country, for twelve joinery applications.
The Building Regulations 1976 Schedule 5, HMSO
The National House-Builders Registration Council Handbook

Specification of timber for joinery

Timber can never be 'free from all defects' and a requirement that it must be 'reasonably free', requires interpretation for various types of joinery. Some guidance is given in:

BS 459 *Doors* Parts 1–4

BS 644 *Wood Windows*

BS 1576 *Wood door frames and linings*

BS 1186: Part 2: 1971 details quality requirements for timber in four 'use classes', ie Class 1S – joinery for clear finishing and Classes 1, 2 and 3 for painting. Rules are given for 'concealed' and 'semi-concealed' surfaces. The Standard must be consulted for details, but the following notes will give guidance:

1 Timber must be free from fungal decay, and from insect damage other than pinhole borer (ambrosia) holes which are permitted in concealed and semi-concealed surfaces, and if the holes are filled, also in Class 1, 2 and 3 surfaces

2 Sapwood is not allowed in hardwood surfaces exposed to the weather.

3 Unsound, dead, and loose knots are restricted to concealed and semi-concealed surfaces and knot sizes are limited.

4 Laminating, finger jointing and edge jointing must not be unduly conspicuous and may be disallowed by the purchaser for Class 1S use. For this use also, the species and character of grain must be the same on all surfaces and be matched as far as possible.

5 For Class 1 timber, checks and shakes are restricted in size and depth. Not less than 8 growth rings per 25 mm is specified and the slope of grain is restricted to not more than 1 in 8 in hardwoods and 1 in 10 in softwoods.

6 Sapwood (except 2), including discoloured sapwood, is allowed.

The recommended moisture contents for all classes of joinery are given in table 2.

Workmanship

The traditional craftsman had great pride in providing a high standard of workmanship, and the expression: 'the work is to be performed in a workmanlike manner' was generally understood in a given context. Today, more precise descrip-

	Moisture content percent + or −2
External joinery	
Heated or unheated buildings	17
Internal joinery	
Heated buildings	
(i) intermittent	15
(ii) continuous, with room	
temperatures of 12–18°C	12
20–24°C	10
(iii) timber in close proximity	
to sources of heat	8

Table 2   Moisture contents for joinery when handed over to the purchaser

tions are necessary and these are provided by – BS 1186: Part 2: 1971 (amended 1976), *Quality of workmanship in joinery.* Requirements are specified for fit of parts and the degree of care in forming joints, including glued joints. At present, only a simple definition is given of an acceptable surface finish. The BS includes: tolerances for joints which permit movement; dimensions of gaps around painted and unpainted doors and sashes; requirements for fit of drawers; laminated wood, and descriptions of *finger joints* which reduce waste by joining short lengths of timber.

Joinery must be protected from exposure and damage during transport and storage on site and during the course of the work. Protection on the site is usually done by the use of strips of hardboard, covering by polythene sheet, or in the case of special work, by 'boxing in' behind a plywood or hardboard covered frame. The contractor should also, in good quality work, ensure that the heat and humidity conditions in the building are suitable for the joinery to be delivered and fixed, so that the conditions are commensurate with the required moisture content of the timber.

Clear seals are available which can be applied to joinery work at the time of manufacture, and which prevent moisture penetration and so protect the work from moisture movement before the final finish is applied.

When timber is framed up, the faces of all the members joined should be perfectly fitted together, with true and flush surfaces in alignment throughout the joint.

Sizes of so-called 'structural' members, the

collapse of which would endanger lives, are always calculated. However, the sizes of other joinery members whether acting as beams, cantilevers, columns or struts have traditionally been based on 'experience'. Actual sizes were then often increased for extra 'safety', for convenience in jointing, or even just to 'fill in spaces'.

To minimise waste, where possible sizes should be based on the standard sawn sizes.

Due to differences in tangential and radial moisture movements, sections which deviate too widely from rectangles are liable to distort, and for this reason built-up sections may be preferred, even for simple sections like door frames with stops. Built-up sections may also be more economical, and complex profiles must be built-up to minimise waste. Externally however, joints which are not glued with waterproof glue present opportunities for water to enter.

The costs of grinding cutters and setting up machines are high, and a large number of operations can only be justified by a very large order.

Normal sources	Thickness[2]	Width[2]								
	mm	75	100	125	150	175	200	225	250	300
Europe	16	X	X	X	X					
	19	X	X	X	X					
	22	X	X	X	X					
	25	X	X	X	X	X	X	X	X	X
	32	X	X	X	X	X	X	X	X	X
	36[1]	X	X	X	X					
	38	X	X	X	X	X	X	X		
	40[1]	X	X	X	X	X	X	X		
	44	X	X	X	X	X	X	X	X	X
	50	X	X	X	X	X	X	X	X	X
	63		X	X	X	X	X	X		
	75		X	X	X	X	X	X	X	X
America	44[3]	X	X	X	X	X	X	X	X	X
	100		X		X		X		X	X
	150			X			X			X
	200						X			
	250								X	
	300									X

[1] These thicknesses are unlikely to be available

[2] The sizes given are for 20 per cent moisture content. For every 5 per cent additional moisture content up to 30 per cent sizes must be 1 per cent greater and for every 5 per cent moisture content less than 20 per cent sizes may be 1 per cent less.

[3] Canadian commerical hemlock (Hem-fir)

Table 3   BS 4471: Part 1: 1969 Basic cross-sectional sizes of sawn softwoods at 20 per cent moisture content

Sizes of softwoods

Metric sizes have been agreed by all the major softwood producing countries and the principal European importing countries. Table 3 shows the BS 4471: Part 1: 1969 *Basic sizes for sawn softwood at 20 per cent moisture content.*

Minus deviations permitted on up to 10 per cent of the pieces in any sample are 1 mm on widths and thicknesses up to 100 mm, and 2 mm on greater sizes.

The standard provides for *precision timber* produced by machining (*regularizing*) at least one face and edge of a section to give a uniform thickness and/or width throughout 1 mm less than the basic sawn size.

Table 4 gives the reductions allowed for planing sawn sections to accurate sizes, ranging in the case of joinery from 7 mm to 13 mm, according to sizes of pieces.

Plus or minus 0.5 mm is allowed on all finished sizes. Lengths of softwoods are from 1.8 m to 6.3 m rising by 300 mm increments.

BS 4471: Part 2: 1971 gives dimensions for small softwood sections as shown in Table 5.

Finished thickness mm	Finished widths mm				
	22	30	36	44	48
6	X		X		
14			X		X
17	X		X		X
22	X	X	X	X	X
30			X	X	X
36			X		X
44					X
48					X

Table 5   BS 4471: Part 2: 1971 Finished widths and thicknesses of small resawn softwood sections

Minus 0.5 mm is permitted off not more than 10 per cent of the pieces in any parcel and plus 3 mm on any proportion of a parcel.

Purpose	Reduction from basic size to finished size for sawn width and/or thickness (mm)				
	15 to and including 22	Over 22 to and including 35	Over 35 to and including 100	Over 100 to and including 150	Over 150
Constructional timber surfaced	3	3	3	5	6
Floorings[1]	3	4	4	6	6
Matchings and interlocking boards[1]	4	4	4	6	6
Planed all round Trim	5	5	7	7	9
Joinery and cabinet work	7	7	9	11	13

[1]   The reduction of width is overall the extreme size exclusive of any reduction of the face by the machining of a tongue or lap joint

Table 4   Reductions from basic sizes to finished sizes to accurate sizes by processing of two opposed faces of softwoods

Sizes of hardwoods

BS 5450: 1977 gives *Sizes of hardwoods and methods of measurement* – as follows:

Thickness mm	Width mm				
	50,63	75	100,125	100,175	200,225 250,300
19		X	X	X	
25	X	X	X	X	
32		X	X	X	X
38		X	X	X	X
50			X	X	X
63				X	X
75				X	X
100					X

Table 6   Basic cross-sectional sizes of sawn heartwoods having 15 per cent moisture content

Hardwoods are not necessarily imported in BS sizes. Availability in any particular species should be checked.

Permitted deviations from the basic sizes are:

Basic size mm	Minus mm	Plus mm
Under 25	1	3
25 – 75	2	6
76 – 125	3	9
126 – 300	4	12

Table 7   Permissible deviations from basic thicknesses or widths of hardwoods at 15 per cent moisture content.

Sizes will be similar for moisture contents less than 15 per cent and greater for moisture contents up to 30 per cent to an extent which can be estimated using the values for radial and tangential movements given in *The Handbook of Hardwoods* PRL, HMSO.

Hardwood in one of the specified thicknesses is often in random widths with either square or waney edges.

The following table gives the reductions allowed for planing sawn sections to accurate sizes, ranging in the case of joinery from 7 mm to 14 mm according to the sizes of the pieces.

End use or product	Reduction from basic size to finished size for basic sawn sizes of width or thickness (mm)				
	15 to 25 mm	26 to 50 mm	51 to 100 mm	101 to 150 mm	151 to 300 mm
Constructional timber, surfaced	3	3	3	5	6
Floorings, matchings and interlocked boarding, planed all round	5	6	7	7	7
Trim	6	7	8	9	10
Joinery and cabinetwork	7	9	10	12	14

Table 8   Reductions from basic sawn sizes to finished sizes by processing two opposed faces of hardwoods.

Finished sizes after processing are allowed plus or minus 0.5 mm deviation.

Lengths of imported hardwoods vary according to species and origin. BS *basic lengths* are any integral multiple of 100 mm but not less than 1 m. No minus deviations are allowed.

Building boards

Plywood, blockboard, hardboard, chipboard and other building boards which may be used in the manufacture of components are discussed in *MBS: Materials*, chapter 3.

JOINTS

BS 1186: Quality of timber and workmanship in joinery Part 2: 1971 *Quality of workmanship* gives detailed requirements for fit, tolerances and general workmanship for the more common joints used in joinery.

The choice of joints depends upon the relationships and shapes of members to be joined. Joints may require to be designed to relate to rebates and mouldings in the members, see figure 55. Other factors include: strength, appearance (including 'secret' methods, see figure 22), need for demounting, see figures 28 and 30, ease of making and cost.

Types of joints	'Flat' sections eg Boards											Thick sections eg Window frames					Movement joints	Demountable joints	'Secret' joints
Typical joint applications	Stile – top rail of panelled door	Stile – middle rail of panelled door	Stile – intermediate rail of panelled door	Shelf–upright	Drawer side – front and back	Door lining head – jamb	Framing	Boards edge – edge	End – end	Moulded sections	Architraves – angles	Post – cill	Curved – straight	Handrails and cills end-end	Other sections end – end	Window sills – angles			
Interlocks																			
Mortice and tenon	16 (b)	16 (c)-(e)	16 (a)-(d)				16(d) (f)-(i)					40	16 (j)						16 (k)
Tongued and grooved								17 (a)-(f)											
Housed				18 (a)-(e)			18 (f)-(j)												
Combed					19 (a)		19 (b)												
Dovetailed				18 (e)	20 (a)-(c)		18 (j)												22 (d)
Lapped						21 (a)-(c)									21 (d)	21 (e)-(f)			
Mitred and scribed										55	22 (a)					22			22 (a)-(d)
Finger									23						23				
Inserts																			
Dowelled	24 (b)	24 (b)	24 (a)	24 (a)				24 (b)											
Loose tongue	25 (a)	25 (a)	25 (a)					25 (a)											
Nails, pins and screws																	43 45	28	28
Bolts													29	29					29
Demountable connectors																		30	
Adhesives								31											

Table 9 Drawings showing common joints for typical joinery applications (figure numbers)

Interlocks may require to be supplemented by Inserts and/or adhesives, but Inserts, demountable connectors and adhesives may be the sole method of fixing.

In recent years, the smaller sizes of many members and the greater cost of forming framed joints, have led to increased use of mechanical methods for joining.

Strength requirements for joints vary considerably in degree, from those which locate members during construction only, to those which are heavily stressed in service in compression, tension, shear and/or torsion, and in one or more directions. The strength of unglued interlocking joints such as mortice and tenon, is related to the reduced sectional area of the weaker member. Nails, screws, bolts and dowels have the disadvantage of concentrating stresses in a limited number of small areas, whereas, adhesives, which are generally stronger than the wood they join, distribute stresses more evenly. Combinations of these forms may be beneficial in service, or in assembly where interlocking shapes or inserts hold members together while glue is setting.

Table 9 suggests examples of types of joints appropriate for stated typical situations. The types are listed in the table, and described under the following headings:

1 Interlocking, eg tongued and grooved
2 Inserts, eg dowels, nails and screws.
3 Demountable connectors
4 Adhesives

1 INTERLOCKING

Mortice and tenon

This is the most common means of joining 'flat' rectangular sections of joinery at right angles. The mortice is a slot cut in, (usually through), one of the members to receive a tenon projecting from the end of the other member. The tenon is glued in the mortice, and in hand work, it is wedged. The tenon and wedges project initially, but when the glue has set the surplus timber is cut off to give a flush face. For mass production, instead of wedges, the joint is secured by non-ferrous metal star-shaped dowels driven from the face through the joint. This, of course, restricts the finishing work which can be done later and hardwood dowels are better in this respect.

The thickness of a tenon should not be more than one third of that of the section, and its depth should not exceed five times the thickness.

(a) *Through tenon*   In its simplest form this joint is used for joining intermediate rails and stiles in doors. The top and bottom edges of the mortice should be cut so that the slot is slightly dovetailed, thus increasing the strength of the joint. This dovetailing effect is obtained by moving the timber slightly from side to side during the machine cutting process.

Joints may be, additionally secured by dowels, particularly in large sections of timber.

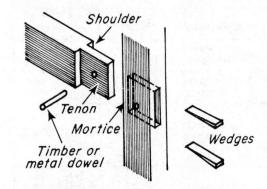

(*a*) *Through tenon*

(b) *Haunched tenon*   This joint is used to connect the stile and top rail of a door, since in order to

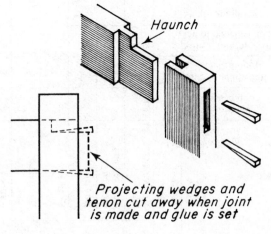

(*b*) *Haunched tenon*

42

wedge the joint is is necessary to retain a thickness of timber above the tenon. The cutting away of the front part of the tenon at the top does this, whilst the retention of the haunch minimizes any loss of strength. In making the joint, the stile is cut so a 'horn' projects beyond the top rail in order to resist the pressure from the wedges when the joint is made. The 'horn' is then cut off level with the top of the door and the wedges trimmed to size.

(c) *Twin tenon* Where the mortice and tenon joint is to be made in a deep rail, say 230 mm and over, there would be a tendency for a single deep tenon to shrink and become loose. To avoid this, two tenons are cut one above the other out of the depth of the rail. In good class work the joint is dowelled as well as being wedged.

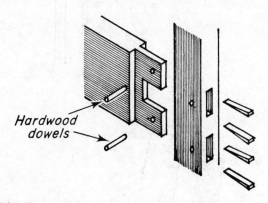

Hardwood dowels

(c) Twin tenon

(d) *Double tenon* Where a rail is more than, say, 65 mm thick two tenons are cut side by side.

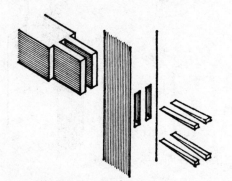

(d) Double tenon

(e) *Twin double* A combination of types c and d, used where the rail is deep and over 50 mm thick. Double and twin tenons can be haunched by leaving shoulders of timber at top and bottom of tenons. This joint allows a mortice lock to be fitted with less weakening of the framework.

Confusion must be guarded against in naming tenons. For example, twin tenons (c) are sometimes called a pair of single tenons and the terms twin and double are interchanged!

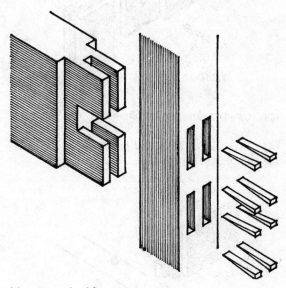

(e) Twin double tenon

(f) *Barefaced tenon* This variation, which is used when the two members to be connected are of different thickness, allows one face of the work to be flush.

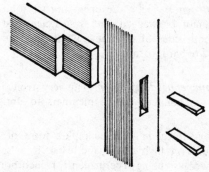

(f) Bare faced tenon

(g) *Open or slot mortice* This joint is easily made. The tenon or tenons cannot be wedged and is secured by gluing and dowelling. It is often used where the framing will be concealed.

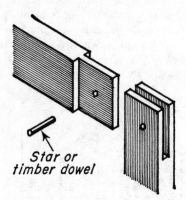

Star or timber dowel

(*g*) *Open or slot mortice tenon*

(h) *Twin double haunched tenon* This is a locating joint only, and therefore it is not wedged.

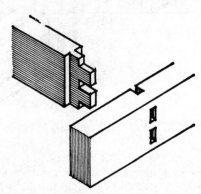

(*h*) *Twin double haunched tenon*

(i) *Stub tenon* Like the open mortice joint this joint cannot be wedged, but is sufficiently strong where both sides of the frame are strengthened by plywood or hardboard.

(j) *Hammer head key tenon* This very strong joint is used to connect curved members to uprights.

(k) *Fox-tail tenon* This complex form of stub tenon used in high class hand work is a 'secret' joint, wedges being (permanently) incorporated in the joint during assembly.

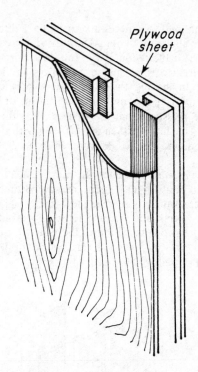

Plywood sheet

(*i*) *Stub tenon*

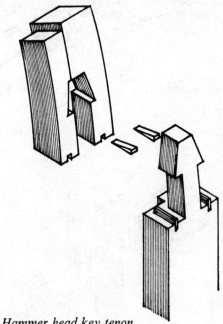

(*j*) *Hammer head key tenon*

16 Mortice and tenon joints

Tongued and grooved

This joint is used principally for joining boards edge to edge, a tongue cut on the edge of one board fitting into a groove cut into the edge of the other. Without glue the joint allows boards to move in their width. With glue the joint locates boards while the glue is setting, although at the cost of extra width equal to the extent of penetration of tongues into grooves. Grooves are often cut slightly deeper than the projection of tongues to ensure a tight joint on the face. Where the reverse face will not be seen and where boards are not to be glued and cramped, the back shoulder can also be cut to remain slightly open.

(a) shows a square edge tongue, characteristic of hand work and (b) and (c) show splayed and rounded tongues which are more suitable for machine work.

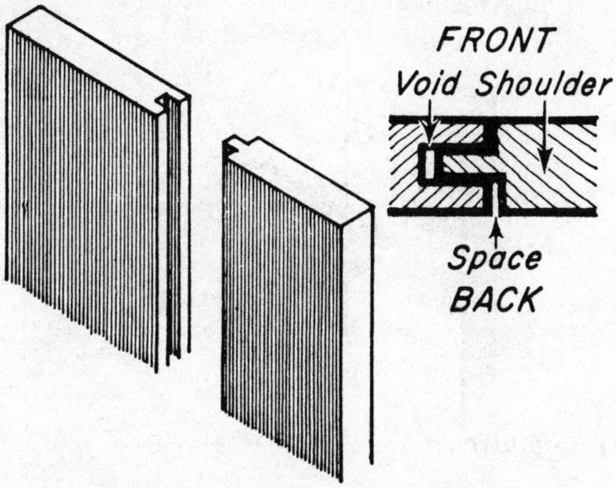

(*a*) *Tongued and grooved – square edge tongue*

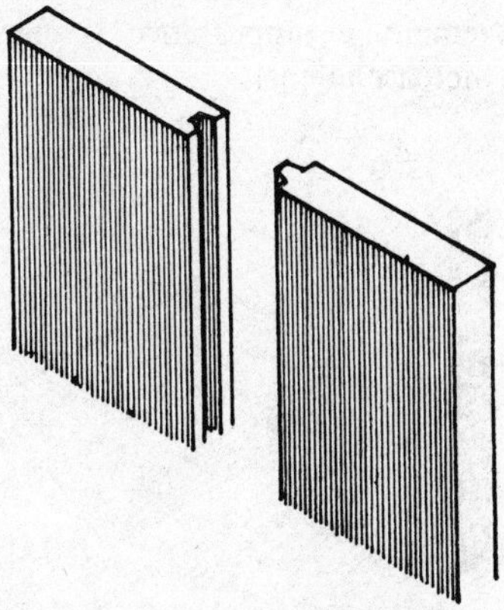

(*b*) *Tongued and grooved – splayed tongue*

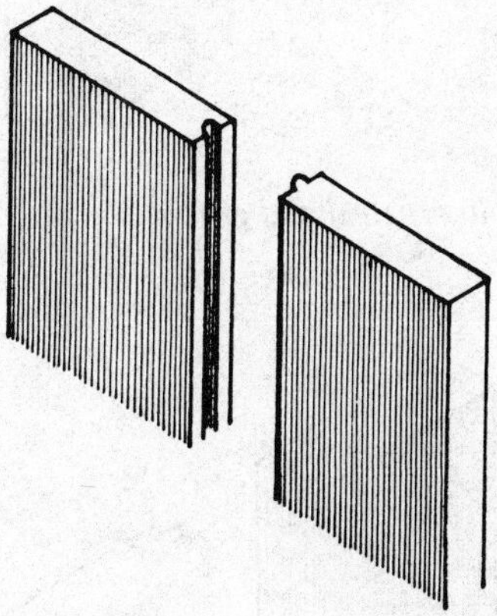

(*c*) *Tongued and grooved – rounded tongue*

(d) *Lindermann* This machine-made joint with an offset dovetail has been used for the strong joints needed for forming deep stair strings.

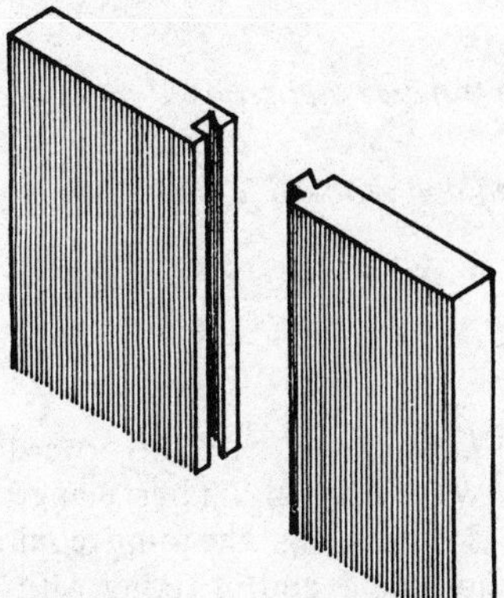

(*d*) *Lindermann*

(e) and (f) These double tongued and grooved machine made joints give a larger gluing surface and are suitable for joining boards of 40 mm and more in thickness.

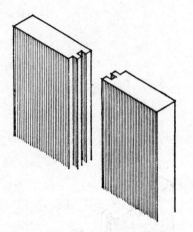

(e)   Double tongued and grooved – square tongue

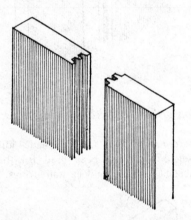

(f)   Double tongued and grooved – spayed tongue

17   Tongued and grooved joints

Housing

(a) *Square housing* A straightforward method of locating two pieces of timber being jointed at right angles as in shelving. The joint requires careful machining and gluing, and/or fixing with screws or nails, punched in and filled.

Other examples of tongued and grooved joints are lapped and rebated corner joints.

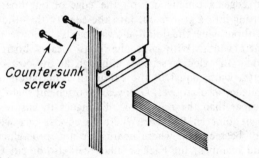

(a)   Square housing

(b) *Shouldered housing* The groove here is less than the thickness of the horizontal member; and will require additional fixing through the face of the vertical member.

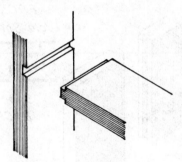

(b)   Shouldered housing

(c) *Stopped housing* The groove is stopped back from the face of the upright. This is done where the improvement in appearance is considered to justify the increase in cost.

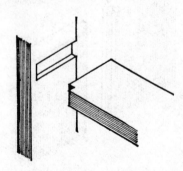

(c)   Stopped housing

(d) *Dovetail housing – single* The groove is cut square on one side and given an upward chamfer to form a single dovetail on the other. The key profile so formed helps to prevent the joint pulling out. This joint can only be assembled by sliding the two parts together, and so the joint is not suitable where the pieces to be connected together are wider than say 300 mm.

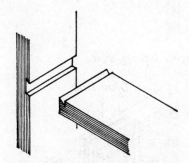

(d) *Dovetail housing – single*

(e) *Dovetail housing – double* The groove is fully dovetailed with a corresponding increase in strength as against the single dovetail housing. There is, of course, a corresponding increase in cost and difficulty of assembly. Additional fixing by screwing or pinning is not so necessary.

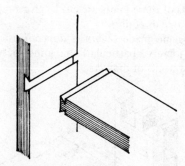

(e) *Dovetail housing – double*

(f) *Rail housing* A form of stopped housing used in framing between rails and end pieces where the rail is not as wide as the end piece.

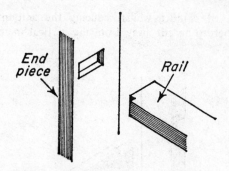

(f) *Rail housing*

(g) *Double stopped housing* Used in skeleton framing where a neat appearance is required; this joint is principally a *locating* joint not having the strength of the other type of housings.

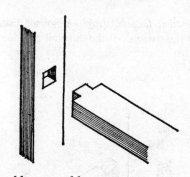

(g) *Double stopped housing*

(h) *Face housing* This easily made joint is used in skeleton framing which is subsequently concealed. In these positions the fixing can be by nails or screws.

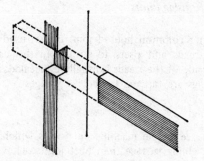

(h) *Face housing*

(i) *Shouldered face housing* This modification of the simple-faced housed joint provides additional

47

area of contact whilst reducing the amount of timber to be cut away from the vertical member.

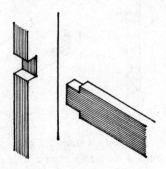

(i)   Shouldered face housing

(j) *Dovetailed face housing*   A housed joint incorporating the strength of the dovetail profile.

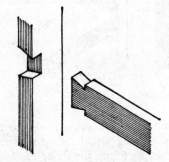

(j)   Dovetailed face housing

18   *Housing joints*

Another common housed joint is that used to join stair treads and risers to strings. In this case, the underside of the treads is usually concealed, and the housings are tapered to receive wedges

Combed

These are simple machine cut joints which have a larger gluing surface than butt joints. They should have a push fit. Figure 19 shows typical combed joints — in the latter, both timber members are shaped identically. In thicker sections the number of tongues and slots can be increased with advantage.

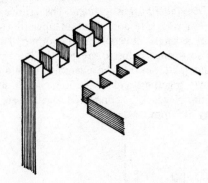

(a)   Corner locking joint

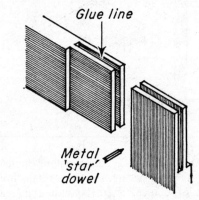

(b)

19   *Combed joints*

Dovetailed

The parts of these joints are cut to give a mechanical 'lock' in one direction.

(a) is a hand made *common dovetail* used in high quality joinery, particularly in joints between the sides and backs of drawers.

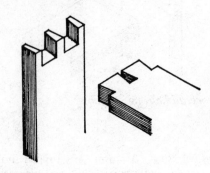

(a) Common dovetail

(b) shows a hand made stopped (and lapped) dovetail joint suitable for joints between the sides and front of drawers. It is hand made and would be used for high quality work only.

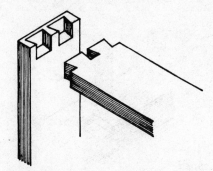

(b)   Stopped or lapped-handwrot dovetail

(c) In this typical version, a special machine cuts tails and sockets together in timber up to about 225 mm wide. All machine cut dovetails are stopped and lapped.

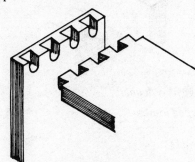

(c)   Stopped and lapped – machine made dovetail

20   Dovetail joints

Other examples of dovetails shown in this chapter are: the hammer head key joint, the lindermann joint, square and face housing joints and a mitre with secret dovetail.

Lapped joints

This principle is used in various forms, including the dovetailed joints figure 20(b) and (c).

(a) *Rebated*   A lapped joint which allows the joining of two pieces of timber at right angles and at the same time conceals the end grain on one face. As with all lapped conditions the joint is secured by pinning or screwing and gluing.

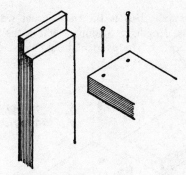

(a)   Rebated joint

(b) *Lapped and tongued*   A joint commonly used between head and jamb of a door lining, it is stronger than the rebated joint but does not conceal the end grain.

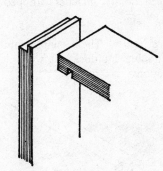

(b)   Lapped and tongued joint

(c) *Rebated and tongued*   This joint is not much used, although it combines the merits of rebated and lapped, and tongued joints

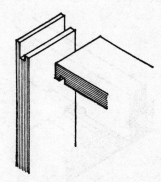

(c)   Rebated and tongued joint

(d) *Half lapped* This is the most usual way of extending the lengths of members where the joint is fully supported. The overlap should be screwed and glued.

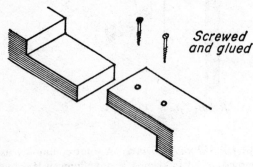

Screwed and glued

(*d*) *Half lapped*

Other lapped joints includes stopped dovetails and lapped mitres.

(e) *Notched joints* These simple joints provide single or double interlocks between lapped rectangular sections.

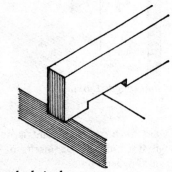

(*i*) *Notched single*

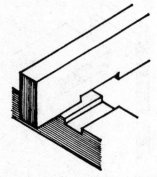

(*ii*) *Notched double*

(f) *Cogged joints* are similar to notched joints and are used in the same circumstances. For joinery, notched and cogged joints would normally be glued while for carpentry they would probably be nailed.

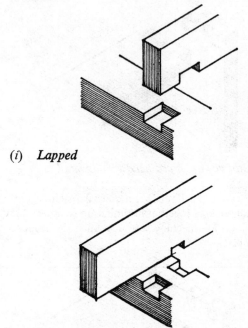

(*i*) *Lapped*

(*ii*) *Cogged – double*

21 *Lapped joints*

Mitred joints

Mitres conceal end grain, the grain runs continuously around the exposed faces and the appearance is symetrical. They are used to connect boards at their edges.

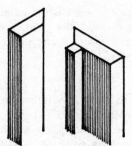

(*a*) *Mitred-plain*

(a) is a plain mitred joint strengthened with a square block screwed to the boards.

50

(b) *Lapped*   A mitred joint which gives a greater gluing area for increased strength. The shoulders ensure a 90° angle.

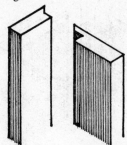

(b)   *Mitre-lapped*

(c) *Mitre with loose tongue*   The tongue, preferably of plywood, locates and strengthens the joint. The groove can be stopped so the tongue is not seen on the surface, although this involves hand work. To ensure a tight fit, the tongue is slightly narrower than the combined width of the grooves.

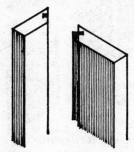

(c)   *Mitre with loose tongue*

(d) *Mitre with secret dovetail*   This mitred joint has the added strength provided by a secret dovetail, but it cannot be cut by machine.

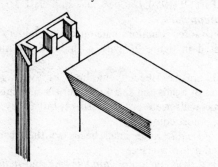

(d) *Mitred dovetail*
22   *Mitred joints*

Finger joint

(a) *The finger joint*   This is a strong end-end joint which can reduce waste of costly timber, by joining short pieces together. The proportions of the fingers vary according to the stresses expected — see BS 1186: Part 2.

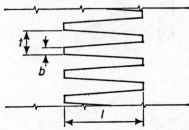

l = Finger length
t = Distance between fingers
b = Width of the finger tip

23   *Finger joint (BS 1186)*

2 INSERTS

These joints employ wood or metal connecting devices such as dowels, loose tongues, nails, screws and bolts either as primary fixings, to reinforce interlocking or glued joints, or to retain members while glue is setting.

Dowelled

Holes for dowels do not weaken timber sections as much as mortices, and properly glued hardwood dowels provide sound joints which usefully reduce the effective length of one member in a joint. The necessary true alignment of dowels and holes is difficult to achieve by hand.

Dowels, with grooves which allow surplus glue to escape, should project about 25 mm, and be a 'push fit' into holes which are very slightly larger in diameter and about 4 mm deeper than dowels, so the shoulders of the joint fit tightly. To help fitting joints, the ends of dowels can be chamfered, although this involves hand work. Shoulders of dowelled joints should also be adequately glued.

(a) and (b) show typical dowelled joints. The dowels are at about 150 mm centres along the edge-edge joint.

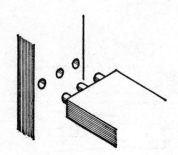

(a)

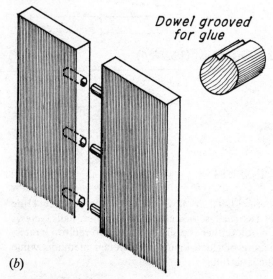

Dowel grooved for glue

(b)

24 *Dowelled joints*

Loose tongue

(a) *Loose tongue* Both pieces of timber forming the joint are grooved and a so called hardwood or preferably a plywood 'loose' tongue is glued in place on one side of the joint to strengthen it. The whole of the joint is then glued and 'cramped up' until the glue is set. This joint is commonly used in table and bench tops.

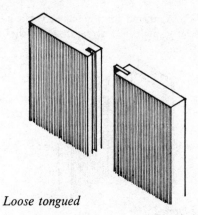

(a) Loose tongued

(b) shows a joint between two members which are sufficiently thick for two rows of dowels as well as a plywood loose tongue. The latter is more easily inserted after the joint has been assembled.

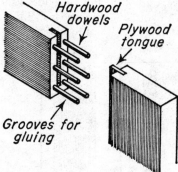

Hardwood dowels

Plywood tongue

Grooves for gluing

(b) Loose tongue with dowels

25 *Loose tongue joints*

Nails and pins

Nails are described in BS 1202: Part 1: 1974 *Steel nails,* Part 2: 1974 *Copper nails* and Part 3: 1974 *Aluminium nails.*

The more common nails used in joinery are illustrated in figure 26 with a guide to the metric sizes.

Nails are described by methods of forming and by types of heads and shanks, materials and finishes.

Some nails were cut from sheet, but today wire nails are most common.

Lost-head nails have small heads so they can be punched below surfaces.

Improved nails, including *annular ring* and *helically threaded* types, resist withdrawal better than round wire nails.

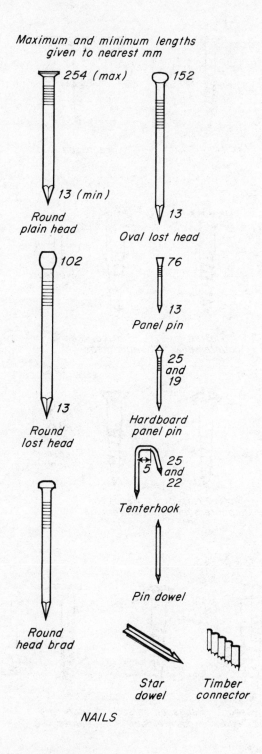

Maximum and minimum lengths given to nearest mm

254 (max)

152

13 (min)

Round plain head

13

Oval lost head

102

76

13

Panel pin

13

Round lost head

25 and 19

Hardboard panel pin

5

25 and 22

Tenterhook

Pin dowel

Round head brad

Star dowel

Timber connector

NAILS

26   Nails and pins

Automatic nails   These nails, which are often resin coated to improve withdrawal resistance, are provided in strips or coils for use in pneumatic guns or manual nailing machines.

Nail heads, in timber which is to be painted or to receive clear treatment, are usually punched below the surface and the hole is filled with proprietary filler. Where a surface is to have a clear finish the filler should be of matching colour.

Externally, steel nails should be zinc coated, but they should be well punched in, as the coating may be damaged. *Panel pins* are used for purposes such as securing sheet materials until non-contact adhesives have set. *Timber connectors* are often called *corrugated wedge fasteners*.

Wood screws
Screws are made in plain, sherardized or galvanized steel, or where corrosion is likely and/or where the screw head will be seen, stainless steel, brass or even bronze screws may be used – the latter metals, however, being less strong than steel.
Screw heads include:
  countersunk   the heads are shaped to fit 'flush' in counter-sinkings in wood, or in metal components such as butt hinges.
  countersunk and raised   the raised heads reduce the danger of damaging surrounding surfaces in driving the screws.
  round   particularly suitable for fixing metals which are too thin to countersink.
  mirror   for fixing glass and other panels, the slots being concealed by screw-on or snap-on domes.
  square   for heavy duty *coach screws*, usually 6 mm diameter or larger, driven with a spanner.
Driving profiles are:
  slot   the standard type
  clutch   the profile prevents removal
  recessed   the *Phillips* and *Pozidriv* heads allow greater purchase to be applied in driving and the specially designed screwdrivers are less likely to slip. Recessed head screws are particularly suitable for mechanical driving.
Thread patterns are:
  single spiral   these traditional screws have two thirds of their length tapered and threaded
  double spiral   twin parallel threads on cylindrical shanks have greater holding power, and they extend over a greater proportion of the length of the screw.

JOINERY

For access panels, glazing beads and similar removable items round or raised head, slotted or recessed heads are appropriate, and brass or other metal, or plastics cups allow screws to be withdrawn and re-driven without damaging the surrounding wood, see figure 27.

Where screw heads are to be concealed, they may be recessed below the surface and the hole filled with a proprietary filler. If the surface is to be clear finished, a *pellet* of the same timber with the direction of the grain following that of the surrounding timber may be glued in, providing a virtually 'secret', but permanent, fixing.

Screws are described in BS 1201:1963 *Wood Screws* and figure 27 shows examples. Approximate sizes of screw gauges are:

Screw gauge	Nominal diameter of screw and unthreaded shank
	mm
0	1.52
1	1.78
2	2.08
3	2.39
4	2.74
5	3.10
6	3.45
7	3.81
8	4.17
9	4.52
10	4.88
12	5.59
14	6.30
16	7.01
18	7.72
20	8.43
24	9.86
28	11.28
32	12.70

Table 10   Screw gauges

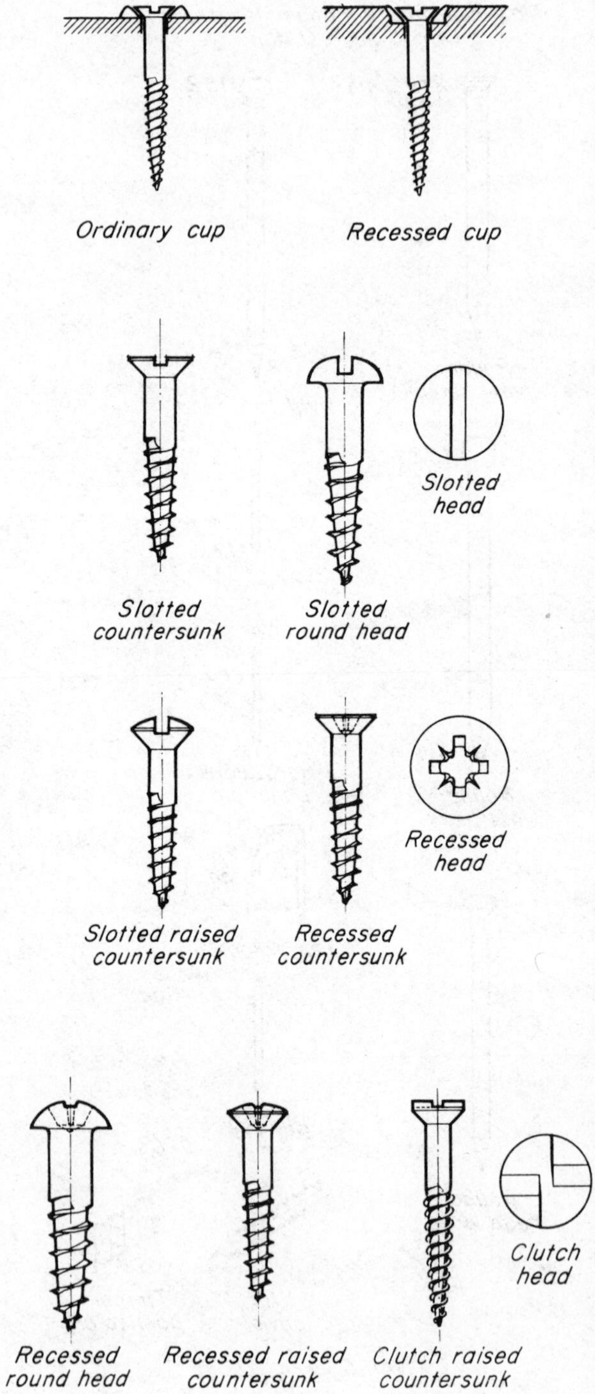

27   *Wood screws and cups*

54

Turn-button Turn-buttons of wood or metal illustrated in figure 43, page 66, are used to fix tops to tables and benches while allowing moisture movement to take place in one direction without attendant distortion or cracking of the tops or frames. In addition, tops can be removed if repolishing or renewal is required.

Slotted angle This method, see figure 45, page 68, also allows movement in one direction but tops cannot be removed so easily.

Slot screw Uses for this joint include joining board edges to form table tops, fixing panelling to framing and hanging cupboards on walls.

A projecting screw on one member is inserted in the circular hole of a 'keyhole' cut in a plate which is fixed to a second member. The members are slid so the screw passes along the slot in the 'keyhole'. The plate then holds the screw head securely, and 'secretly', although, as glue is not used the joint is demountable.

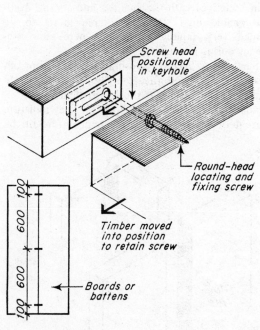

28   *Keyhole joint*

Bolts with suitable washers are used for heavy-duty work.

Handrail bolt This joint secures the ends of timber to make up a continuous handrail. A bolt threaded at both ends when tightened produces a very strong joint which is difficult to detect in use. The slots on the underside of the timber are filled with matching timber and cleaned off smooth.

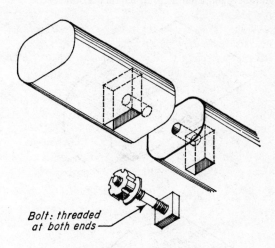

29   *Handrail bolt*

3   DEMOUNTABLE CONNECTORS

These enable preformed members to be rapidly located and joined. In addition to angle plates which allow moisture movement (figure 45) and 'keyhole plates' which allow dismantling (figure 28), connectors include the following types:

Corner plates — with slots shaped so they draw parts together.

Two-part components — which clip together, but which can be dismantled, others which draw parts together by a cam action, and plates fixed to table tops with wood screws, threaded for metal screws in the tops of table legs.

Figure 30 shows a two-part plastics connector which holds members, usually boards, rigidly at right angles without the need for a housing or other framed joint, or for glue. If required, these joints are easily 'knocked down', although in fact, their chief use is for rapid assembly of furniture components by purchasers.

Using a template, the two members to be joined are each marked with two positions for screws. (a) shows the smaller part of the connector, with a nut placed in a recess in its upper surface, screwed to a horizontal board. (b) shows the larger part of the connector screwed to a vertical member, locked over the smaller part already fixed on the horizontal member, and then secured to it by a bolt.

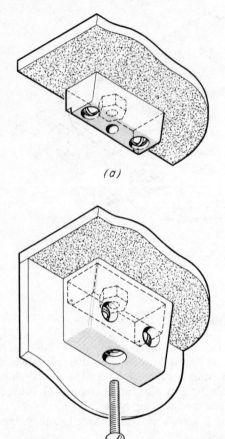

(a)

(b)

30   Connector[1]

4   ADHESIVES

References
MBC: Materials chapter 13
BRE Digest 175 *Choice of glues for wood*
BRE Digests 211 and 212 *Site uses of adhesives*
Requirements and properties of adhesives for wood,
PRL Bulletin 20: 1971 HMSO

[1]   Plasplugs Ltd., Burton-on-Trent, Staffordshire, (Patent no. 1912/73)

There is an extremely wide range of adhesives available, having very different properties, suitable uses, and requirements for their use.

Adhesives must be suited to both the substrate and adherend, eg, in relation to their perviousness. Resins and oils in timber and preservative and fire retardant salts can present problems in adhesion. Some adhesives stain wood, and synthetic resin adhesives tend to blunt cutting tools.

It is interesting to note that BRE Digest 212 has a checklist of thirty-four items! Manufacturers' recommendations should be followed.

The need to prepare surfaces so they are dry and clean and matched to give a thin *glue line*, for controlled curing conditions, and with the exception of light duty contact adhesives the need to clamp members together until the adhesive has set, limits the use of adhesives on the building site to work such as applying plastics laminates to existing surfaces. In workshops PVA and casein adhesives which are clean and easy to use have supplanted animal glues. In factories one or two part synthetic resin adhesives with the facilities and control available enable high strength durable joints to be formed very rapidly especially where radio frequency curing is used.

Surfaces to receive glue must be free from oil, grease or dust, and the glue film must be evenly applied. The manufacturer's particular recommendations should be followed. The moisture content of the timber and the temperature of the

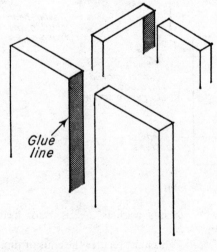

Glue line

31   Butt joints

room and of the glue are of paramount importance. To attempt to joint wet timber in a cold damp workshop is to invite failure.

Correct application and mixing of the catalyst glues are also vital, as is the observation of the correct procedure in bringing the pieces into perfect contact and cramping up.

Figure 31 shows simple *butt* or *rubbed* joints. Table 11 shows adhesives which are suitable for five exposure categories.

The description 'WBP' applied to plywood refers only to the bonding agent and although the adhesive is suitable for hazardous exposures, for equivalent durability the timber must either be heartwood of a durable species or be treated with a compatible preservative.

JOINERS' SHOP PRODUCTION

In addition to mass-production joinery factories, joinery workshops are run by specialist firms and by contractors. Specialist firms and the larger contractors maintain substantial timber stocks, and in some cases drying kilns. Some firms specialize in very high quality work for prestige buildings. In such workshops timber is thicknessed, planed, moulded, sanded, and the joints are cut by machine. The parts will then be fitted together, wedged, glued, cramped and finished by hand.

A typical sequence of operations in the manufacture of timber components in a well-equipped joiner's shop will be as follows: The shop foreman 'takes off' the quantities of timber required for a

Category	Examples of exposure	Recommended adhesives	Durability of adhesive
Exterior high hazard	full exposure to weather	RF RF/PF PF (cold setting)	WBP WBP WBP
low hazard	inside roofs of porches	RF, RF/PF, PF MF/UF	WBP BR
Interior high hazard	laundries	RF, RF/PF, PF MF/UF	WBP BR
low hazard	inside dwelling houses, heated buildings, halls and churches	RF, RF/PF, PF MF/UF UF Casein	WBP BR —
Chemically polluted atmospheres	swimming baths	RF, RF/PF, PF	WBP

Key MF melamine-formaldehyde
     PF phenol-formaldehyde
     RF resorcinol-formaldehyde
     UF urea-formaldehyde
     WBP weather and boil proof
     BR boil resistant
     MR moisture resistant and moderately weather resistant
     INT interior

Table 11 Adhesives for exposures (Information from BRE Digest 175)

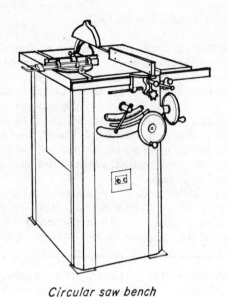

Circular saw bench

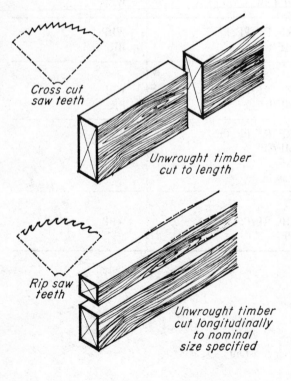

Cross cut saw teeth

Unwrought timber cut to length

Rip saw teeth

Unwrought timber cut longitudinally to nominal size specified

32   Sawing

component, from the architect's large scale working details or from the workshop setting out rod, and from these quantities prepares a cutting list. The information contained in the cutting list for each project is used when choosing the timber required from the storage racks. The amount of timber used will be set down on a *cost/value sheet*.

MACHINING

The basic processes are illustrated in figures 32-41.

(a) The timber is first cut to length by means of a *circular cross cut saw*. Then a *circular rip saw* is used to cut the timber to width and thickness. The timber is cut 'oversize', allowance being made at this stage for planing the finished timber, say 3 mm on each face. The *Standard Method of Measurement* allows a maximum of 3 mm. The sawn timber than passes to the *surface planer* to provide a true *face* and *edge*, and to remove any twist or irregularity. The timber then passes to a *thicknesser* which reduces the timber to the right size.

(b) The *surface planer* and a *thicknesser* is often combined as one machine as illustrated.

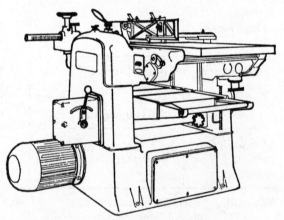

Combined planer and thicknesser

At this stage the timber goes either to the site for fabrication, or to the setting-out bench for further machining.

The setting out is done by the shop foreman, who draws the vertical and horizontal sections of the components full size on a plywood sheet or

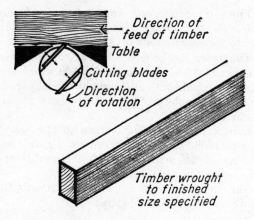

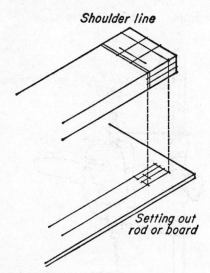

Direction of
feed of timber

Table

Cutting blades

Direction
of rotation

Timber wrought
to finished
size specified

33   Planing and thicknessing

Shoulder line

Setting out
rod or board

34   Setting-out

marked on the timber from the setting-out rod. Since proportions and types of joints should be to accepted standards, it is not always necessary to specify setting out details of joints on working drawings.

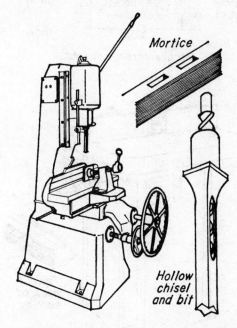

Mortice

Hollow
chisel
and bit

35   Mortising machine

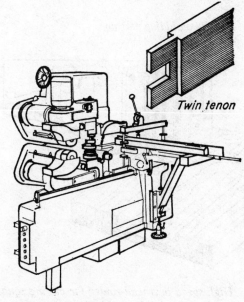

Twin tenon

36   Tenoning machine

setting-out board, say 225 mm wide x 12 mm thick. This board is also known as a *setting-out rod*.

As an alternative to drawing direct on to plywood, full size drawings can be prepared in negative form on transparent material such as tracing paper. This has the advantage that prints can be taken to provide a record of the work.

The setting-out rods, being full-size working drawings conventionalized by the shop foreman, go to the marker out, who transfers the relevant lines on to the timber. The dimensions from the setting-out rod can also be used by the shop foreman to produce the cutting list.

Lines of joints, and cuts with depths and type are

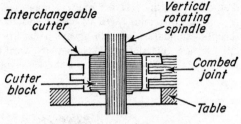

Interchangeable cutter

Vertical rotating spindle

Cutter block

Combed joint

Table

Section through cutter

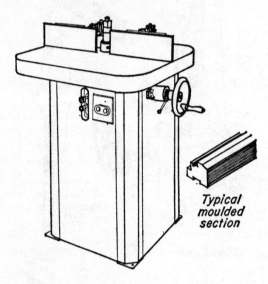

37 Spindle moulding machine

Typical moulded section

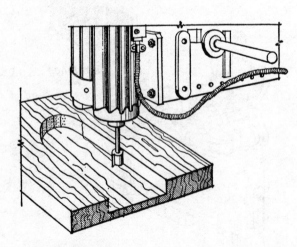

38 High speed overhead router for cutting square or curved housings

From the *setting-out bench* (34) the timber travels to the *morticer* (35) or the *tenoner* (36), then to the *spindle moulder* (37).

The timber can be rebated, moulded, grooved or chamfered on the spindle moulder. Standard profiles are available but cutters can be specially made to any reasonable profiles, and circular work can be carried out.

Surface planer, thicknesser and spindle moulding operations can be combined on a *planer and moulder*. If this machine is used, the mortice and tenon operations are carried out later.

The following machines are ancillary to the main production line machinery.

Router for recessing to any profile as shown in figure 38.

Boring machine for drilling holes in series.

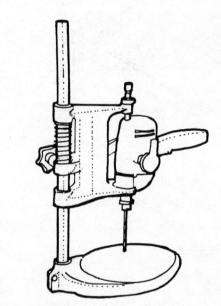

(a) Drill and stand

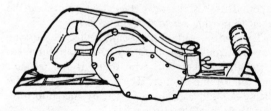

(b) Planer

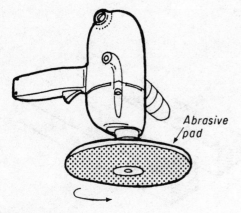

(c) *Disc sander*

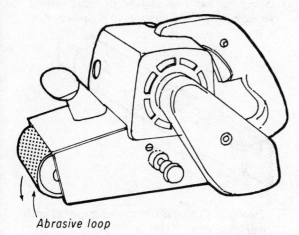

Abrasive loop

(d) *Orbital sander*

Reciprocating action abrasive pad

(e) *Reciprocal sander*
39 *Portable electric power tools*

Dovetail machine for fabrication of dovetail joints, mainly used for drawer construction. It cuts front and sides together.
Panel saw (or dimension saw) for cutting sheet materials, such as hardboard, plywood, etc, to size.
Band saw for cutting circular work.

Sanding machines
(a)*Belt sander,* which consists of a belt of abrasive sheet under which the timber is passed.
(b) *Drum sander,* which consists of a number of drums covered with abrasive sheet over (or under) which the timber passes, on a moving bed.

After machining, the timber passes forward for fabrication. Portable power tools, such as a planer, drill and hand sanding machines — disc or orbital — will be used during this part of the work. See figures 39(a)-(e).

FACTORY PRODUCTION

Large firms mass-produce windows, doors and door sets, cupboard fittings, staircases and sections such as skirtings and architraves. Machinery is similar to that used in joiners' shops, but handwork is almost eliminated and production is large and rapid. There is likely to be an increasing demand for fully finished components, glazed, painted and complete with locks, hinges and fastenings.

The main processes of production are briefly: Timber, bought up to twelve months in advance, requires a large storage area. Scantlings are sorted automatically into equal lengths, and after selection for quality, into 'sets' of say 160 pieces of 100 mm x 50 mm. These are stacked under cover for further air drying and then kiln drying takes from 2 to 18 days according to the species and sizes, with careful control of temperature and humidity throughout. Sawn sections of the appropriate sizes are cut to lengths to make the most economic use of the scantlings available.

Figure 40 (a)-(c) shows the processes for machining the sills and jambs of windows:
(a) The cut lengths passed on a conveyor, are planed to size and the initial cuts are made to form the required profile. Sill and jamb sections then go on separate lines.
(b) Mortice slots are cut in sills, and tenons are formed on the ends of jambs.
(c) A moulder completes the cutting of the profile,

Sill section → 　　　　　　Jamb section →

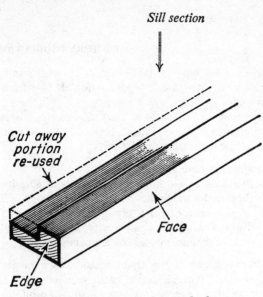

Cut away portion re-used

Face

Edge

(a) Planer and moulder to face and edge

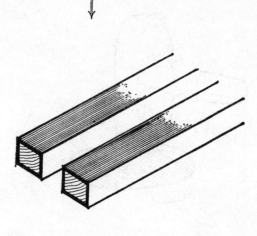

(a) Scantling, cut into section size and passed through planer and moulder to face and edge

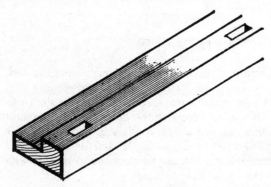

(b) Morticer – cuts mortice slots as required

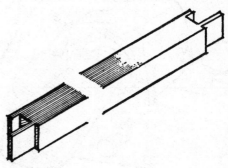

(b) Double end tenon cutter shapes tenons at each end of section

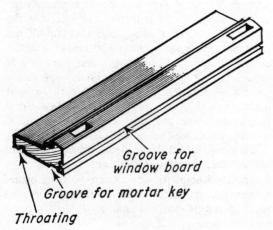

Groove for window board

Groove for mortar key

Throating

(c) Moulder – completes sill profile

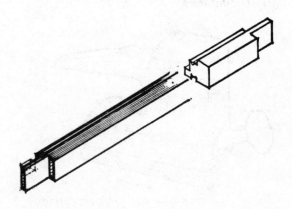

(c) Moulder completes jamb profile

40　Machine fabrication of sill and jamb sections

with grooves, throats and chamfers, as required. Sections are batched so as to minimise the changing of cutters. The maintenance and repair of woodworking machinery and the sharpening of cutters is done, wherever possible automatically, in a separate workshop.

Random lengths of moulded sections can be cut to non-standard lengths to form 'special' windows, which being out of the main production line are more expensive, although not always prohibitively so.

Sections for external joinery may be vacuum impregnated with preservative before assembly. See *MBS: Materials* chapter 2.

In addition to random checks, parts are inspected at several stages.
1 Length sorting
2 Cross cutting
3 Cleaning off
Finishing moulder

Figure 41 (a)-(k) shows stages in the manufacture of the standard window shown in figure 42.

The frames, sashes or casements and vents, are fabricated separately.

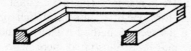

(a) The timber sections are machined to form rebates to receive the glass, and then cut to length. The ends of the top rails, stiles and bottom rails of the casement are then machined to form combed joints. The loosely assembled casement is placed in a jig with a cramping device which squares and lines up the joints, glues them with synthetic resin glue and automatically drives a pin or star dowel at the corners.

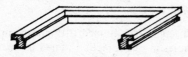

(b) The assembled casement is passed through a *drum sander* and then through a *moulder* which profiles the outer edges.

(c) Recesses are cut for cadmium plated hinges. The hinge consists of two interlocking cranked portions, and a separate pin, The single knuckle part of the hinge is dropped in place in the recess and machine screwed into position by zinc plated screws.

The casement is dipped in preservative. The vacuum process cannot, in this instance, be used since the face profile is cut after assembly.

(d) The double knuckle part of the hinge is screwed into position on the jambs of the frame.

(c) The transomes are fitted into the jambs to form H frames, which are then glued.

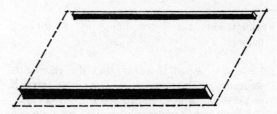

(f) The head and sill are placed in position on an automatic cramp bed.

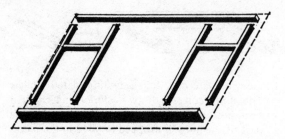

(g) The H frame is set down, on the cramp bed, the joints between the H frame and the head and sill being open and spaced slightly apart.

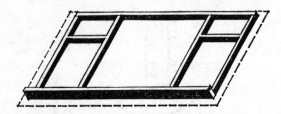

(h) The tenons are glued from a hand dispenser and the frame is cramped up.

(i) The component is passed through a drum sander.

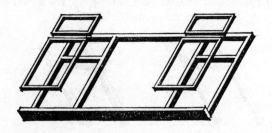

(j) Pre-assembled casements are placed in position on the frame.

(k) Hinge pins are driven home by a vibrating hammer.

(l) Knots are sealed (*knotted*) and the casements wedged open by metal dogs. The whole frame is immersed in primer and passed through a dryer. Casements are temporarily secured by plywood battens and the windows are stacked before delivery.

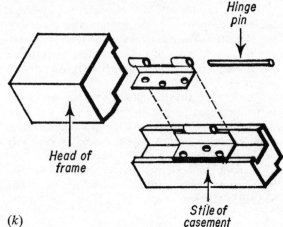

Hinge pin

Head of frame

Stile of casement

(k)

41 *Manufacture of standard window*

Figure 42 shows a typical standard timber window with the parts and joints named.

JOINERY FITTINGS

Fittings such as benches and cupboards can either be made mainly from suitably thick boards which provide general solidity and make for easily formed joints, or with frames infilled with, or covered with, relatively thin sheets. The first method may be economical for 'one-offs' but for batch or mass production the second method is likely to be more economic and it is illustrated here with three-dimensional drawings which, incidentally, are best able to show the implications of three way intersections between members.

Fittings should be designed so as much fabrication as possible can be carried out in the joiner's shop and site labour and time in fitting is minimised.

In public buildings special consideration must be given to wear on table tops and the effect of kicks and floor cleaning operations on bases to fittings, for which timber is not always a suitable finish.

Cupboard units

It is best to consider a framed fitting as comprising vertical frames in one direction joined by members in the other direction. Thus, figure 43 shows front and back frames joined by cross members. These frames stand on a base, part of which is infilled to form the bottom of a cupboard. A top of cross-

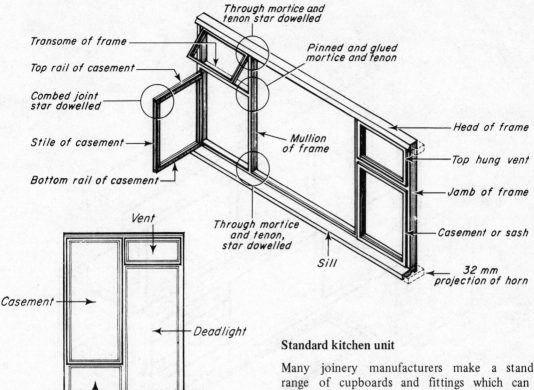

Through mortice and
tenon star dowelled

Transome of frame

Pinned and glued
mortice and tenon

Top rail of casement

Combed joint
star dowelled

Head of frame

Stile of casement

Mullion
of frame

Top hung vent

Bottom rail of casement

Jamb of frame

Casement or sash

Through mortice
and tenon,
star dowelled

Sill

32 mm
projection of horn

Vent

Casement

Deadlight

Sublight

42   Standard casement windows

tongued boards or veneered blockboard would be
fixed, either with 'buttons', or with screws in
slotted angles — methods of fixing which allow
differential movement. Buttons also permit easy
removal and replacement of the top. Ends and
vertical divisions are formed by panels with stiles
and rails either infilled with plywood or covered
with plywood to give a 'flush' appearance.

Figure 44 shows (1) cross section frames to
receive longitudinal rails and drawer sides, (2)
separate units below a top.

A further method shown in figure 45 is to make
the fittings with solid ends and panels, out of 19
mm or 25 mm nominal blockboard with edges
lipped by machine or veneered, with a thin plywood
back for bracing. A light framework is made for the
front and back. The cupboard units to be fitted complete with all furniture in the joiner's shop.

Standard kitchen unit

Many joinery manufacturers make a standard
range of cupboards and fittings which can be
supplied from stock for kitchen units. The British
Woodwork Manufacturers issue standards for this
type of fitting which is manufactured under licence.
A typical fitting is shown in figure 46.

Cupboard fitting

The cupboard and drawer fitting shown in figure
47 is a single item of joinery for fixing *in situ* after
fabrication in the joiner's shop. It is built up of
blockboards with all exposed edges lipped and
cupboards and door faces of a veneered blockboard. The blockboard horizontal members would
be housed and glued to the side panels.

Counter fitting

The counter with glass screen shown in figure 48
is an example of a basic framework built out of
75 x 50 mm softwood and covered with 18 mm
plywood. The top is also of 18 mm plywood veneered with plastics sheet. The framing of small
members under the counter will give support to the
hardwood nosing which itself helps to stiffen the
construction.

65

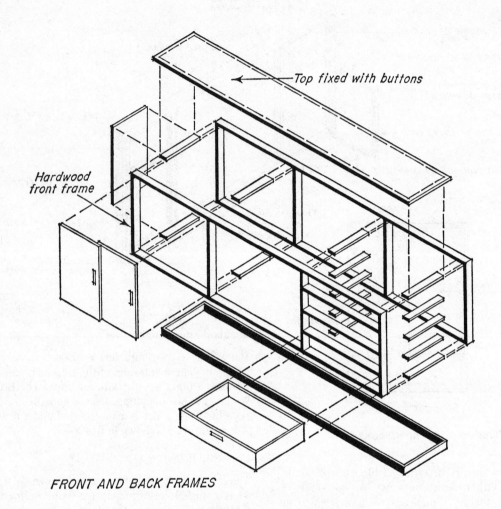

Top fixed with buttons

Hardwood
front frame

FRONT AND BACK FRAMES

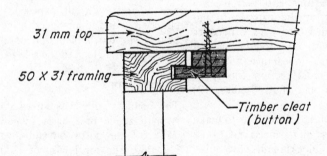

31 mm top

50 X 31 framing

Timber cleat
(button)

BUTTON FIXING

43   Cupboard units – with front and back frames

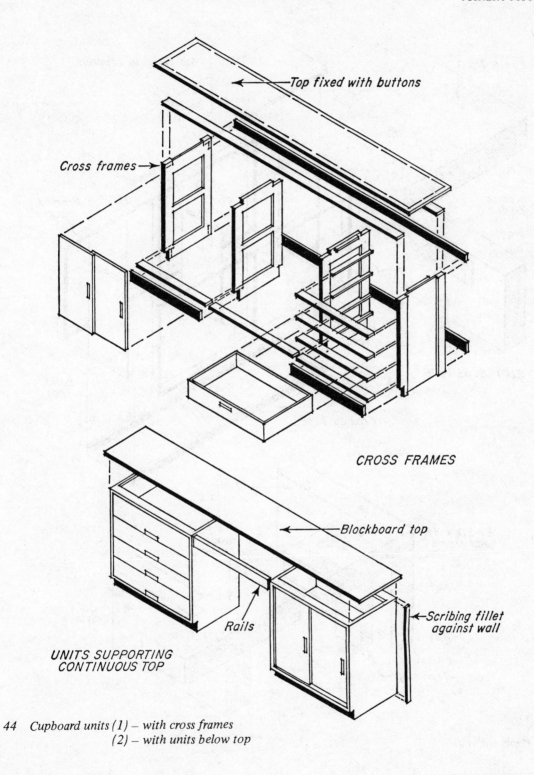

Top fixed with buttons

Cross frames →

CROSS FRAMES

Blockboard top

Rails

Scribing fillet against wall

UNITS SUPPORTING
CONTINUOUS TOP

44   Cupboard units (1) – with cross frames
        (2) – with units below top

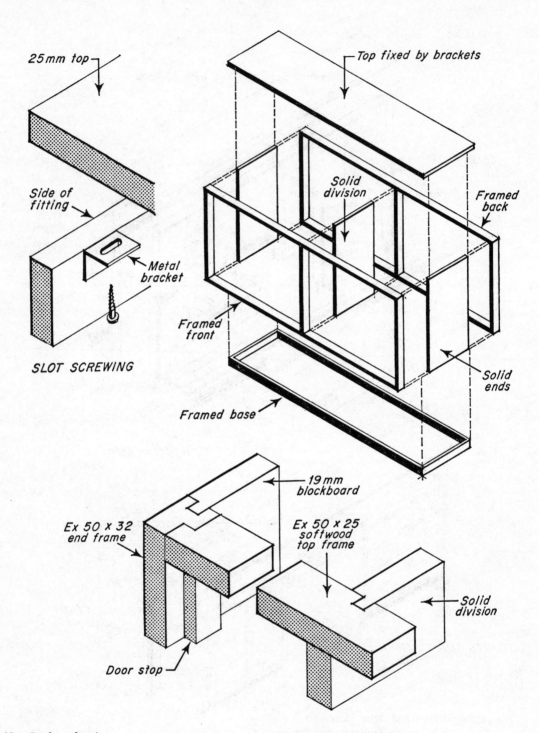

25mm top

Side of fitting

Metal bracket

SLOT SCREWING

Top fixed by brackets

Solid division

Framed back

Framed front

Solid ends

Framed base

19 mm blockboard

Ex 50 x 32 end frame

Ex 50 x 25 softwood top frame

Solid division

Door stop

45   Cupboard units

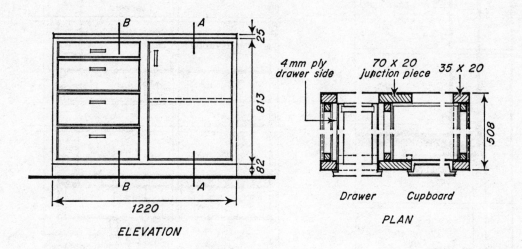

B   A

25

813

82

B   B   A   A

1220

ELEVATION

4 mm ply
drawer side

70 X 20
junction piece

35 X 20

508

Drawer   Cupboard

PLAN

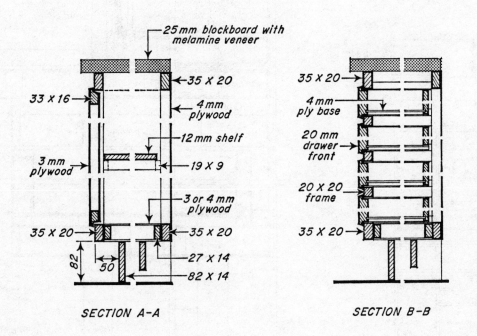

25 mm blockboard with
melamine veneer

35 X 20

33 X 16

4 mm
plywood

12 mm shelf

3 mm
plywood

19 X 9

3 or 4 mm
plywood

35 X 20

35 X 20

82

27 X 14

50

82 X 14

SECTION A-A

35 X 20

4 mm
ply base

20 mm
drawer
front

20 X 20
frame

35 X 20

SECTION B-B

46   Standard kitchen cupboard unit

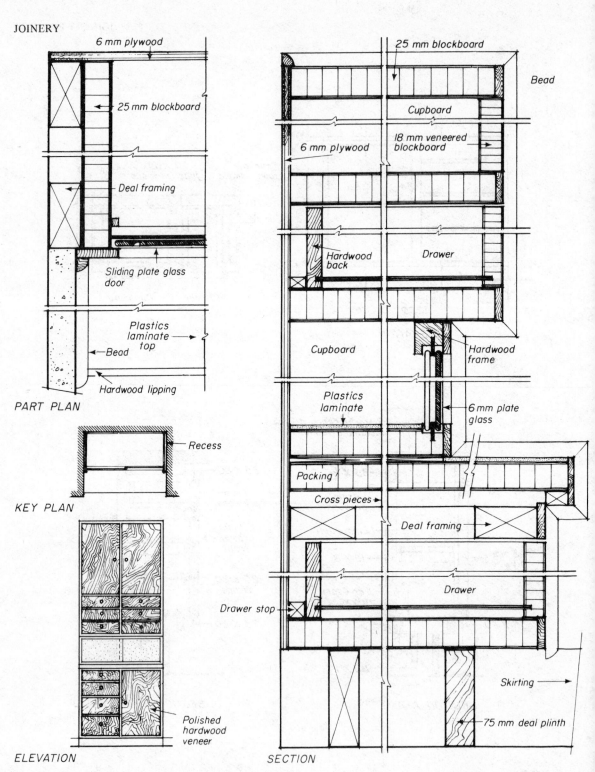

6 mm plywood

25 mm blockboard

Deal framing

Sliding plate glass door

Plastics laminate top

Bead

Hardwood lipping

PART PLAN

Recess

KEY PLAN

Polished hardwood veneer

ELEVATION

25 mm blockboard

Bead

Cupboard

18 mm veneered blockboard

6 mm plywood

Hardwood back

Drawer

Cupboard

Hardwood frame

Plastics laminate

6 mm plate glass

Packing

Cross pieces

Deal framing

Drawer

Drawer stop

Drawer

Skirting

75 mm deal plinth

SECTION

47   Cupboard fitting

70

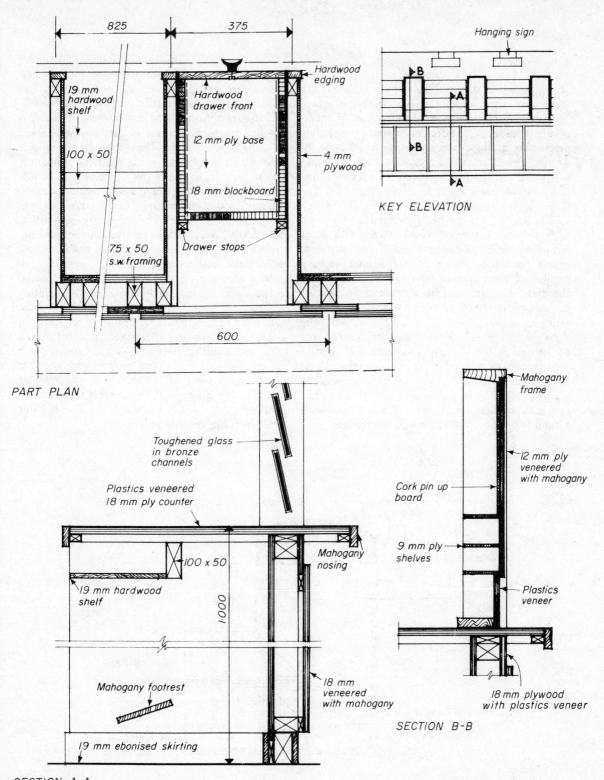

825

375

19 mm
hardwood
shelf

100 x 50

Hardwood
edging

Hardwood
drawer front

12 mm ply base

4 mm
plywood

18 mm blockboard

75 x 50
s.w. framing

Drawer stops

600

PART PLAN

Hanging sign

KEY ELEVATION

Toughened glass
in bronze
channels

Plastics veneered
18 mm ply counter

100 x 50

1·000

Mahogany
nosing

19 mm hardwood
shelf

Mahogany footrest

18 mm
veneered
with mahogany

19 mm ebonised skirting

SECTION A-A

48 Counter fitting

Mahogany
frame

12 mm ply
veneered
with mahogany

Cork pin up
board

9 mm ply
shelves

Plastics
veneer

18 mm plywood
with plastics veneer

SECTION B-B

Shop fronts

Shop fitting is a specialized trade with certain techniques which are not general joinery practice. The shop front details in figures 49 to 54 incorporate a variety of different materials including metals, to produce a comprehensive selection of details. The fascia is framed out of 50 x 50 mm soft wood and finished with 100 x 25 mm tongued and grooved and splayed hardwood boarding. The frame to the shop windows is of 100 x 50 mm hardwood, the glazing being secured in this case with internal hardwood beads fixed with brass screws in brass countersunk cups. The showcase frames shown in figure 54 are formed from a small steel angle screwed on a hardwood surround, the glass being retained by another angle finished in bronze and fixed reversed. Note how condensation is carried away by a groove in the sill. The sliding access panels behind the display are made of 19 mm softwood framing covered with perforated hardboard, and with hardwood edging. Metal angle guides hold the top and a fibre guide secured to the panel slides in a groove in the sill. The blind box is the normal wood framed box zinc lined with a blind lath in hardwood to match the fascia.

Metal members for window frames and similar parts, are often preferred to wood. Solid metal sections are expensive and not easy to joint but extruded aluminium sections are now commonly used for shopfronts. The appearance of metal is provided by brass, bronze or stainless steel sheet on moulded wood cores. The section drawn through a die which presses the metal onto the timber. A typical section is shown in figure 49. It is less expensive and lighter than a solid metal section, but rigid and comparatively easily jointed. There are limits, however, to the complexity of profiles, and clearly, very sharp external angles are not possible. Large sections may be built up by joining two or more smaller ones together.

Note that the edge of the metal strip is secured to the wood by turning it into a groove. Jointing of these metal-on-wood sections is done by mortice and tenon in the timber core, but on the external angles metal is mitred and brazed, soldered or just filled and polished over. The wood core at such angles is jointed by cutting back in each member and fitting a piece of timber across the mitre as shown in the diagram. If the metal is to be brazed a shielding strip should be behind the face and this would be set in the wood block.

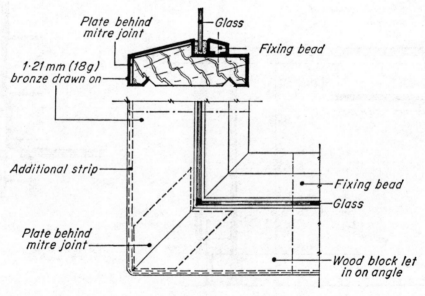

49 *Metal on wood sections*

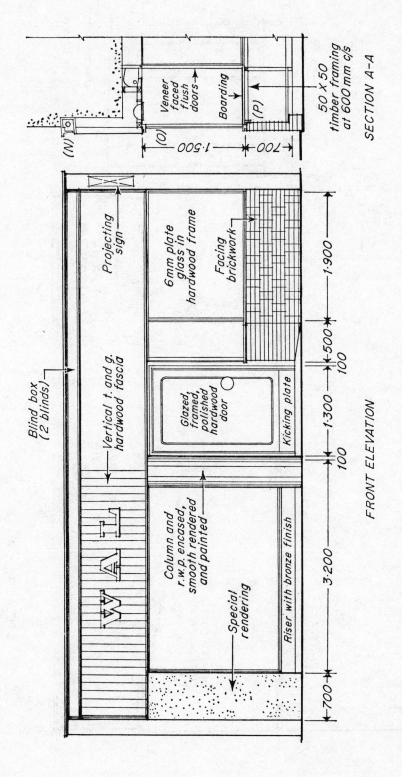

SECTION A-A

Veneer faced flush doors

Boarding

(N)

(O)

(P)

50 x 50 timber framing at 600 mm c/s

1·500

700

FRONT ELEVATION

Blind box (2 blinds)

Projecting sign

Vertical t. and g. hardwood fascia

6mm plate glass in hardwood frame

Facing brickwork

Glazed, framed, polished hardwood door

Kicking plate

WALL

Column and r.w.p. encased, smooth rendered and painted

Special rendering

Riser with bronze finish

1·900

500

100

1·300

100

3·200

700

50   Shopfront (1)

73

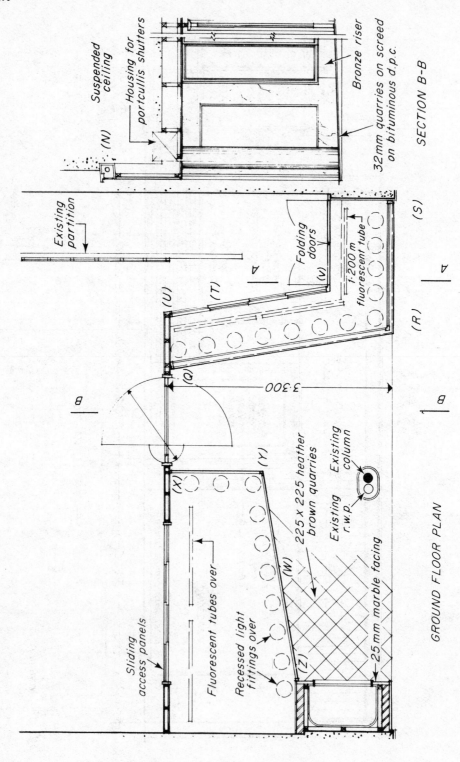

Suspended ceiling

Housing for portcullis shutters

(N)

Bronze riser

32 mm quarries on screed on bituminous d.p.c.

SECTION B-B

Existing partition

Folding doors

(U)

(T)

(V)

1·200 m fluorescent tube

(S)

A

(R)

A

B

(Q)

3·300

B

(X)

(Y)

225 x 225 heather brown quarries

Existing column

Existing r.w.p.

25 mm marble facing

Sliding access panels

Fluorescent tubes over

Recessed light fittings over

(W)

(Z)

GROUND FLOOR PLAN

51 Shopfront (2)

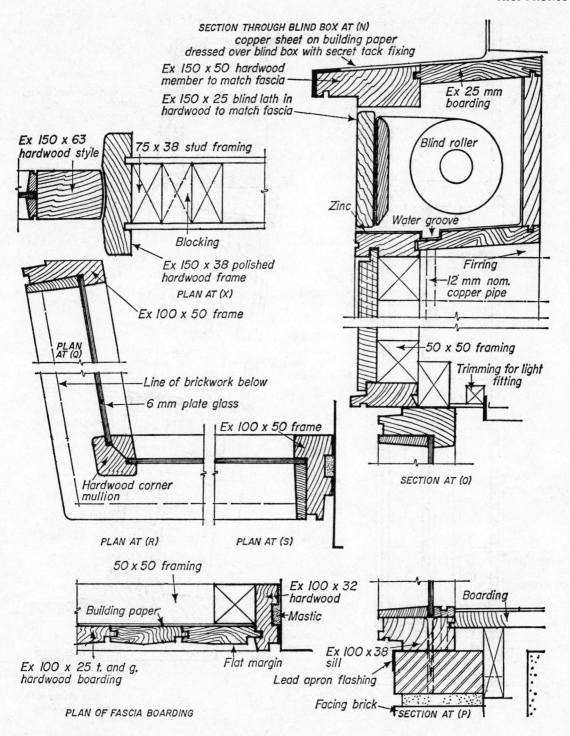

SECTION THROUGH BLIND BOX AT (N)
copper sheet on building paper
dressed over blind box with secret tack fixing

Ex 150 x 50 hardwood
member to match fascia

Ex 150 x 25 blind lath in
hardwood to match fascia

Ex 25 mm
boarding

Ex 150 x 63
hardwood style

75 x 38 stud framing

Blind roller

Blocking

Zinc

Water groove

Ex 150 x 38 polished
hardwood frame

PLAN AT (X)

Ex 100 x 50 frame

Firring

12 mm nom.
copper pipe

PLAN
AT (Q)

Line of brickwork below

6 mm plate glass

50 x 50 framing

Trimming for light
fitting

Ex 100 x 50 frame

Hardwood corner
mullion

PLAN AT (R)   PLAN AT (S)

SECTION AT (0)

50 x 50 framing

Ex 100 x 32
hardwood

Boarding

Building paper

Mastic

Ex 100 x 25 t. and g.
hardwood boarding

Flat margin

Ex 100 x 38
sill

Lead apron flashing

Facing brick

SECTION AT (P)

PLAN OF FASCIA BOARDING

52 Shopfront (3) – details

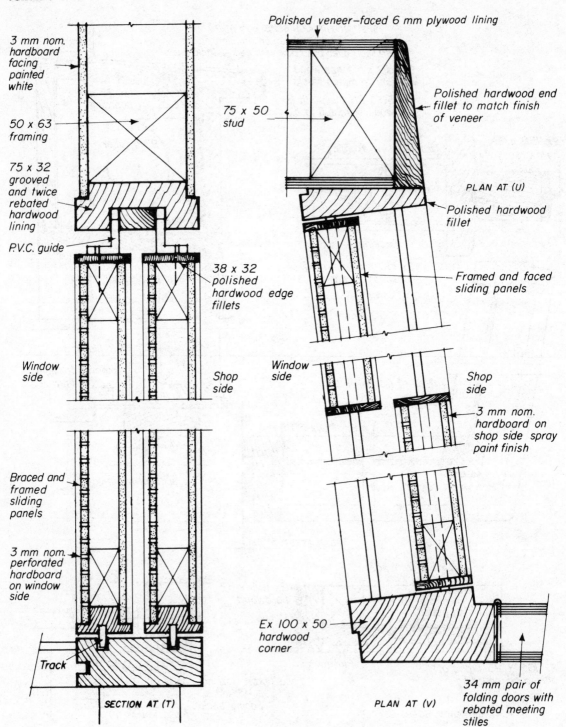

3 mm nom. hardboard facing painted white

50 x 63 framing

75 x 32 grooved and twice rebated hardwood lining

P.V.C. guide

38 x 32 polished hardwood edge fillets

Window side

Shop side

Braced and framed sliding panels

3 mm nom. perforated hardboard on window side

Track

SECTION AT (T)

Polished veneer-faced 6 mm plywood lining

75 x 50 stud

Polished hardwood end fillet to match finish of veneer

PLAN AT (U)

Polished hardwood fillet

Framed and faced sliding panels

Window side

Shop side

3 mm nom. hardboard on shop side spray paint finish

Ex 100 x 50 hardwood corner

PLAN AT (V)

34 mm pair of folding doors with rebated meeting stiles

53   Showcase details (1)

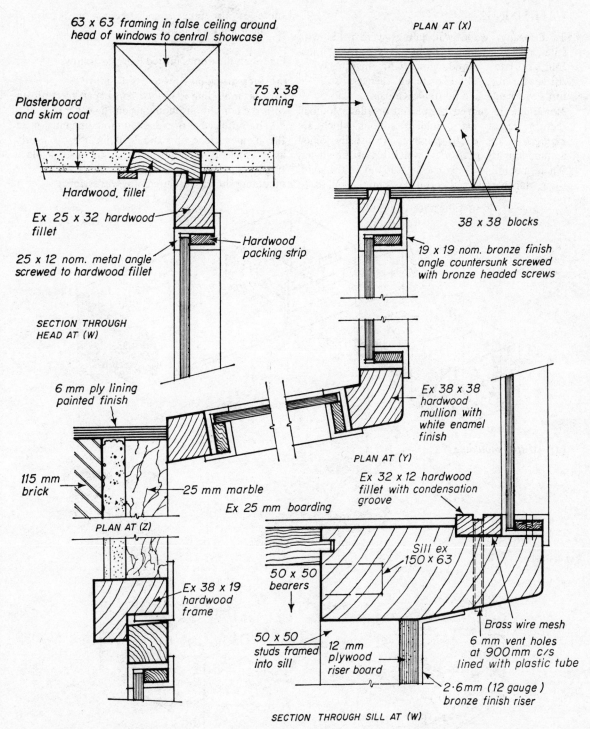

63 x 63 framing in false ceiling around head of windows to central showcase

PLAN AT (X)

75 x 38 framing

Plasterboard and skim coat

Hardwood, fillet

Ex 25 x 32 hardwood fillet

Hardwood packing strip

25 x 12 nom. metal angle screwed to hardwood fillet

38 x 38 blocks

19 x 19 nom. bronze finish angle countersunk screwed with bronze headed screws

SECTION THROUGH HEAD AT (W)

6 mm ply lining painted finish

Ex 38 x 38 hardwood mullion with white enamel finish

PLAN AT (Y)

115 mm brick

25 mm marble

Ex 25 mm boarding

Ex 32 x 12 hardwood fillet with condensation groove

PLAN AT (Z)

Sill ex 150 x 63

50 x 50 bearers

Ex 38 x 19 hardwood frame

Brass wire mesh

50 x 50 studs framed into sill

12 mm plywood riser board

6 mm vent holes at 900mm c/s lined with plastic tube

2·6mm (12 gauge) bronze finish riser

SECTION THROUGH SILL AT (W)

54   Showcase details (2)

WALL LININGS

Traditionally, wood wall linings were made with stiles, rails and panels. The panels were plain, linenfold, or later, raised, inset with marquetry or surfaced with, often matched, veneers such as birds eye maple and quarter sawn oak.

Mouldings are shaped or splayed profiles. Moulded picture frames and moulded sections which are *planted*, ie applied to framing, are usually joined at junctions by mitre cuts which bisect the angles. Where mouldings are *stuck*, ie 'cut out of the solid' their thicknesses and positions should relate to those of any rebates and tenons, or 'leaves' of combed joints.

Figure 55 illustrates mitred joints as follows:

(a) stuck mouldings cut to form a mitre.
(b) one moulding is *scribed* i.e. shaped to conform with the continuous moulding on the other member.

The outer edge of a scribed moulding must meet the main surface of a moulded member as nearly as possible at right angles – in order to avoid a fragile 'feather edge', which would result if the moulding shown in figure 55(a) was scribed.

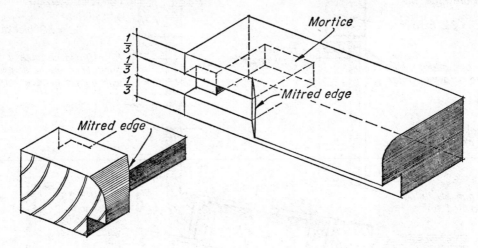

(a) *Mitred moulding*

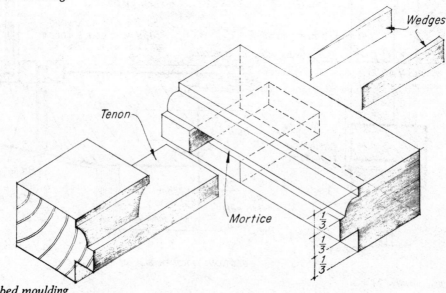

(b) *Scribed moulding*

(c) shows a combed joint with a splay on one member scribed to fit the splay on the other member.

(d) shows a stopped splay and a rounded angle cut with a machine router on one member, and a square stopped splay on the other — a method which, however, exposes end grain. A similar joint formed by hand is called a *mason's mitre*.

Today, wall linings usually have softwood frames which are concealed, and the superficial appearance of woods such as sapele, teak and rosewood is provided by veneers bonded to plywood or blockboard. Panels must be rigid when in position. Generally 6 mm or 9 mm plywood is used and this is glued to a light framework in units which can easily be prepared for jointing, trans-

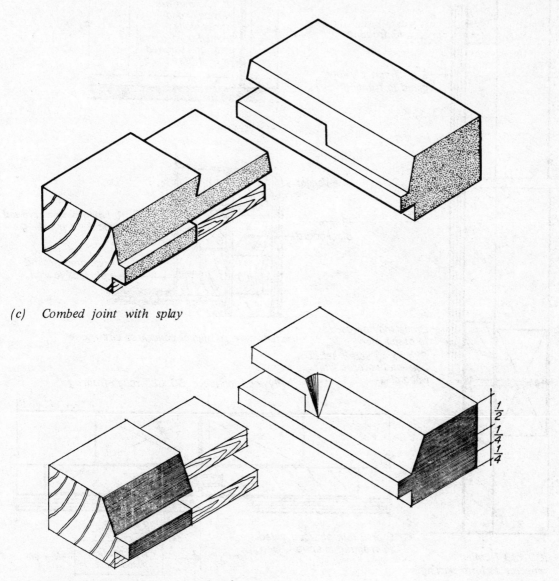

(c)   Combed joint with splay

(d)   Combed joint with splay formed with a router

55   *Mouldings*

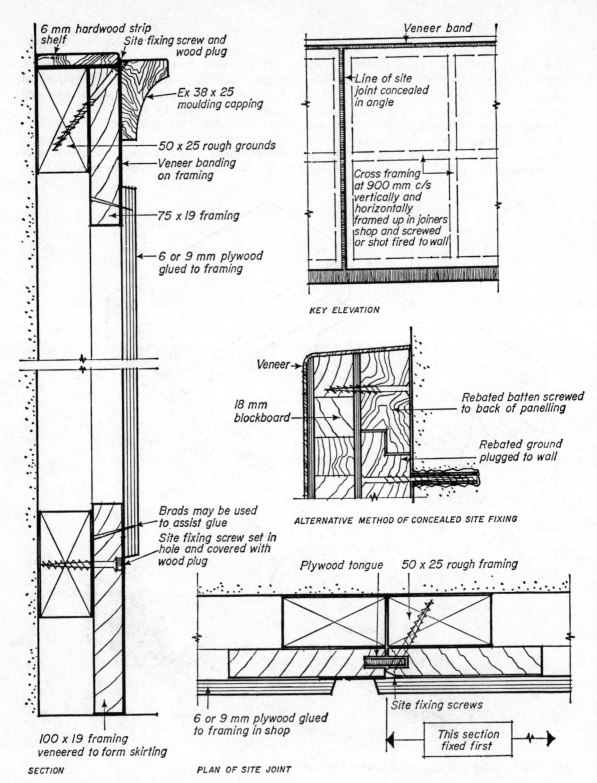

6 mm hardwood strip shelf

Site fixing screw and wood plug

Ex 38 x 25 moulding capping

50 x 25 rough grounds

Veneer banding on framing

75 x 19 framing

6 or 9 mm plywood glued to framing

Brads may be used to assist glue

Site fixing screw set in hole and covered with wood plug

100 x 19 framing veneered to form skirting

SECTION

Veneer band

Line of site joint concealed in angle

Cross framing at 900 mm c/s vertically and horizontally framed up in joiners shop and screwed or shot fired to wall

KEY ELEVATION

Veneer

18 mm blockboard

Rebated batten screwed to back of panelling

Rebated ground plugged to wall

ALTERNATIVE METHOD OF CONCEALED SITE FIXING

Plywood tongue   50 x 25 rough framing

Site fixing screws

This section fixed first

6 or 9 mm plywood glued to framing in shop

PLAN OF SITE JOINT

56   Flush plywood panelling

ported to the site and fixed. Normally a length of 3.600 m is the maximum but smaller units are more easily handled and convenient, provided that the increased number of site joints are acceptable.

Figure 56 shows a typical panel of 9 mm ply on a framing of 19 mm softwood. The framing projects beyond the plywood to form a recess and skirting. There is also a recessed band below the capping and at the vertical joints. The frame members will be jointed up, so that the plywood can be glued and secured to the framing from behind. In this example the ply is on the face of the framing so that its edge is exposed. This can be sanded down and when the whole surface is polished or clear finished will give a neat appearance. In the example shown each unit is completed, including the capping, in the joiner's shop. Site fixing is to 50 x 25 mm grounds plugged or shot fired to the wall. Screws are driven in along the top edge, down the free side and along the bottom. Those along the top edge are covered with a hardwood strip, those down the free sides are hidden by the next section and those on the base will not show if set in and covered with a plug. An alternative method of fixing is to have rebated grounds screwed to the back which interlock with similar grounds plugged to the walls.

A door is a moving part of a building and will be subjected to constant use and often abuse throughout its life. Therefore it must be carefully designed and detailed and well made from good materials. It must also be remembered that conditions of temperature and humidity will often be different in the rooms or spaces on each side of the door, which will produce a tendency for the door to warp or twist. The detailing must counteract this.

A door will either be of unframed, framed, or flush construction. The unframed door, consists of tongue and grooved boarding suitably jointed. Framed construction consists of an outer frame of timber, with infill either solid or glazed, to the various panels outlined by the framing. A flush door is formed by the application of sheet material such as hardboard or plywood on a suitable core.

PERFORMANCE SPECIFICATION

Function

A door is a moveable barrier to an opening in a building. Doors may be hung to swing, to slide, to fold or to revolve and the various arrangements as shown in plan form in figure 57.

Durability

Proper maintenance allied to the choice of good materials with good design and workmanship will ensure satisfactory durability throughout the life of the building, and these criteria also apply to all building components, including doors. Timber doors may need special consideration, in particular, external doors, and regular painting or clear treatment is necessary.

Weather protection

In the case of external door, this is concerned with the exclusion of air and water. Penetration tests are often carried out by manufacturers and new British Standards are under consideration which will include this requirement. The top and bottom of the door is particularly vulnerable and special precautions in the form of throating and provision of weather bars should be taken. Figure 58 shows details of an external pre-hung door set suitably detailed.

Outward opening doors should, wherever possible, be set back into the opening and be provided with a projecting weather fillet to the head of the frame. Where possible the edges of the meeting styles of doors hung in pairs should be rebated. Doors should, as far as possible, be draught proof, and the use of some form of additional protection in the form of weatherstripping at the rebate is a wise precaution.

Sound and thermal insulation

The loss of heat through a door can be high although the provision of weather seals may improve the situation. However, metal doors are available which incorporate a cavity filled insulation and provide excellent thermal characteristics. For good sound insulation doors must be 'solid' with tight seals at all edges. Special doors are required if the criterion is high, and more important, the passage of sound between the door and frame must be restricted. Where the specification requirements are high for both sound and thermal insulation then two sets of doors with an intervening space, or vestibule, will be necessary.

Fire resistance

Precautions in respect of an outbreak of fire fall into three categories.

1 Structural fire precautions: being concerned with restricting the spread of the fire within the building. A door is regarded as a weak point in respect of fire resistance and for this reason the position and construction of doors is controlled by the Building Regulations in respect of fire resistance. Specially constructed timber doors will resist the spread of fire for periods up to 1 hour. See figure 75, page 100.
2 Means of escape: to enable the occupants to

For side hung doors, determine the inside and outside faces, then, in relation to this, describe the direction of opening as clockwise or anti-clockwise.

For sliding doors, many variations are possible, the arrangement being determined by the choice of track as indicated.

Outside

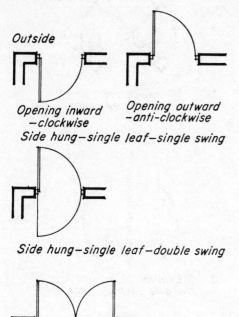

Opening inward
—clockwise

Opening outward
—anti-clockwise

Side hung—single leaf—single swing

Side hung—single leaf—double swing

Side hung—double leaf—single swing
—opening outwards

Side hung—double leaf—single swing
— opening inwards

Side hung—double leaf—double swing

Outside

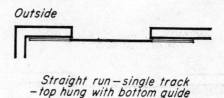

Straight run—single track
—top hung with bottom guide

Straight run—single track
—sliding in cavity

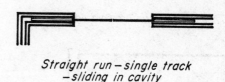

Straight run—double track—top hung

Straight run—triple track—top hung

Curved track—sliding on return wall

The sliding door can also be arranged to fold by pivoting the doors in pairs. A range of sliding, folding, internal doors is sometimes referred to as a folding partition.

(a) Pass doors
57 Method of hanging doors (1)

(b) Sliding doors

DOORS

Outside

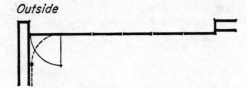

*Curved track sliding on return wall
—with pass door*

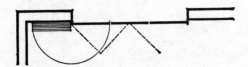

Three leaf—sliding folding door

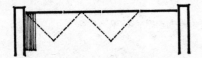

Four leaf—sliding folding door

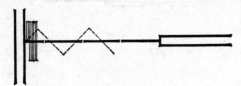

*Centre hung folding sliding door
with half leaf*

Folded
position

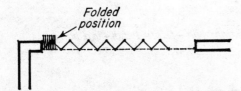

*Collapsible; on top track and bottom guide
as for a metal folding shutter gate.*

*Flexible; on top track—used as an
internal partition or space divider*

(c)   Folding doors

57   *Methods of hanging doors (2)*

84

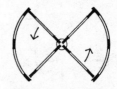

1   *Revolving position
—for draught exclusion*

2   *Leaves folded flat
to give clear passage*

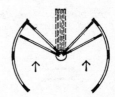

3 *Leaves collapsing against
pressure from crowd*

Revolving doors are used to form a draught-proof
lobby and are collapsible by hand to form a clear
opening. They can also be made automatically
collapsible by pressure from a crowd in case of
panic through fire or disturbance.

(d)   Revolving doors

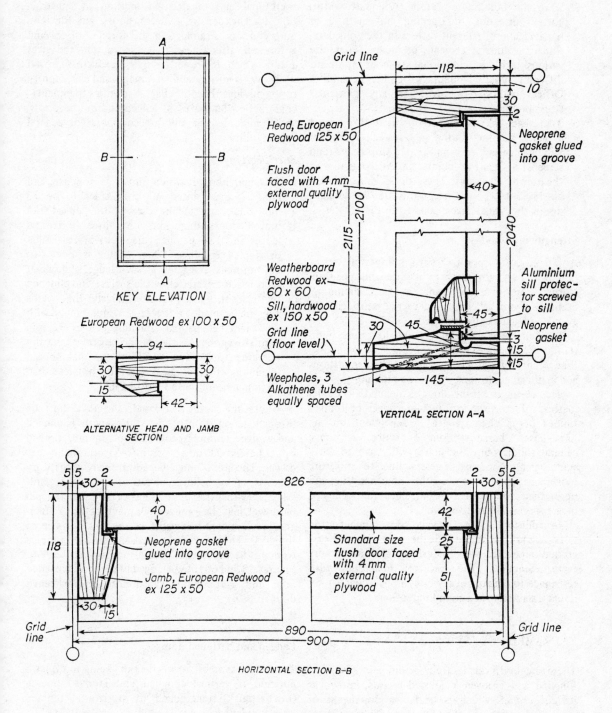

A

B — — — B

A

KEY ELEVATION

European Redwood ex 100 x 50

94

30 | 30

15

42

ALTERNATIVE HEAD AND JAMB
SECTION

Grid line

118

10

30

2

Head, European
Redwood 125 x 50

Neoprene
gasket glued
into groove

Flush door
faced with 4 mm
external quality
plywood

40

2100

2115

2040

Weatherboard
Redwood ex.
60 x 60

Sill, hardwood
ex 150 x 50

Grid line
(floor level)

Aluminium
sill protec-
tor screwed
to sill

30

45

45

Neoprene
gasket

3

15

15

Weepholes, 3
Alkathene tubes
equally spaced

145

VERTICAL SECTION A–A

5 5

2

826

2

30 5 5

40

30

Neoprene gasket
glued into groove

Jamb, European Redwood
ex 125 x 50

42

25

Standard size
flush door faced
with 4 mm
external quality
plywood

118

51

30

15

Grid
line

890

900

Grid line

HORIZONTAL SECTION B–B

58 *External prehung door set to satisfy air and water penetration test*

leave the building in safety. Adequate width, correct direction of opening and method of hanging are all relevant factors in the consideration of a door as a means of escape. There are various legislative requirements appropriate to different types of buildings and the Local Fire Officer will always advise on any particular situation.

3 To restrict the movement of smoke throughout a public building during an outbreak of fire, it will be necessary to install *smoke-stop* doors (and screens) at strategic points, and in particular at the top of stairways. These doors must be self-closing but need not necessarily be *fire resistant* doors; they must have a good fit in the rebates.

Strength and stability

A door is called upon to resist a number of stresses that will vary according to its use and position. Normal closing and opening, banging, slamming, bumping from articles being carried through and even kicking are to be expected.

In addition to these factors, the door must withstand stresses due to the variation in humidity that occur through changes in weather conditions and artificial conditions within the building.

The strength of the door is dependent on its method of construction and in respect of framed timber doors the strength is dependent on the joints used. Large sections of timber will give general solidity but the jambs will have to withstand greater internal stresses due to moisture movement. Flush doors on the other hand depend upon their total construction, since the facing is in the form of a *stressed skin*.

In addition to the air and water penetration tests already mentioned further research is being carried out with a view to devising tests for a future British Standard. The tests are concerned with resistance to torsion, heavy body impact, hard body impact, slamming and sound reduction.

UNFRAMED DOORS

These are doors made from a number of vertical tongued and grooved V jointed boards, known as *matchboarding*, which is held firm by means of horizontal members called ledges and strengthened by diagonal members known as braces. They are a traditional and much used method of construction for inexpensive exterior doors and for temporary doors. Framing, in the form of styles and a top rail, strengthens the construction and gives a door which, if properly made, has further proved itself by tradition and is much used for factory type buildings. BS 459: Part 4 specifies the quality, construction and sizes of ledged and braced doors, and framed ledged and braced doors for general use, as follows:

Specification

The matchboard which must be tongued and grooved and jointed on both sides to be 16 mm thick and in the case of the ledged and braced doors there must be three horizontal ledges and two parallel (diagonal) braces nailed or stapled together. When nailing is used, two 50 mm nails, staggered at each ledge, and one at each brace driven below the surface and clinched tight, must be used. Alternatively the boards may be stapled to the ledges and braces with 1.63 mm (16 gauge) clinching staples 32 mm long driven below the surface by mechanically operated tools. The width of the matchboard (excluding the tongues) must be not less than 70 mm and not more than 114 mm.

Where the door is framed, the rails must be through tenoned into the styles, with haunched and wedged tenons to top and bottom rails, pinned by a hardwood dowel or non-ferrous metal star dowel. The joints must be additionally secured by adhesive or by bedding in red or white lead paint. Where weather resistant adhesive is used, the pin or dowel may be omitted. A manufacturing tolerance of 2 mm is allowable in the finished size of the door. The vertical tongued and grooved timbers forming the matchboard are also known as *battens*. Figures 59 and 60 show a ledged braced and battened door and a framed ledged braced and battened door to BSS.

Ledged and battened doors

This is the simplest form of door, being in effect a number of vertical tongued and grooved boards (or battens) strengthened by horizontal timbers known as ledges.

The ledged and battened door is mostly used for

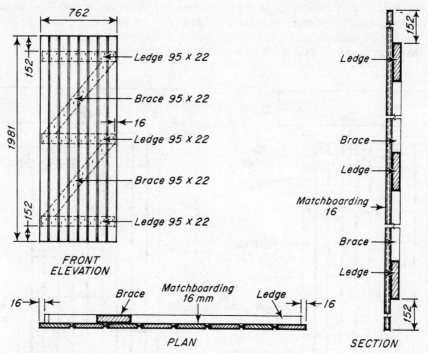

57 *Details of ledged, braced and battened door to BS 459: Part 4*

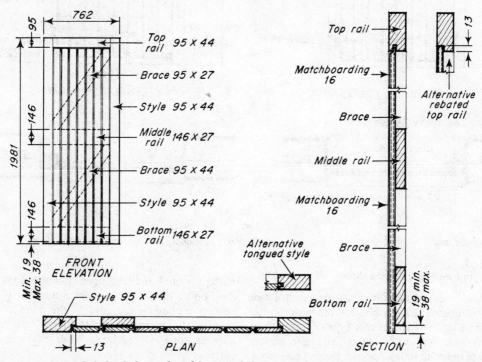

59 *Details of framed, ledged, braced and battened door to BS 459: Part 4*

temporary work since after a time, if subjected to heavy use, it would tend to distort diagonally. This type of door is shown in figure 60 in heavier construction than the minimum laid down in the BS.

so that the outer end of the brace supports the top free corner of the door. This is because the brace works in compression (not in tension) and if it is put on the other way round the joints between the

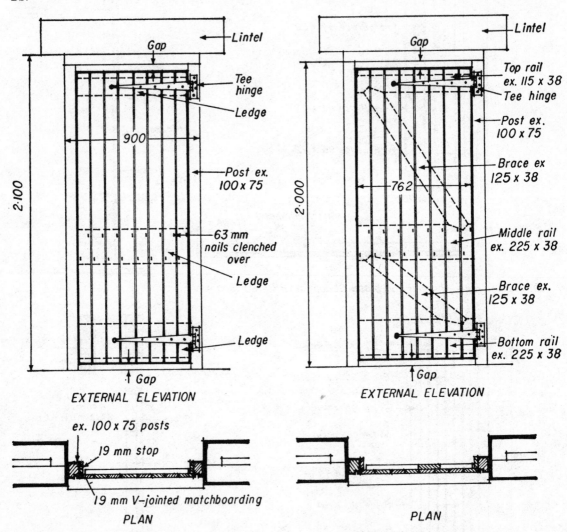

60 Ledged and battened door

61 Ledged, braced and battened door

Ledged, braced and battened door

This is a more satisfactory form of construction since the diagonal braces prevent the distortion of the door. Figure 61 shows this type of door, which is often used for out-buildings. The direction of the brace must be upwards from the hanging style,

battens would tend to open and the door would drop on its hinges. Since there is not enough thickness of timber on the edge of the door to accommodate the screws for butt hinges, this type of door is hung on tee hinges over the face of the battens.

FRAMED DOORS

Framed, ledged, braced and battened door

This is a refinement of the ledged and battened type and has the addition of styles, framed to top, bottom and middle rails. An example is shown in figure 62. The styles and top rail are the same thickness. Bottom and middle rails plus the thickness of the *battens,* are the same total thickness as the styles. The bottom and middle rails are cut with barefaced tenon, the top rail being fixed with a through, haunched tenon. The battens extend from the top rail to the ground over the middle and bottom rails in order to shed water from the face of the door. The door can be hung on strap or tee hinges, but since there is an outer frame the door can also be hung on butt hinges. Large garage or warehouse doors are made using the same principles of framing, battening and bracing shown for this type of door. The illustrations of these types of doors are of heavier construction than the minimum specified in the British Standard.

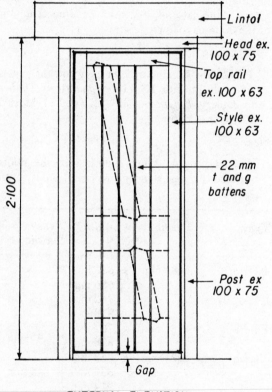

EXTERNAL ELEVATION

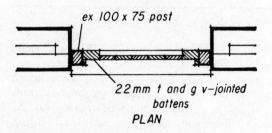

PLAN

62   *Framed, ledged and braced door*

INTERNAL ELEVATION

The timber sizes shown are nominal

Framed panelled doors

A framed or panelled door is a traditional form of construction. Its success depends on the correct proportions of the framing, the use of good quality well seasoned timber, and accurate framing up with properly made joints. The proportions of the panels must be carefully considered so that the door contributes to the architectural qualities of the building.

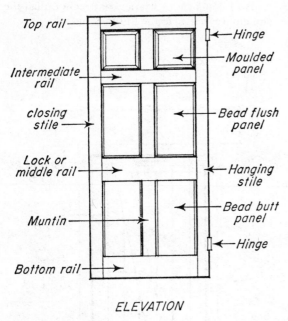

Top rail

Hinge

Moulded panel

Intermediate rail

closing stile

Bead flush panel

Lock or middle rail

Hanging stile

Bead butt panel

Muntin

Hinge

Bottom rail

ELEVATION

63 Panelled door

The door illustrated in figure 63 has a *composite* elevation to illustrate the various forms of panel to be found in doors of this type. The horizontal rails are framed into the styles using various types of mortice and tenon joints fully illustrated in figure 16 and described on page 42.

The vertical middle rail or *muntin* is stubtenoned into the horizontal rails. To prevent any tendency for the rails to deform, the styles are grooved and the tenons haunched into them.

The styles (or stiles) should not be too narrow, or difficulty may be experienced in fitting suitable furniture without destroying the framing effect, and the bottom rail must be deep enough to allow

proper jointing. Any excessive cutting away of the framing, particularly at the joints to fit bolts and locks, will seriously weaken the construction and these points should be checked at the design stage, by the designer considering the application of the furniture, at the same time as the method of framing.

Standard panelled and glazed wood doors

Minimum standards for framed, panelled and glazed factory made interior and exterior wood doors are set down in BS 459: Part I: 1954 (amendments up to 1967). The specification provides for the patterns, dimensions and construction of the doors as follows:

Specification

Timber for framing and the plywood for panels to conform with BS 1186: *Quality of Timber in Joinery. Exterior* quality plywood to be used for exterior doors.

Sizes

A guide to the types and sizes of the doors covered by the standard specification is given below:

Type	Height	Width	Finished thickness
Interior	1981 mm	x 610 mm 686 mm 762 mm 838 mm	35 mm
Exterior	1981 mm	x 762 mm 838 mm	45 mm
Glazed	1981 mm	x 762 mm 838 mm 914 mm	45 mm
Garage	1981 mm	x 2134 mm	45 mm

Table 12   Sizes of Standard BS doors

NB   In all references to BS 459, approximate metric equivalents correct to the nearest mm are given in the text. Until the appropriate British Standards are revised, however, the imperial units (given in the Standard) must be regarded as the correct dimension. See also additional British Standards relating to doors listed on page 39.

Framing

The option of dowelled or mortice and tenon joints is given for framing. The Standard specifies the finished sizes of the framing and the thickness of the plywood panels for all the types listed in the schedule. Where dowels are used they are to be of hardwood, minimum 16 mm diameter, equally spaced at not more than 57 mm centre to centre, with a minimum of three dowels in bottom and lock rail and a minimum of two for the top rail.

Where the framing is morticed and tenoned the doors must have through haunched and wedged tenons to top and bottom and one other (middle) rail. If there are more intermediate rails these are stub-tenoned (minimum 25 mm) into the styles.

For solid panels, the plywood is framed into grooves to fit tightly, the panels being cut to fit, 2 mm less in width than the grooved opening.

For glazed panels for exterior doors the opening is rebated out of the solid one side; with mitred glazing beads loosely pinned in position for delivery. All mouldings are scribed at the joints.

The adhesive used must comply with either BS 745: *Animal glue;* BS 1204: *Synthetic Resin Adhesive;* or BS 1444: *Cold Setting Casein Glue.* A manufacturing tolerance of 2 mm is allowed on the heights and widths of the finished sizes of component parts. The diagrammatic form of each of the joints mentioned is shown in 'Joints' starting on page 40.

Furniture

The doors can be supplied fitted with locks to the requirements of the purchaser, and the exterior doors prepared to receive a standard letter plate to BS 2911: *Letter Plates.*

The standard positions for butt hinges is specified.

Finish

The British Standard relates to joinery 'in the white', and if the doors are delivered unprimed they should be handled carefully and stored in dry conditions. Knotting and priming should be carried out as soon as possible and before fixing in position.

Figure 64 illustrates the BS designs for single panel interior door and a standard exterior glazed

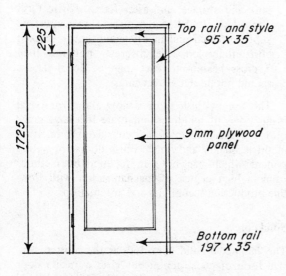

INTERIOR UNGLAZED DOOR No.1

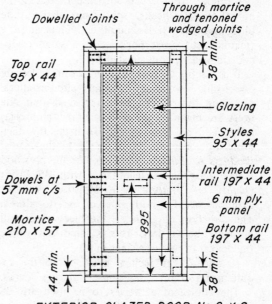

EXTERIOR GLAZED DOOR No.2 X G

63 *Panelled and glazed wood doors: BS 459*

door. In addition to the two types illustrated the Standard includes three and four panelled doors and exterior doors with glazing bars. The standard garage doors have six panels.

It will be seen that the British Standard specifies minimum requirements and the panelled and framed doors described are used generally for low cost buildings.

FLUSH DOORS

BS 459: Part 2: 1962 (amendments to 1968) sets down the requirements for exterior and interior factory made flush doors in timber, in terms of standard strength or stability, since the Standard does not require any particular form of construction. Thus the reputation of, and method of construction used by the manufacturer is all important in respect of quality.

Specification

The quality (though not the type) of timber to be used is specified in detail with regard to the following matters: moisture content, amount of sapwood that may be accepted; freedom of the timber from decay and insect attack; the limitation of checks, splits and shakes; the plugging of knot holes and other defects, and the treatment of pitch pockets, ie a small cavity containing a resinous substance.

It is useful to note that pin-worm holes are permissible — under certain circumstances, providing that it can be established that the holes are made by the pinhole borer (ambrosia) beetle and no other insect. To make the diagnosis, reference should be made to the *Forest Products Research Leaflet No.17.* The plywood facing must be in accordance with BS 1186: *Quality of Timber:* with Moisture resistant exterior type for both sides of exterior doors. The direction of grain on the face veneer will normally be vertical. This is important where the door is to receive a clear finish.

Hardboard for facings must be to the requirements of BS 1142: *Fibre Building Boards.*

The choice of adhesives to be used are BS 745: *Animal Glue* or BS 1444: *Cold Setting Casein Glue* or BS 1204: *Synthetic Resin Adhesives.*

Where lippings are provided, they are to be solid, fixed to both vertical edges of the door, and measure at least 7 mm on face.

Sizes

The standard sizes are given below:

Type	Height	Width	Finished thickness
Interior	1981 mm	610 mm 686 mm 762 mm 838 mm	35 mm
Exterior	1981 mm	762 mm 838 mm	44 mm

Table 13   Sizes of Standard BS Flush Doors

Furniture

Provision for locks, letter plate and hinges are standardized.

Finish

The Standard specification relates to the doors, at the time of despatch from the factory, with an untreated surface. The doors should be protected from exposure to the weather to prevent deterioration during transport and storage, and after fixing. Where flush doors have to be stored on site, they must be kept protected and in dry condition — stacked horizontally on level bearers, not less than 3 cross bearers to each pile of doors. Doors should not be stacked leaning.

The use of flush foors is now almost universal in all types of buildings and there is a large range of types available reflecting considerable variation in price, quality and finish. Flush doors are a component which can be manufactured by methods using a high degree of mechanization with flowline production techniques and automation.

Solid core

The laminated solid core door is the most expensive form of construction but gives a quality door of high sound insulation which will withstand heavy use over a long period of time. It is illustrated in figure 65. The core laminations are laid

92

alternately to balance stresses, and thus reduce the risk of distortion. Western red cedar is a suitable timber for use in the core since it has a small moisture movement which is an important advantage where the door is subjected to changing temperature and humidity. Hardwood veneers for this class of door would be specially selected and matched for figure of grain.

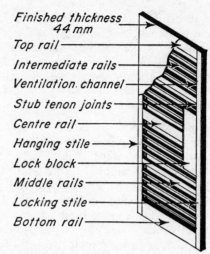

66 Semi-solid core flush door

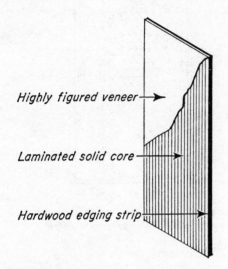

65 Solid core flush door

Semi-solid core

The semi-solid framed core medium cost door should contain 50 per cent timber, and is best constructed on the *stressed skin* principle, using the plywood to give a construction of great strength and rigidity. The edges of the door are normally lipped in hardwood to protect and cover the edges of the plywood. This type of door will also probably be veneered in hardwood, and a typical example is shown in figure 66.

Skeleton frame

The skeleton frame door shown in figure 67 is a less expensive method of framing which produces a door suitable for low cost contracts. This class of door would be faced with hardboard or plywood for painting.

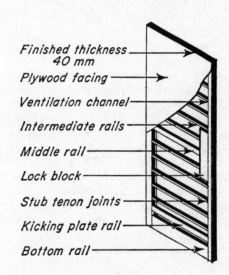

67 Skeleton framed flush door

Cellular core

There are various proprietary methods of producing a suitable cellular core such as a hardboard 'eggbox' or lattice construction. Both of these are illustrated in figures 68 and 69. Expanded cellular paper-board, extruded wood chipboard, flaxboard, and a method of utilizing timber 'shavings' in the form of precision cut spirals, are also commonly used for the core. Whichever form of construction is used it must avoid the defect of surface undulation where the 'ripple effect' reflecting the construction of the core is seen on the face of the door. The cost of these doors is related to the type of facing that is used, and in ascending order of cost the range is as follows:

1 Painted hardboard.
2 Inexpensive plywood facing for painting.
3 A medium cost plywood facing finished at the factory with a clear finish. This type of clear finish has the double advantage of sealing the timber and enhancing the grain of the facing.
4 A sliced cut figured hardwood veneer plywood of timbers such as sapele, teak, oak, walnut and afrormosia, finished and protected at the factory by a clear lacquer.

The technique of utilizing a grain printing process to reproduce hardwood figure, either on hardboard or an inexpensive plywood is now also used in the manufacture of flush doors. The technique is also used in the furniture industry. The method and type of lipping is also a guide to the cost of the door; the cheapest range will be unlipped, the medium range will be lipped on the vertical edges, either with parana pine or hardwood, and the most expensive range will have a matching hardwood lipping to all edges. It is in any case necessary to lip exterior doors on all edges for weather protection. It is important that a highly finished component such as a flush door, manufactured under strictly controlled conditions, should be carefully stored and handled on site. Manufacturers will not usually guarantee doors unless they are stored flat and dry, protected until ready for use, and not hung in a damp or freshly plastered building.

DOOR FRAMES AND LININGS

Doors are hung on either frames or linings within an opening, the difference being that a lining provides a covering to the reveals (sides) and soffit (upper surface) of an opening. A frame should always be strong enough to support the door without help from the main structure of the building; a lining on the other hand is supported to a certain extent by the construction surrounding the open-

ing. Neither frame nor lining must support any construction other than the door.

The size of the opening within the frame should allow between 2 mm and 3 mm clearance for hang-

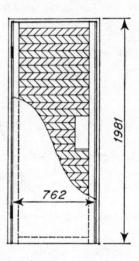

35 MM INTERIOR FLUSH DOOR
–expanded cellular board infill

68   *Cellular core*

Dimensions correct to nearest mm

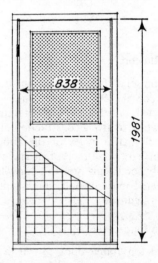

44 MM EXTERIOR FLUSH DOOR
– hardboard lattice core

69   *Lattice core*

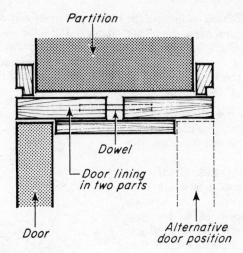

Partition

Dowel

Door lining
in two parts

Door

Alternative
door position

70   Dowelled door lining to allow adjustment
for various thicknesses of partition

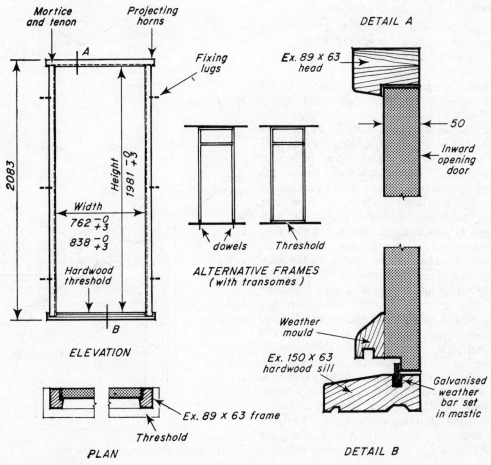

Mortice
and tenon

Projecting
horns

Fixing
lugs

DETAIL A

Ex. 89 x 63
head

50

Inward
opening
door

2083

Height
1981 $^{-0}_{+3}$

Width
762 $^{-0}_{+3}$

838 $^{-0}_{+3}$

Hardwood
threshold

dowels   Threshold

ALTERNATIVE FRAMES
(with transomes)

ELEVATION

Weather
mould

Ex. 150 x 63
hardwood sill

Galvanised
weather
bar set
in mastic

Ex. 89 x 63 frame

Threshold

PLAN

DETAIL B

71   Timber door frames

95

ing and adjusting the door. Rebates to receive the door should be minimum 12 mm deep, the rebate can either be recessed into a frame from the solid, or usually formed by a planted stop on the surface of a lining. A planted stop has the following advantages:

1 It makes a more economical use of timber.
2 Providing it is only temporarily pinned in position it can be adjusted on site to suit the door after it is hung.
3 Doors can be hung on either side of the stop, making the 'handing' of linings unnecessary.
4 Linings can be prefabricated in two separate halves, loosely dowelled together so that they can be adjusted on site to fit varying widths of partition. The planted stop fixed on site will then cover the gap between the two parts of the lining. An example of this construction is shown in figure 70.

Frames and linings appropriate to panelled and flush standard doors are described in BS 1567: 1953 and standard sections for an inward opening external door shown in figure 71.

The backs of frames should be protected against moisture penetration by priming paint before fixing.

Frames are now usually 'built in' as the work proceeds. Temporary strutting is necessary until the walling is built and metal cramps or lugs, as shown in figure 72, should be screwed to the back of the frame so as to coincide with the joints in the masonry, say three lugs to each side of the opening. Projecting 'horns' on the frame can also be built in to assist in restraining the frame. If a threshold is not fitted, metal dowels protruding from the foot of the post should be let into the step. The joint between door frame and the masonry opening should be raked out to a depth of say 12 mm and pointed with a suitable mastic. The mastic will probably be gun applied, and the width of mastic filling to the joint should be at least 6 mm or it will be ineffective. A detail is shown in figure 73.

Linings, on the other hand, must be fixed after the opening is formed. Timber pallet pieces (elm ie preferable) are built into the brickwork or blockwork joints and the lining screwed or nailed to these. In good class work the screws would be counter sunk and pelleted in timber matching the frame to conceal the screw head. It may be neces-

sary, particularly if the opening is wide, to fix the lining at the soffit also.

If the wall is plastered it is necessary to provide architraves (cover strips) to cover the joint between the lining and the plasterwork.

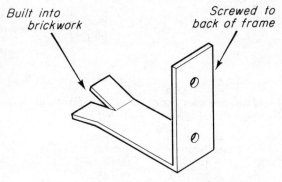

Built into brickwork   *Screwed to back of frame*

72 Fixing cramp

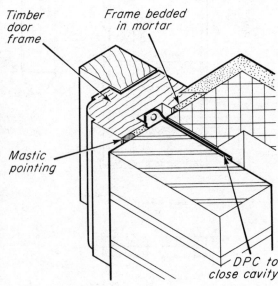

Timber door frame   *Frame bedded in mortar*

Mastic pointing

DPC to close cavity

73 External door in timber frame

STANDARD TRIM

For low cost contracts *standard trim* sections as covered by BS 584: 1967: *Wood trim (soft wood)*, would be of suitable section. The architrave sections are shown in figure 74.

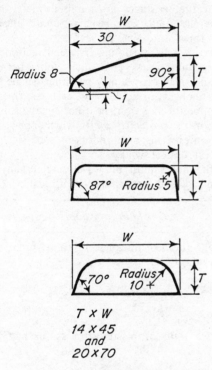

T × W
14 × 45
and
20 × 70

All dimensions in mm

74 *Standard architraves: BS 584*

Architrave details are shown in figures 85 and 86. Care should be taken to ensure that the thickness of the architrave is greater than the thickness of the skirting in order to avoid an awkward detail at the architrave-skirting junction. Traditionally a block of timber known as an architrave block was fixed at this point, against which both architrave and skirting butted.

The BS trim can be specified to be delivered at one of two alternative levels of moisture content, (a) 14 to 17 per cent where the conditions are such that the moisture content can be substantially maintained until completion of the building, or (b) not greater than 20 per cent.

The lower moisture content will be preferabel since it will reduce the risk of movement and twisting of the trim after fixing.

FIRE DOORS

The spread of fire through buildings may be limited by dividing them into horizontal or vertical *compartments* by fire resisting construction. The volumes of these compartments is govered by the anticipated calorific value of their contents, the chosen method of extinguishing fire, and the ease of egress for occupants in the event of fire. These factors relate directly to the use of the building, its volume and area, and to the height of individual floors above ground level. *The Building Regulations 1976*, Part E, give pricise requirements for the compartmentation of buildings, and further information is given in *MBS: Structure and Fabric*, Part 2, Chapter 10.

All openings in compartment walls and floors, including those to escape routes, must have one of the following types of doors,[1] or shutters:
Smoke stop doors resist the passage of smoke and other combustion products during the early stages of a fire and are not intended to withstand the full force of a fire. They can be normal doors in wood frames with 25 mm rebates or in metal frames with 20 mm rebates, both incorporating metal draught excluders.

Door type	Stability[1] Minutes	Integrity[2] Minutes
Half-hour fire-check	30	20
Half-hour fire-resisting	30	30
One-hour fire-check	60	45
One-hour fire-resisting	60	60

1 *Stability* Failure is deemed to occur when collapse of the specimen takes place.
2 *Integrity* Failure is deemed to occur when cracks or other openings exist through which flames or hot gases can pass or when flaming occurs on the unexpected face.

Table 14 *Fire-check and fire-resisting doors*
(Information from BRE Digest 155)

[1] *The Building Regulations* 1976 refer to all fire doors as being fire resisting doors.

Fire-check doors provide a barrier to fire for a stated time, without allowing excessive quantities of smoke to escape. They must: comply with the constructional specification given in BS 459: Part 3: 1951, or give an equivalent performance in fire tests.

Fire-resisting doors provide a higher standard of *integrity* than fire-check doors. See table 14 Integrity in fire-resisting doors is provided by intumescent strips set in their edges and in the frame rebates. These foam at high temperatures and effectively seal the gaps.

Tests for *Integrity* and *Stability* are carried out in accordance with BS 476: Part 8: 1972, but the test for *Insulation* in that BS is waived for all fire doors.

In order to avoid any confusion between the terms 'fire check' and 'fire resisting' doors, *BRE Digest 220: Timber fire doors* refers to both as being fire resisting doors but each type is also designated according to the periods of *stability* and *integrity*, ie Half hour (30/20) fire resisting door; One Hour (60/45) fire resisting door; Half hour (30/30) fire resisting door; One hour (60/60) fire resisting door. Where doors with more than one-hour fire resistance are required, metal doors are generally used. Fire resisting doors must be hung on three butt hinges per leaf.

Doors in walls separating flats and maisonettes from common access areas, and doors between houses and small garages may be either: single leaf, opening one way, or double leaf, each leaf opening in the opposite direction. In other types of buildings, doors in *protected shafts* which open onto escape routes, halls or corridors may be single or double leaf, double swing.

All fire doors must be self-closing, usually by means of a metal mechanism – with leaf selectors

Half hour type doors	One hour type doors
Minimum finished thickness 45 mm. Styles, top and bottom rails to be not less than 38 mm thick and 95 mm wide rebated both sides 25 mm to receive the protective plasterboard infill.	Minimum finished thickness 54 mm. Framing as for half hour type.
Middle rail 38 mm thick and 165 mm wide.	
Intermediate rails not less than 45 mm wide. Protective infill panels of 9 mm thick plasterboard fitted into the rebates and nailed to the framework.	Protective infill of plasterboard as for half hour type.
	Asbestos wall board or insulating board 5 mm thick glued over the whole area of the face of the door. The board to be applied in one piece and no metal fastenings to be used.
Plywood or hardboard facing 3 mm thick glued over the whole area of the face of the door – no metal fixings to be used.	Plywood or hardboard facing as for half hour type.
Doors may be used without lippings, but where these are required they must be no more than 9 mm on face and glued to the styles and rails. The lippings may be either tongued and grooved or straight profile on cross section – no metal fixings to be used. Lipping can be on one or both vertical edges, or all four edges.	Lippings as for half hour type, but must be tongued and glued, into grooves in the styles and rails.
External doors must be lipped on all four edges.	

Table 15   Fire doors (BS 459: Part 3: 1951)

for rebated-stile doors, and these must resist the pressure exerted by fires. In less hazardous conditions such as housing, rising butts of approved specification may be allowed. Metal doors are likely to be very heavy to close, and typically assistance is given by hanging them on an inclined overhead track. The door is normally held open by a counter-weight connected to a wire which incorporates a fusible link and this breaks when a critical temperature is reached.

Glazing in half-hour and one-hour fire doors is permitted subject to the limitations stated in table 16.

Door		Maximum size of 6 mm wired glass	Beads
Smoke stop		Any	—
Fire-check	½ hour	1.2 m²	13 x 13 mm minimum wood
Fire-resisting	½ hour	1.2 m²	ditto, but encased in non-combustible cover strip
Fire check	1 hour	.5 m²	non-combustible sub-frame
Fire resisting	1 hour	.5 m²	ditto

Table 16   Requirements for glazing in fire doors (information from CP 153: Part 4: 1972)

Further requirements for timber fire doors are given in *BRE Digest* 220.

Specification

Timber and plywood in accordance with BS 1186: *Quality of Timber in Joinery;* plasterboard to comply with BS 1230: *Gypsum Plasterboard;* Asbestos wall board or asbestos insulating board is permitted in accordance with BS 3536: *Asbestos insulating boards and asbestos wallboards.* However, it must be noted that ordinary asbestos sheeting to BS 690: *Asbestos-cement slates and sheets* is not suitable. Hardboard must be in accordance with BS 1142: *Fibre Building Boards;* Adhesives to be BS 745: *Animal Glues* or BS 1204: *Synthetic Resin Adhesives* or BS 1444: *Cold Setting Casein Glue.* For external doors, either gap-filling or close contact synthetic resin adhesives must be used.

Sizes and construction

838 mm or 914 mm are standard widths, with a standard height of 1981 mm.

Doors are to be marked on the hanging style to BS 459: Part 3: *Half Hour* or *One Hour* as appropriate. Typical details of fire-check doors and frames to BS 459 is shown in table 15 and figure 75. The dimensions are given to the nearest mm.

Frames in wood to have 25 mm rebate as shown in the diagram, and if this is formed by a stop, it is to be fixed by 38 mm long No. 8 screws spaced 76 mm from each end and not more than 610 mm apart. The one hour type door must have the frames rebated out of the solid, and pressure impregnated with 15 to 18 per cent solution of monoammonium phosphate in water. Maximum clearance between door and frame when hung to be 3 mm. Metal frames to BS 1245: *Metal Door Frames*, with one pair of hinges for half hour doors but 1½ pairs of hinges for 1 hour doors.

The type of fastening to be used will be determined by the use of the door. Where locks are required the large rebate of the frame must be borne in mind, since locks with a small back set will be unsuitable. Since, to be effective, fire-check doors must be kept closed, self-closing springs, or rising butt hinges must be specified.

The British Standard specifies two types of timber fire-check doors which can be mass produced reasonably easily, but any door in its frame, which has been shown by test in accordance with BS 476: Part I: *Fire Tests on Building Materials* to give a similar performance to the doors described in the Standard, can be used as a fire-check door for the appropriate period.

SOUND RESISTANT DOORS

A type of flush door which would be expected to give a sound reduction of 37 decibels (dB) is shown in figure 76. To achieve this reduction the door must be hung as shown with sealing strips at the rebate of the frame, and the frame must be adequately secured to the walling, which should be at least 190 mm thick solid masonry to achieve the reduction indicated. The dB reduction required to eliminate a normal conversation from one side of

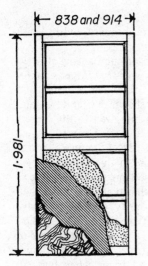

838 and 914

1·981

ELEVATION with facing
materials cut away

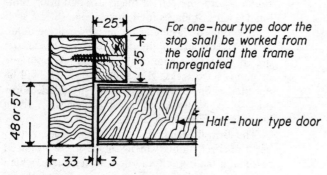

25

35

48 or 57

33 ⊢ 3

For one-hour type door the
stop shall be worked from
the solid and the frame
impregnated

Half-hour type door

TIMBER DOOR FRAME
minimum dimensions

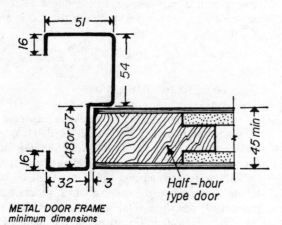

51

16

54

48 or 57

16

32 ⊢ 3

45 min

Half-hour
type door

METAL DOOR FRAME
minimum dimensions

75 *Fire check doors: BS 459: Part 3*

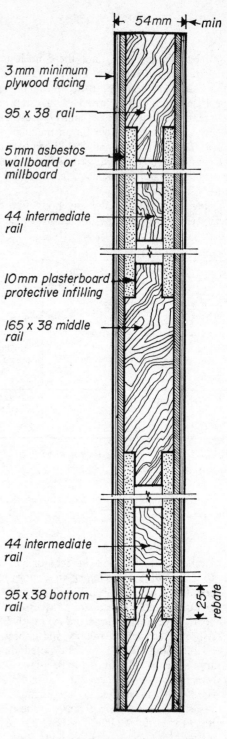

54mm ⊢ min

3 mm minimum
plywood facing

95 x 38 rail

5 mm asbestos
wallboard or
millboard

44 intermediate
rail

10 mm plasterboard
protective infilling

165 x 38 middle
rail

44 intermediate
rail

95 x 38 bottom
rail

25
rebate

SECTION one-hour type check
flush door

a construction to another would be 28 dB. This is a normalized level difference represented by the door in its frame as shown, well fitted in the wall. The figure takes into account the combination of, and the different dB ratings for door and wall.

by neoprene gaskets in extruded aluminium sections at the threshold, and the extruded aluminium weather stripped door stops. Further details of this type of weatherstripping are given on pages 122 and 123.

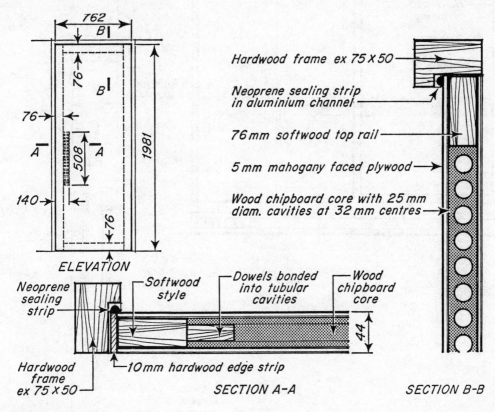

762
B
76
B
76
A — A
508
1981
140
76

ELEVATION

Hardwood frame ex 75 × 50

Neoprene sealing strip in aluminium channel

76 mm softwood top rail

5 mm mahogany faced plywood

Wood chipboard core with 25 mm diam. cavities at 32 mm centres

Neoprene sealing strip

Softwood style

Dowels bonded into tubular cavities

Wood chipboard core

44

Hardwood frame ex 75 × 50

10 mm hardwood edge strip

SECTION A-A

SECTION B-B

76   Sound resistant door

GLAZED DOORS

In addition to the standard panelled glazed door previously described, purpose made glazed doors are very much used so that persons passing through can see if anyone is coming from the opposite direction. Where these doors are used in entrances, as they often are, a very heavy use is made of them and sound construction is essential. Figure 77 shows an example of a pair of glazed doors in hardwood as part of a glazed entrance screen detail. Points to emphasize are the weather stripping

Since this type of door will be in constant use it is sensible to use a floor spring as a means of controlling the movement. The floor spring can be fitted with a device which checks the doors open at 90°.

Another example of glazed door construction is shown in figure 78. This is a range of doors formed from extruded aluminium sections and is suitable for an hotel or department store entrance. The profiles are neat and points to note are the draught-proofing by woven pile strips and the different methods of securing the glazing in the door and fanlight.

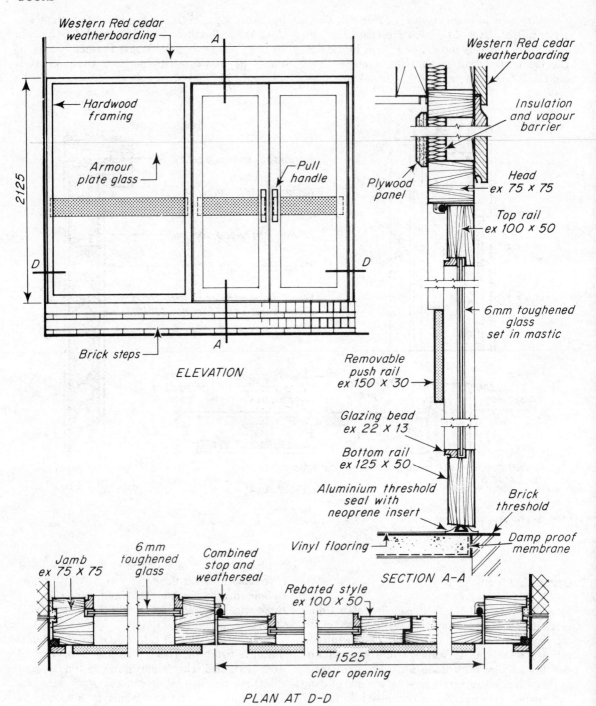

Western Red cedar weatherboarding

Hardwood framing

Armour plate glass

Pull handle

2125

D

D

Brick steps

ELEVATION

A

A

Western Red cedar weatherboarding

Insulation and vapour barrier

Plywood panel

Head ex 75 x 75

Top rail ex 100 x 50

6mm toughened glass set in mastic

Removable push rail ex 150 x 30

Glazing bead ex 22 x 13

Bottom rail ex 125 x 50

Aluminium threshold seal with neoprene insert

Vinyl flooring

Brick threshold

Damp proof membrane

SECTION A-A

Jamb ex 75 x 75

6mm toughened glass

Combined stop and weatherseal

Rebated style ex 100 x 50

1525 clear opening

PLAN AT D-D

77   *Hardwood glazed doors*

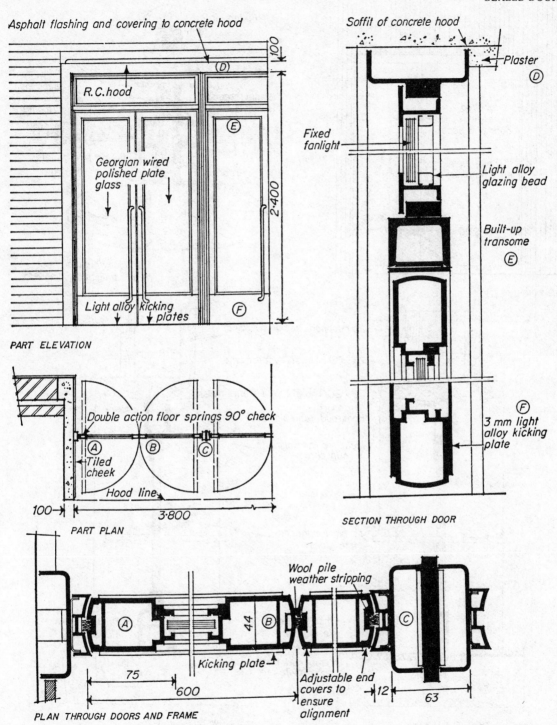

Asphalt flashing and covering to concrete hood

100

R.C. hood

Georgian wired
polished plate
glass

2·400

(D)

(E)

Light alloy kicking plates

(F)

PART ELEVATION

Double action floor springs 90° check

(A)   (B)   (C)

Tiled cheek

Hood line

100→   3·800

PART PLAN

Soffit of concrete hood

Plaster   (D)

Fixed fanlight

Light alloy glazing bead

Built-up transome   (E)

(F)   3 mm light alloy kicking plate

SECTION THROUGH DOOR

Wool pile weather stripping

(A)   44   (B)   (C)

Kicking plate

75

600

Adjustable end covers to ensure alignment

12   63

PLAN THROUGH DOORS AND FRAME

78   *Glazed aluminium doors*

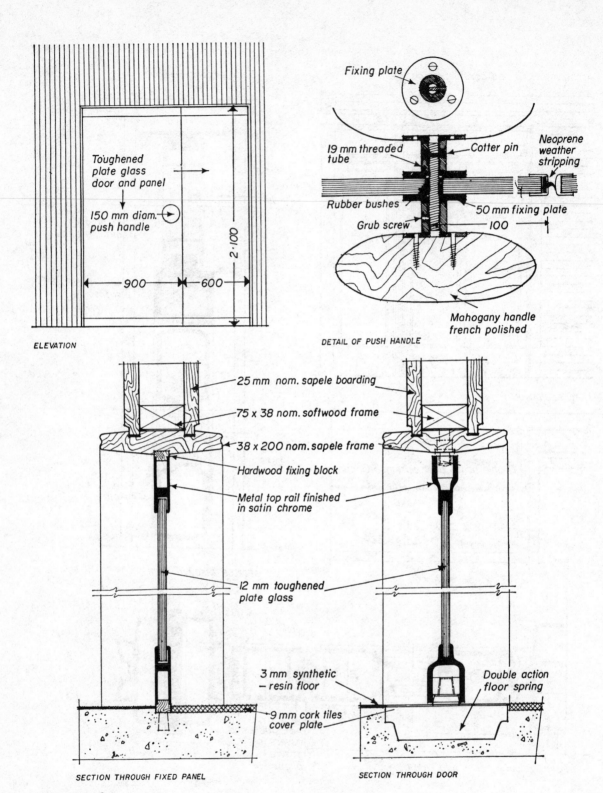

ELEVATION

DETAIL OF PUSH HANDLE

Toughened plate glass door and panel

150 mm diam. push handle

900

600

2·100

Fixing plate

19 mm threaded tube

Cotter pin

Rubber bushes

Grub screw

Neoprene weather stripping

50 mm fixing plate

100

Mahogany handle french polished

25 mm nom. sapele boarding

75 x 38 nom. softwood frame

38 x 200 nom. sapele frame

Hardwood fixing block

Metal top rail finished in satin chrome

12 mm toughened plate glass

3 mm synthetic – resin floor

9 mm cork tiles cover plate

Double action floor spring

SECTION THROUGH FIXED PANEL

SECTION THROUGH DOOR

79   *Glass door*

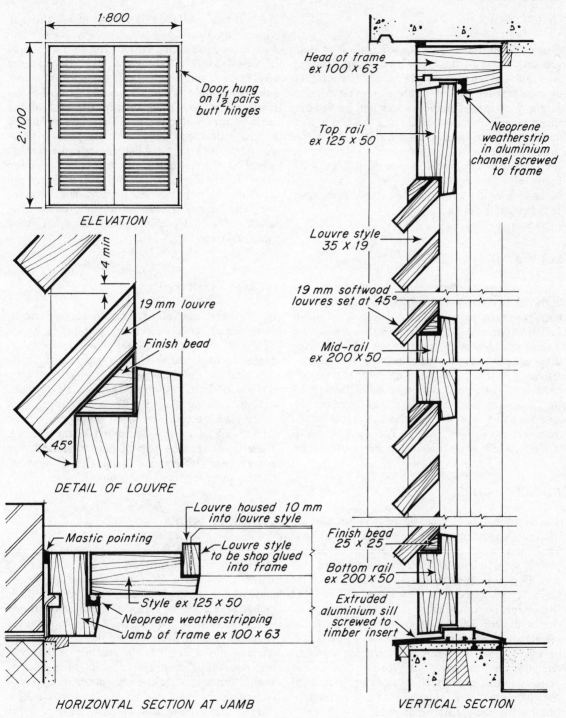

1·800

2·100

ELEVATION

Door, hung on 1½ pairs butt hinges

Head of frame ex 100 × 63

Neoprene weatherstrip in aluminium channel screwed to frame

Top rail ex 125 × 50

Louvre style 35 × 19

19 mm softwood louvres set at 45°

Mid-rail ex 200 × 50

4 min

19 mm louvre

Finish bead

45°

DETAIL OF LOUVRE

Finish bead 25 × 25

Bottom rail ex 200 × 50

Extruded aluminium sill screwed to timber insert

Louvre housed 10 mm into louvre style

Louvre style to be shop glued into frame

Mastic pointing

Style ex 125 × 50

Neoprene weatherstripping

Jamb of frame ex 100 × 63

HORIZONTAL SECTION AT JAMB

VERTICAL SECTION

80 *Timber louvre door*

GLASS DOORS

Figure 79 illustrates a toughened plate glass door and side screen of the type fitted at the entrance to shops and showrooms. The door is controlled by an adjustable top centre pivot hung on a double action floor spring. A special lock will be fitted in the top and bottom metal rails with the lock keepers set into the hardwood frame and concrete floor. The attractive feature of this type of door is its transparency, but it is sometimes difficult to know when the door is open, and for this reason some form of decoration may be fixed to the door to indicate its position.

LOUVRED DOORS

This is a form of door which is now much used both internally for decorative purposes and externally where permanent ventilation is required. In the example shown in figure 80 the louvres are housed into a vertical louvre style which is then shop glued within the panel formed by the main framing of the door. The edges of the ouvres, because of their projection in front of the face of the door, are chamfered off at the corners. The louvre slats are set at 45° and fixed so that there is a minimum overlap of 3 mm. The door is shown closing against an extruded aluminium threshold.

FLEXIBLE DOORS

This type of door is used where it is not possible for the user to open the door in the normal way. The most usual applications are in industrial buildings, warehousing or hospitals where the user may be pushing or driving a trolley or carrying bulky packages. It is a comparatively inexpensive alternative to installing automatic opening and closing devices. The door is composed of a flexible membrane of either reinforced rubber or neoprene, or where complete vision is desired for safety in operation, and the use is not excessive, transparent or translucent plastic sheet. In any case, because of the risk of collision, this type of door would be fitted with a clear plastic vision panel.

The door is designed to open on impact, the flexibility of the sheeting taking the force out of the 'collision', and allowing the user to pass through. The doors then close automatically, being controlled by jamb spring hinges. The door illustrated in figure 81 is a lightweight door formed by a steel angle supporting frame at the head and hinged side, from which is hung a flexible sheet of 8 mm reinforced rubber clamped into the heel of the angle by means of a steel flat. The hinges are double action vertical spring type. For larger doors up to say 4.000 m high by 4.000 m wide the framing would be of steel tubing with the spring mechanism made as a separate detachable unit, and arranged to slide inside the vertical tube framing from the top. The heaviest doors are suitable for openings which are used by large vehicles and other heavy industrial transport.

BRONZE DOORS

In complete contrast a pair of purpose made, monumental cast bronze doors is shown in figures 82 and 83. The doors are set round a rolled steel chanel framing which is *rawlbolted* into the main structure of the building. The doors swing on single action floor springs. The separate moulded sections forming the door frame are clipped back to the main steelwork by metal straps, and are also 'tucked in' to the stone surround to the opening. These doors are examples of fine craftsmanship in a traditional setting and would be a dominant element in any architectural composition.

VESTIBULE DOORS

Figures 84 and 85 show the application of a pair of purpose made hardwood doors to close off a vestibule for extra security when the building is shut up for the night. Teak would be a suitable timber to use in this instance. A pair of hardwood glazed doors form the main entrance doors to the building. A special feature of these doors is the *rounded corner* detail at the junction of the styles and rails. Toughened glass should, of course, be used in this situation. The *night doors* are a form of folding door. Each side of the opening having a pair of doors hung leaf on leaf. Note that the method of hanging is devised so that the edges of the doors do not show and the outer door forms

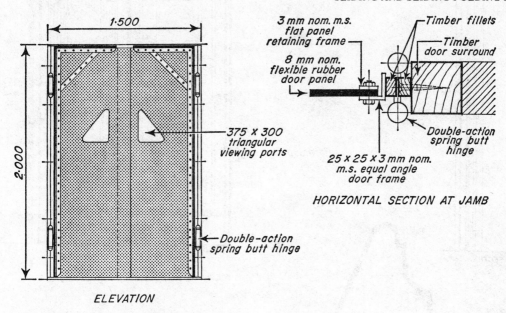

ELEVATION

81   *Lightweight flexible rubber doors*

a decorative hardwood lining to the sides of the vestibule during the day. The entrance doors are hung on double action floor springs to allow the doors to act as a means of escape in the case of fire during the dime that the building is in use, and the fact that the line of swing impedes the outer doors does not matter since the two sets of doors will not be in use at the same time. Each of the night doors will be hing on 1½ pairs (3 to each door) of substantial brass hinges. The doors are an example of good class joinery work and will have to be carefully made and well hung to avoid trouble in use, since the stress on the hinges to the outer doors will be considerable.

SLIDING AND SLIDING-FOLDING DOORS

These types of doors are now much more used and providing that the problems of manipulation and maintenance are understood the doors will work satisfactorily throughout their life. It must be emphasized, however, that the working parts of the doors must be treated like machinery and must be regularly maintained. It should also be borne in mind that the more complex the mechanism the greater chance of failure. A straight sliding single

leaf door is the simplest and cheapest but takes up most space when open. Increasing the number of leaves saves space but complicates the mechanism. Folding systems take up the least space of all but require the most complex hanging gear. The weight of the doors can be taken on wheels or rollers at the base or alternatively suspended from hangers on a track at the had of a door. A neater finish can usually be obtained by the bottom rollers but general openion is that top track is the most efficient method of hanging.

Straight track sliding: single leaf

The track system chosen as an example of this type of action is suitable for interior doors not exceeding a width of 1200 mm and operating on a 'ball runner' principle. The details are shown in figure 86. The linear ball bearing motion is provided by a sliding inner bar grooved to receive chrome steel ball bearings and running between a vee section galvanized steel outer track. The ball bearings are located by a retainer cage. This type of gear, which will operate on doors weighing between 55 Kg and 90 Kg, is very reliable and prevents lifting or rocking of the doors when in use. The illustration shows an internal door in a house and this type of gear is often used where there is

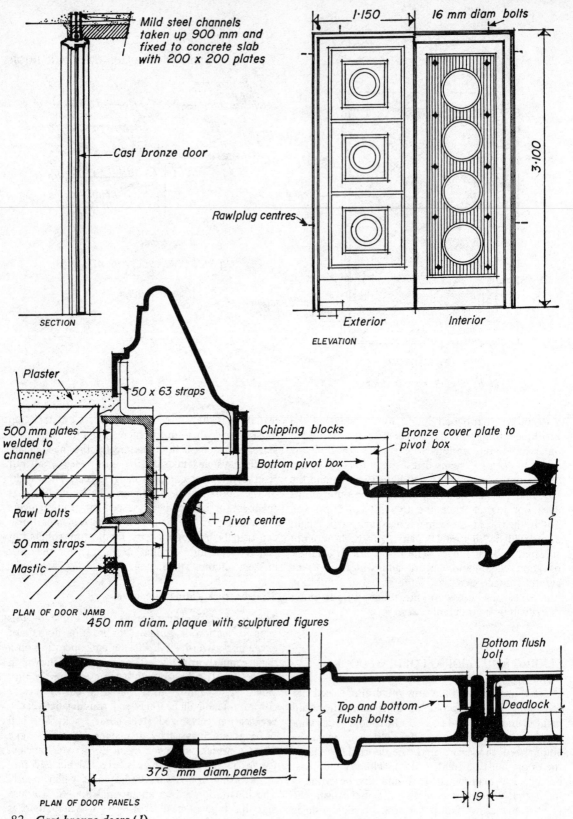

Mild steel channels taken up 900 mm and fixed to concrete slab with 200 × 200 plates

Cast bronze door

SECTION

1·150   16 mm diam bolts

3·100

Rawlplug centres

Exterior   Interior

ELEVATION

Plaster

50 × 63 straps

Chipping blocks

Bronze cover plate to pivot box

500 mm plates welded to channel

Bottom pivot box

Rawl bolts

+ Pivot centre

50 mm straps

Mastic

PLAN OF DOOR JAMB

450 mm diam. plaque with sculptured figures

Bottom flush bolt

Top and bottom flush bolts

Deadlock

375 mm diam. panels

19

PLAN OF DOOR PANELS

82   *Cast bronze doors (1)*

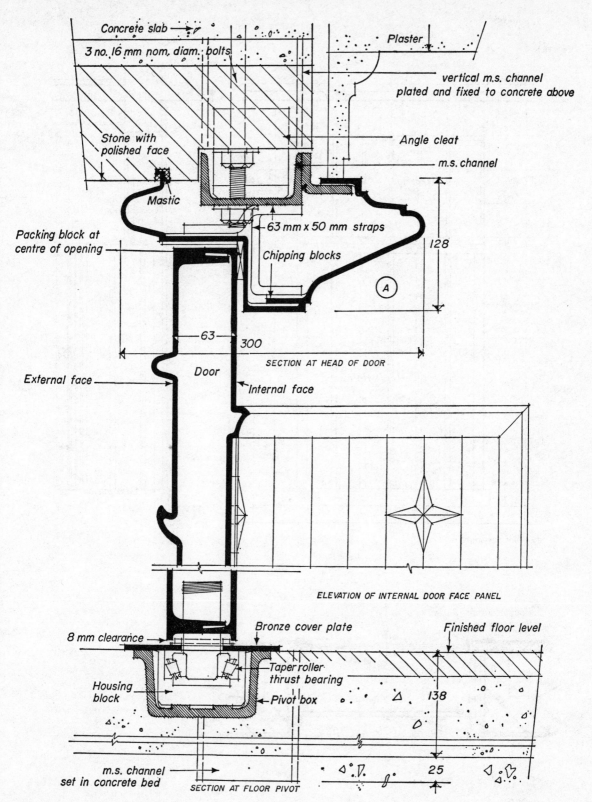

Concrete slab

3 no. 16 mm nom. diam. bolts

Plaster

vertical m.s. channel plated and fixed to concrete above

Stone with polished face

Angle cleat

m.s. channel

Mastic

Packing block at centre of opening

63 mm x 50 mm straps

Chipping blocks

128

A

63

300

External face

Door

Internal face

SECTION AT HEAD OF DOOR

ELEVATION OF INTERNAL DOOR FACE PANEL

8 mm clearance

Bronze cover plate

Finished floor level

Housing block

Taper roller thrust bearing

Pivot box

138

m.s. channel set in concrete bed

SECTION AT FLOOR PIVOT

25

83   Cast bronze doors (2)

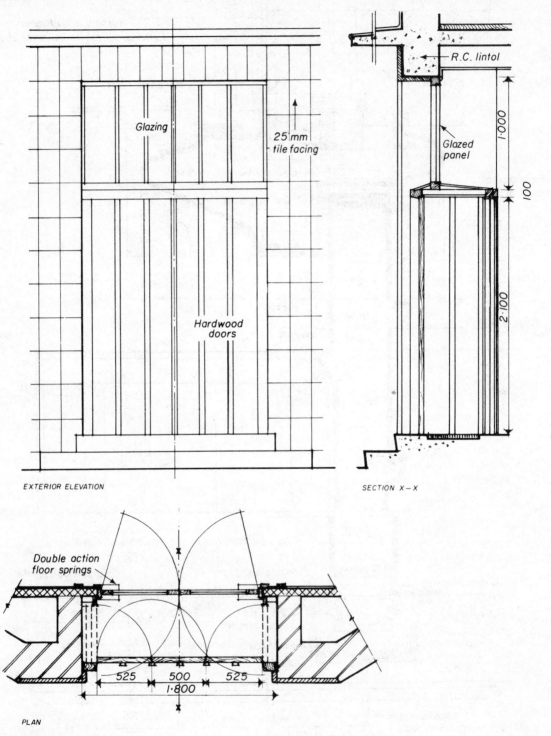

Glazing

25 mm
tile facing

Hardwood
doors

EXTERIOR ELEVATION

R.C. lintol

Glazed
panel

1·000

100

2·100

SECTION X — X

Double action
floor springs

525   500   525

1·800

PLAN

84   Vestibule doors (1)

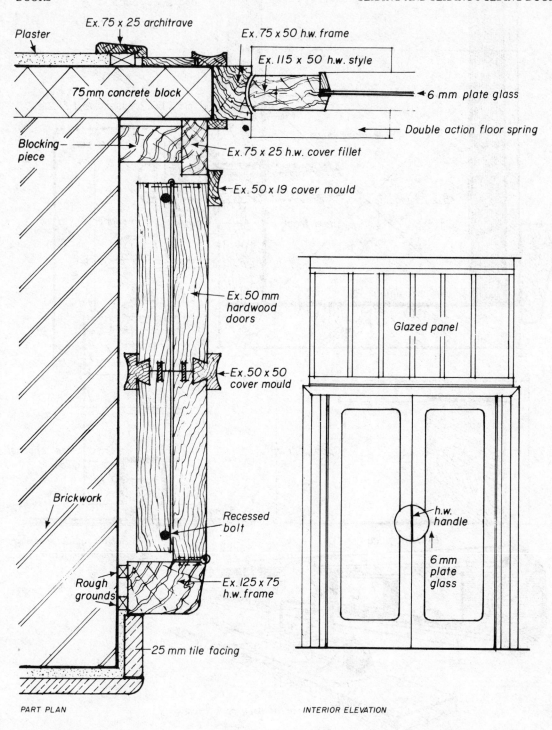

Plaster

Ex. 75 × 25 architrave

Ex. 75 × 50 h.w. frame

Ex. 115 × 50 h.w. style

75 mm concrete block

6 mm plate glass

Double action floor spring

Blocking piece

Ex. 75 × 25 h.w. cover fillet

Ex. 50 × 19 cover mould

Ex. 50 mm hardwood doors

Glazed panel

Ex. 50 × 50 cover mould

Brickwork

Recessed bolt

h.w. handle

6 mm plate glass

Rough grounds

Ex. 125 × 75 h.w. frame

25 mm tile facing

PART PLAN

INTERIOR ELEVATION

85 *Vestibule doors (2)*

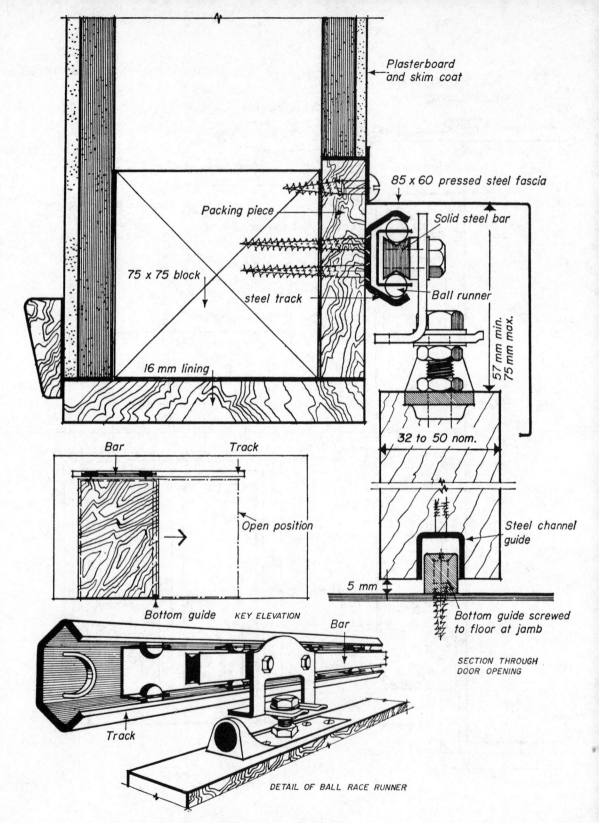

Plasterboard
and skim coat

85 x 60 pressed steel fascia

Packing piece

Solid steel bar

75 x 75 block

steel track

Ball runner

57 mm min.
75 mm max.

16 mm lining

32 to 50 nom.

Bar   Track

Open position

Steel channel
guide

5 mm

Bottom guide   KEY ELEVATION

Bottom guide screwed
to floor at jamb

Bar

SECTION THROUGH
DOOR OPENING

Track

DETAIL OF BALL RACE RUNNER

86   *Sliding gear for internal door. Straight track, single leaf*

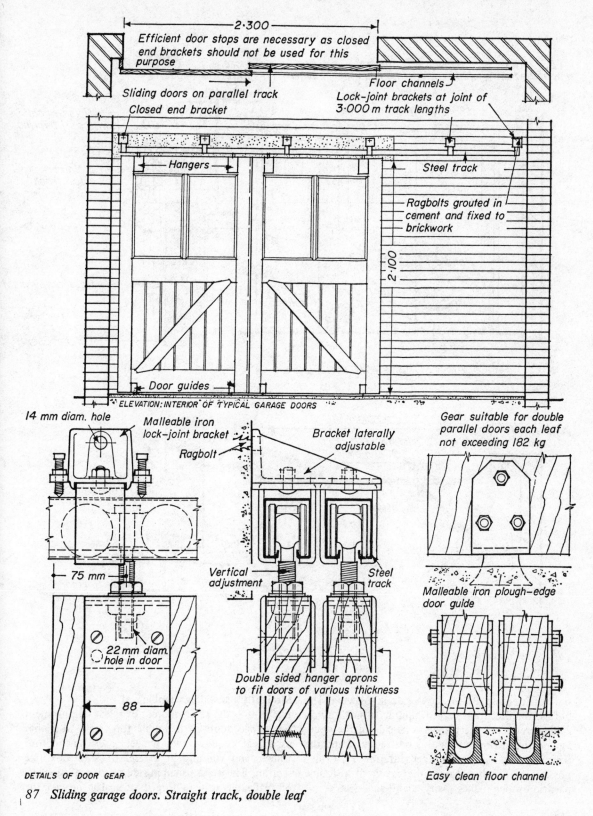

2·300

Efficient door stops are necessary as closed end brackets should not be used for this purpose

Sliding doors on parallel track

Closed end bracket

Floor channels

Lock-joint brackets at joint of 3·000 m track lengths

Hangers

Steel track

Ragbolts grouted in cement and fixed to brickwork

2·100

Door guides

ELEVATION: INTERIOR OF TYPICAL GARAGE DOORS

14 mm diam. hole

Malleable iron lock-joint bracket

Ragbolt

75 mm

22 mm diam. hole in door

88

DETAILS OF DOOR GEAR

Bracket laterally adjustable

Vertical adjustment

Steel track

Double sided hanger aprons to fit doors of various thickness

Gear suitable for double parallel doors each leaf not exceeding 182 kg

Malleable iron plough-edge door guide

Easy clean floor channel

87 *Sliding garage doors. Straight track, double leaf*

113

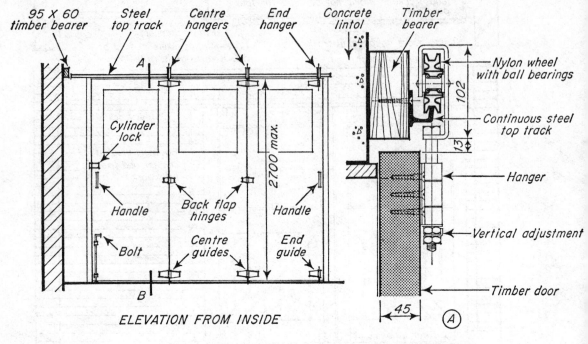

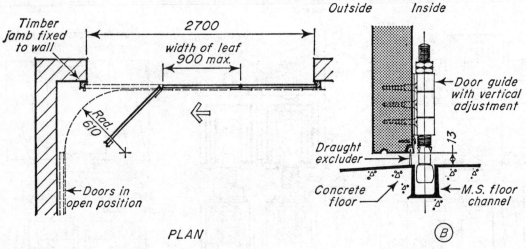

88 *Top hung sliding doors*

not sufficient space to allow a door to swing. The bottom of the door is controlled by a small nylon guide screwed to the floor at one side of the opening, so that a floor channel is not required and the fixing is suitable for carpeted interiors. It is also possible to fix this gear in the cavity of a double partition which makes a very neat detail.

Straight track sliding: double leaf
Figure 87 shows a simple two leaf arrangement for garage doors with double top track. Note that each leaf requires two hangers each having four wheels and running in a steel track of box like section. The track is supported on special brackets of malleable iron or forged steel. The heavier the

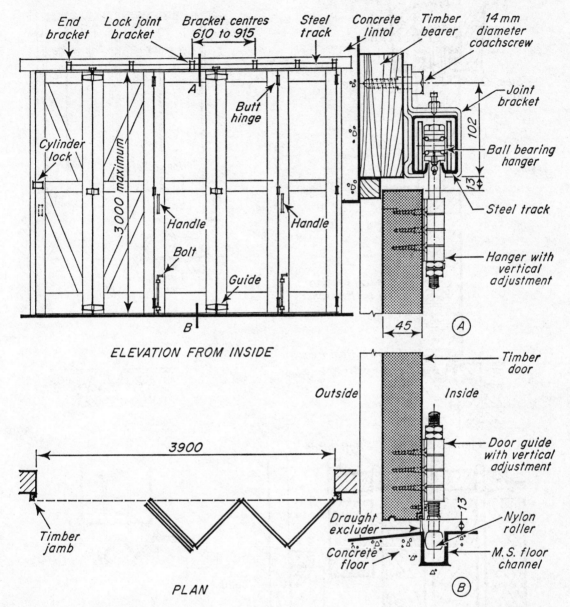

89 *Top hung folding doors*

door the larger the track. The biggest being 150 mm by 125 mm, nominal, which would be capable of supporting doors weighing up to about 1500 Kg. There should be about 13 mm clearance between the doors and between the door and the wall. The bottom of the doors is held in place by malleable iron guides running in a steel channel let into the floor. The design of the track should prevent outward movement and so avoid any tendency for the doors to jam. The bottom rollers should also be so arranged that any dirt that gets into the channel will be ploughed out rather than pressed down. There are many alternative designs for track and channel guides. The leaves of the door are nor-

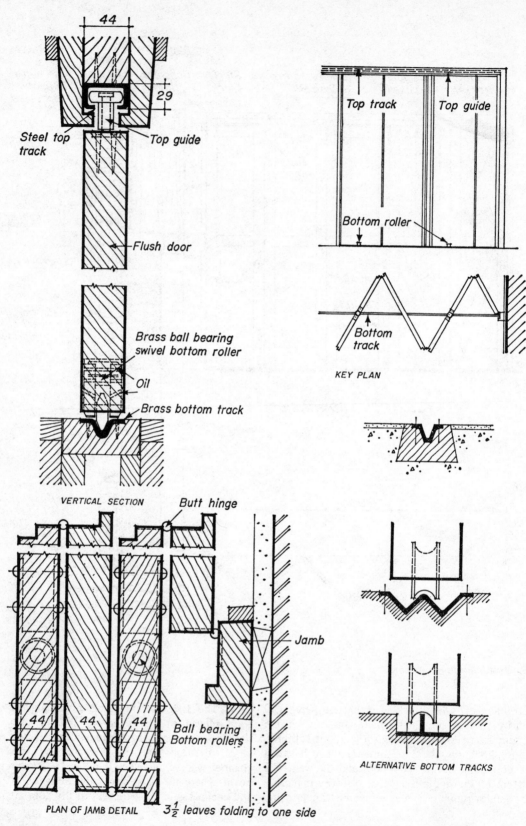

44

29

Steel top track

Top guide

Flush door

Brass ball bearing swivel bottom roller

Oil

Brass bottom track

VERTICAL SECTION

Butt hinge

Jamb

44 44 44

Ball bearing Bottom rollers

PLAN OF JAMB DETAIL

3½ leaves folding to one side

Top track

Top guide

Bottom roller

Bottom track

KEY PLAN

ALTERNATIVE BOTTOM TRACKS

90 Folding partition

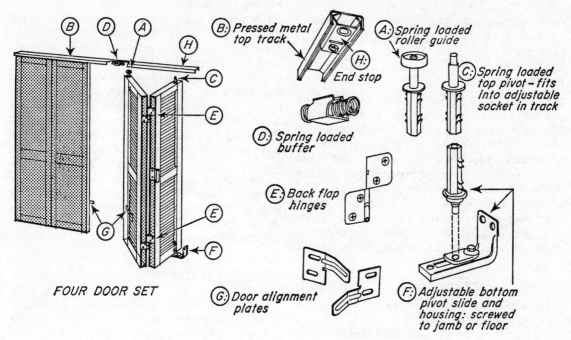

FOUR DOOR SET

B: Pressed metal top track

H: End stop

A: Spring loaded roller guide

C: Spring loaded top pivot – fits into adjustable socket in track

D: Spring loaded buffer

E: Back flap hinges

G: Door alignment plates

F: Adjustable bottom pivot slide and housing: screwed to jamb or floor

DOOR FURNITURE

91   Louvred folding partition

mally secured with bolts into the floor with an outside fastening on the end leaf by means of various kinds of locking bar or jamb bolt used with a padlock. Special cylinder locks are also available. In the example shown there is no frame or timber trim owing to the necessity for adequate clearance, but a wooden fastening post is screwed to the wall to close the gap between wall and inner door when in the closed position. The clearance required between the faces of the straight track doors can cause difficulties in respect of draught proofing and weathering.

Curved track

Here the doors are all in one plane and can fit close to each other and be rebated – see figure 88. One disadvantage, however, is that an area of the side walls of a width equal to the door opening has to be kept free to allow the doors to slide over the face. Hangers and guides as used with straight tracks are combined with back flap hinges to control the movement of the doors. The width of the doors

should be restricted to a maximum of 900 mm. The minimum curve of track for light doors is in the region of 600 mm. The end leaf can be free swinging for use as a pass door and can be secured with an ordinary cylinder lock to a rebated door post. This makes a convenient arrangement where the suite of doors is used mainly for pedestrian traffic and only occasionally for vehicular access. Figure 87 illustrates a set of doors on a curved track suitable for a garage door opening. The top track is secured to a timber bearer plugged to the inside face of the lintel spanning the door opening. The hangers which are attached to the back flap hinges have nylon wheels and a ball bearing action. the curved section of the track must be supported across the corner and this is usually done by packing out a short straight length of timber bearer at the correct angle. The radius of the curved track is governed by the distance between the return wall and the jamb of the opening and various radius curves can be fitted. A finished door thickness of 45 mm is the most suitable and the doors are located at floor level in the bottom channel by means of adjustable

117

nylon rollers. A swing or pass door is shown, and a roller bolt steers the swing door round the corner. To fasten the doors, the swing door is secured by a cylinder lock.

Folding doors

The sliding, folding systems are the most sophisticated in terms of track and hanging — see figure 89. They take up less space and can be made to fit more closely at the head. The track, hangers and guides are all similar in principle to those used for the sliding curved type of door except that each pair of doors swings inwards from the hanger. Framed and filled in sliding doors should be of robust construction and should not be less than 45 mm finished thickness. The top rail should be at least 150 mm deep to allow adequate fixing for the hangers. In the case

of very large garage or warehouse doors and doors for industrial use, greater thickness and strength is often necessary. If the sliding folding range of doors is designed with an odd number of leaves, one leaf can swing and be used as a pass door. Figure 89 shows a set of top hung doors of framed, ledged and braced construction and suitable for industrial use in say a warehouse or factory. The top track is of U section galvanized stell and the runners or hangers have ball bearing action. The door is restrained at the fllor level in the usual way by nylon rollers running in a shallow floor channel. Note also the draught stripping at the threshold. Back flap hinges are usual but will be seen at alternative joints on the outside elevation and if this is to be avoided then (100 mm) butt hinges can be used as shown.

FOLDING PARTITION

The sliding folding system of doors is often used in the construction of a room divider. Figure 90 shows a centre hung sliding folding partition used for this purpose. A half leaf is necessary against the frame on one side. The particular example illustrates the use of bottom track and rollers with a top guide. The requirements for bottom track are, however, contradictory since the track giving the least break in the floor surface is least likely to restrain the door properly.

LOUVRED FOLDING PARTITION

This type of partition shown in figure 91 has become popular for use as a room divider or decorative screen. Many firms make this type of door as standard at much less cost than doors of similar construction could be purpose made. Decorative timbers such as North American clear pine or Luan mahogany are used. The rails are dowelled and the louvre slats notched into the styles. This type of door is also suitable for built-in storage units and wardrobes, where maximum access is required.

The use of top and bottom pivots leaves the threshold completely clear, and a spring loaded roller guide is fixed to the top leading corner of each pair of doors to ensure smooth running in the track. Special back flap hinges are used and door

280 mm (max)
Leather cloth stretched over hinge sections
Extruded aluminium hinged supporting plate
Aluminium angle
5 mm self-tapping screws
125x25 timber insert full height of opening

FIXING. JAMB DETAIL

Aluminium plate
Handle

CLOSING JAMB DETAIL

Timber pelmet
Overhead track

HEAD DETAIL

92 Collapsible partition

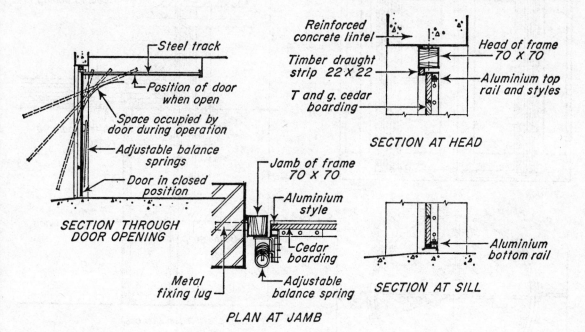

93   Overhead door

alighment plates guide the doors together on the closing style of each pair of doors. If the four panels shown were hung to fold one way, then a different type of track would be required.

COLLAPSIBLE PARTITION

This type of collapsible sliding door or partition has almost become standard construction for use as a space divider in houses, and small community buildings. The partition illustrated in figure 92 is made up of an aluminium alloy collapsible frame over which is stretched leathercloth or similar material. These partitions are top hung and do not require a floor fixing or channel, and an important point to note is the minimum amount of space taken up when the doors are folded back.

OVERHEAD DOORS

This type of door is known colloquially as an *up and over* door. It opens into a horizontal position overhead and is particularly useful for garages and wherever floor space is restricted. The type illus-

trated in figure 93 pivots on a balance spring, and is formed by cedar weatherboarding in an aluminium edge frame. The maximum sixe opening for a door of this type is in the region of 2.500 m wide and 2.100 m high. As the door moves from the vertical to the horizontal position, nylon wheels which are fitted to the top corners of the door run along the steel track at high level, the action of the door being balanced by special springs positioned as shown.

REVOLVING DOORS

Since this type of door requires special fittings and mechanism it is manufactured by specialist firms. The designer has freedom in the design of the leaves of the door and the curved casing. There are various patent methods of collapsing these doors so that a direct through access is possible when desired. The leaves should always be made to collapse in an outward direction in an emergency, and the door should be glazed, using safety glass. For a four compartment door an overall diameter of 1.800 m to 2.100 m is usual. Where luggage has to pass through the doors as in hotel entrances the

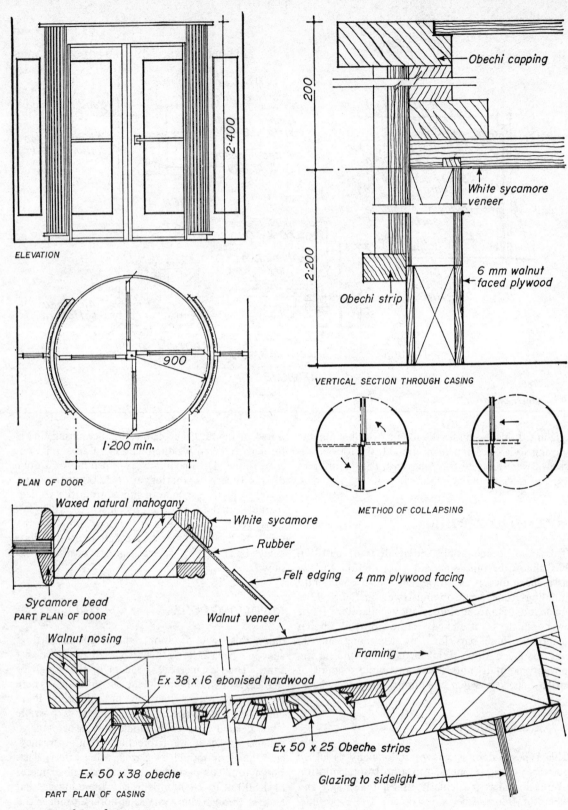

ELEVATION

2·400

200

2·200

Obechi capping

White sycamore veneer

6 mm walnut faced plywood

Obechi strip

VERTICAL SECTION THROUGH CASING

PLAN OF DOOR

900

1·200 min.

METHOD OF COLLAPSING

Waxed natural mahogany

White sycamore

Rubber

Felt edging

4 mm plywood facing

Sycamore bead
PART PLAN OF DOOR

Walnut veneer

Framing

Walnut nosing

Ex 38 x 16 ebonised hardwood

Ex 50 x 25 Obeche strips

Ex 50 x 38 obeche
PART PLAN OF CASING

Glazing to sidelight

94 *Revolving door*

120

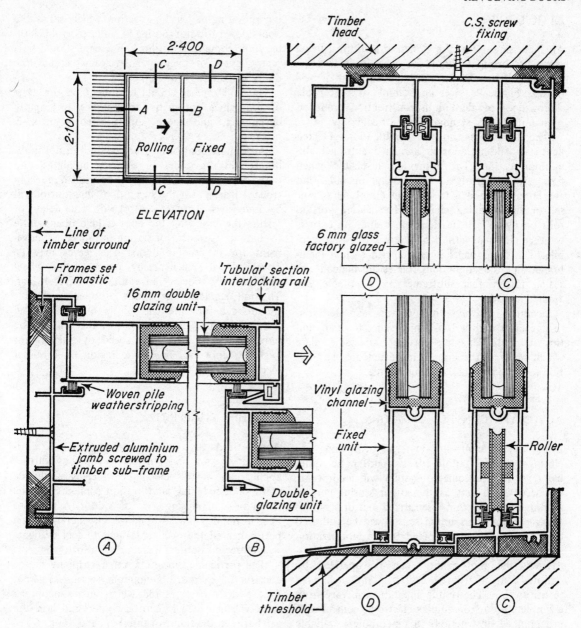

2·400

2·100

C   D

A   B

Rolling   Fixed

C   D

ELEVATION

Timber head

C.S. screw fixing

6 mm glass factory glazed

D   C

Line of timber surround

Frames set in mastic

16 mm double glazing unit

'Tubular' section interlocking rail

Woven pile weatherstripping

Extruded aluminium jamb screwed to timber sub-frame

Double glazing unit

A   B

Vinyl glazing channel

Fixed unit

Roller

Timber threshold

D   C

95   Patio door

large diameter is essential. A four compartment door with associated joinery work is shown in figure 94. Where space is limited a three compartment revolving door can be used and in this case the diameter can be reduced to 1.500 m. It is good practice to place an auxilliary swing door in close proximity to the revolving door and where the revolving doors are used in association with steps at an entrance the first riser should be at least 1.000 m away from the sweep of the doors.

PATIO DOOR

An increasing use of the garden as additional living space has brought about the need for a well designed and draught proof sliding door for domestic use. Figure 95 gives an example of a reversible sliding door of aluminium construction produced to manufacturers' standard sizes for economy.

The illustration shows a combination of fixed light and sliding door in anodized extruded aluminium section. The doors are 'reversible' when fixing for either right or left hand opening, and are factory glazed with a sealed double glass unit set in vinyl glazing channel. The sliding portion rolls on nylon ball bearing rollers and the door is weather stripped with silicone treated woven wool pile. The fixed panel is sealed with a vinyl membrane, and the aluminium frames are bedded and sealed into timber subframes by a suitable gun applied mastic.

Security is always an important consideration, in particular with a door which slides to open, and this particular example has an adjustable plate which prevents the door being lifted out, in addition to a cylinder lock and pull handle.

AUTOMATIC CONTROL OF DOORS

Doors can be controlled in terms of opening and closing by use of various types of automatic equipment. A fully automated system will incorporate a device which acts as the initial sensing control such as a bush-button, a sensitized mat or a photo-electric beam. This initial sensor will be followed by a timing device connected to the motorization apparatus which causes the doors to move. Alternatively the motorization can be operated by remote control from a central point such as a security cabin. The timing apparatus can vary from a simple cut-out to complex electronic control with programmed instructions to incorporate variable time delays for closing and opening doors in series as circumstances or security requires. It is essential that all automatic control devices allow the doors to be moved by hand in the event of a power failure. The motor gear usually takes its initial power from electricity which is then used to generate hydraulic or pneumatic pressure to cause the doors to move as signalled. The equipment should be capable of incorporating a checking action which slows the doors down towards closing in order to avoid clashing and rebound. A further refinement should be a repeat cycle of opening and closing should the door meet any obstruction.

Specialist advice should be sought on this type of gear since automation techniques are rapidly developing, and more sophisticated control is possible.

Automatic control may be required in hospitals, hotels, shops, offices or security buildings, and both swing doors and sliding doors can be controlled. Briefly, for the swing door the control will be as follows, a master control with time delay for setting the time that the door is held open, and a regulating resistance for setting the speed of movement for the sliding doors. The leaves may be driven electro mechanically by a driving wheel attached to a moving rail at the top of each leaf. The rail regulates the width of opening, brakes the door before the end of its movement, and makes electrical disconnection at the end of the movement. The maximum speed of opening for a sliding door will be in the region of 1 m per second.

WEATHER STRIPPING

Apart from the weather stripping details illustrated in the drawings, figures 96-100 show further applications of this technique which is a valuable method of reducing air filtration (draughts) at the threshold and closing style of a door. A point to bear in mind is that as buildings in general become better heated the occupants tend to feel draughts where previously there was no discomfort.

The particular type of weather stripping shown consists of extruded aluminium sections secured to the door or threshold which grip a neoprene strip or pad which in turn is compressed into the gap between the frame or threshold and door.

A double swing external door is a particularly difficult situation since the weather stripping must not impede the smooth action of the door. Figure 96 shows a method of weather stripping the meeting styles of a pair of double swing timber doors. The neoprene insert is available with tongues suitable to seal gaps from 4 mm to 10 mm wide. The neoprene tongue closes and compresses against a strip of PVC in a similar extruded aluminium channel section, both extrusions being fitted into a groove in the face of the styles. Weather stripping on the top rail of the door can also be carried out by using this type of weather stripping. Figure 97 shows a method of weather stripping at the threshold. This will withstand very heavy foot traffic and is ideal provided the 13 mm upstand is not inconvenient. An alternative is shown in figure 98 where the upstand is reduced by cutting a rebate in the threshold. This detail gives a small under-door gap and gives an unobstructed threshold. Toughened glass doors can be weather stripped by fixing an extruded channel with neoprene insert around the closing edges of the doors. The channel is secured by adhesive and is cut away

to accommodate locks or a kicking plate to the base of the door. The neoprene tongue would seal against the glass, but the plain channel provides a symmetrical detail, as shown in figure 99.

A combined stop and compression seal is shown in detail in figure 100. This type of seal is used where an airtight or dust proof seal is required as in a computer room. The door must be sealed all round and top and bottom bolts should be fitted to hold the doors close against the seal.

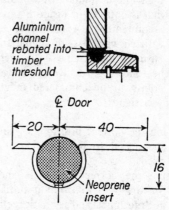

98 *Timber door with rebated threshold*

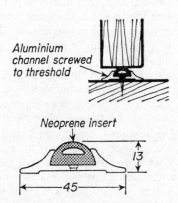

96 *Timber swinging doors*

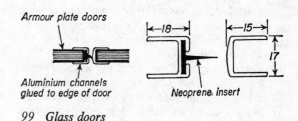

99 *Glass doors*

97 *Timber door with flush threshold*

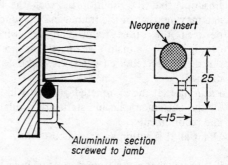

100 *Timber door stop*

4 Windows

DESIGN

A window is an opening designed primarily to let light and/or air into a building. It will also provide a view of what is outside, or inside if this is part of the design requirements. A window opening will normally be fitted with glass or similar transparent material – usually in a frame – to keep out the weather. The following list gives, in broad outline, the main points to be considered in connection with window design:

(a) Choosing the correct positions of the opening with due regard to both aesthetic and functional needs.

(b) Choosing the correct materials and proportions for the frame, so that it fulfils satisfactorily both technical and aesthetic requirements.

(c) Choosing correctly the weight and type of glass for the infil.

(d) Arranging the right part of the window to open, both in respect of proportion of opening and position and type of sash in order to admit any desired amount of fresh air for adequate ventilation.

(e) Determining whether or not the window opening when glazed will have any special requirements in respect of sound or heat insulation.

(f) Making sure that the method of manufacture and jointing will satisfactorily withstand the elements for an agreed period of time.

(g) Ensuring that the junction between the fixed and moving parts of the frame, and the junction between the outer frame and the window opening will remain weathertight throughout their expected life (which should be defined).

(h) Ensuring that the completed product will fulfil all the current applicable statutory regulations and requirements.

(j) Doing all this within an agreed cost limit.

It will be seen that a large number of technical and aesthetic decisions must be correctly taken to pro-
duce a satisfactory component and that windows are a most important building element in respect of giving architectural character to a facade, and controlling the comfort conditions in the room which they light and ventilate. The more important design points are summarized in the following paragraphs.

PERFORMANCE STANDARDS

Lighting

The matter of lighting, both natural daylight and artificial lighting, is part of the fundamental design procedure for a building. Work should be carried out in greater detail at each stage of the design so that the lighting effect of each window has been fully considered before production drawings are made.

The window must light a room efficiently by providing the right amount of daylight in the right place with due regard to the use of the room. Where illumination of the room is a critical factor, the amount of light falling on the working surface at any given point should be calculated. Calculation of illumination levels in respect of daylight is a complex matter and students are referred to *MBS: E and S,* chapter 4, 'Daylighting'.

It is however, not only a matter of providing the right area of window, but the shape and position also affect the distribution of light in the room, together with the amount of obstruction caused by the mullions and transomes.

The contrast between the light area of the window and the dark area of the wall in shadow, in which the window is placed, is an important factor. Too sharp a contrast creates glare. A good illustration of these points, which may be helpful, is to consider the traditional Georgian arrangement of tall windows with wide-splayed internal reveals painted a light colour, which reflect the light well and lessen the contrast between the window and wall. The windows, if they go down to the floor, distribute light over a large area of floor, which

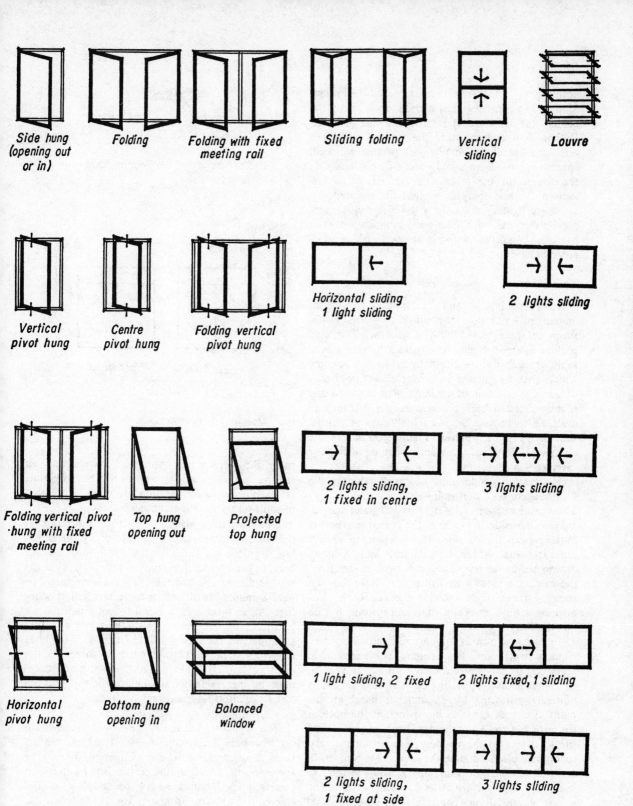

Side hung
(opening out
or in)

Folding

Folding with fixed
meeting rail

Sliding folding

Vertical
sliding

Louvre

Vertical
pivot hung

Centre
pivot hung

Folding vertical
pivot hung

Horizontal sliding
1 light sliding

2 lights sliding

Folding vertical pivot
·hung with fixed
meeting rail

Top hung
opening out

Projected
top hung

2 lights sliding,
1 fixed in centre

3 lights sliding

Horizontal
pivot hung

Bottom hung
opening in

Balanced
window

1 light sliding, 2 fixed

2 lights fixed, 1 sliding

2 lights sliding,
1 fixed at side

3 lights sliding

100   Types of window casements

again gives valuable reflection into the room. Similarly, when they are carried up to near the ceiling, the same effect is produced at high level. Rather than concentrating the window area into one wide opening, a number of openings are used, spaced out so as to avoid areas of deep shade in the corners of the room. Glazing bars of narrow section are also splayed, so that the inclined surfaces are lighted and only a thin edge is in complete shade and dark. The good illumination given by these windows, without an excessive window area, should be noted.

Ventilation

Window openings should be arranged to give an amount of ventilation most suited to the use of the room or space served by the window. This may require a large amount of opening, to give a very rapid change of air or alternatively a small opening which gives a regulated and controlled slow change of air. The question of air movement is considered in more detail in *MBS: E and S,* chapter 3. It may be desirable to provide one or more types of ventilation in the same window. Figure 100 shows the alternative ways of providing opening lights, or casements in a window.

In *handing* a side hung casement window the following convention is followed:
The opening casement is right or left hand according to the side on which the casement occurs looking from the *outside*. The casement is always hinged on the outside of the frame. Most working drawings show a view of the casement as seen from the outside as shown in figure 101. Note that the apex of the triangle showing the convention for opening always indicates the hinged side of the opening light.

In terms of ventilation the vertical sliding sash window is efficient. The opening which is variable according to the position of the sash given ventilation at high level by letting out the used air and is normally protected by an arch or lintel at this point. The sash can also be opened at the bottom for letting in fresh air, the opening being up to half the total area of the window. The opening is easy to operate provided that the window is well made and well balanced. Bottom hung, *opening in* and top hung, *opening out* windows are also an efficient means of ventialtion. The side hung opening casement does not provide draught proof ventilation

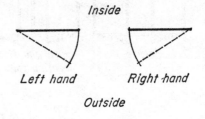

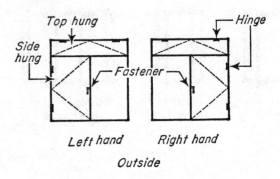

102 Handing of casements

since the vertical slit causes a concentrated air stream. In most windows a small top hung opening is usually provided for slow or night ventilation in addition to the side hung casements.

One particular aspect of natural ventilation — that of habitable rooms — is covered by the Building Regulations. The term *habitable room* in this context includes all living rooms, bedrooms, kitchens and sculleries. A habitable room is required to have a minimum of one or more ventilation openings whose total area is equal to not less than one twentieth of the floor area of the room and that some part of the area is not less than 1.75 m above the floor. The ventilation must be direct to the open air, and an unobstructed 'zone of open space' must be maintained to a window for this purpose (see Regulation K1, paragraph 3).

The regulations make it clear that windows are not the only acceptable means of natural ventilation. A door, for instance, if opening directly to the open air, and fulfilling certain other conditions (see Building Regulations K4, paragraph 4) is considered to be a ventilation opening.

Mechanical ventilation is also permitted, apart

from window openings. The Building Regulations also deal with the ventilation of larders in detail.

Apart from empirical data quoted in the *Building Regulations 1976*, it is not easy to say in precise terms how much opening should be provided to give a certain ventilation rate because this is dependent on wind pressure and *stack effect*. Stack effect occurs mainly in winter, when warm air escapes from the upper part of the room and is replaced by cold, and therefore heavier air from outside.

Appearance

The pattern of windows on the facade is known as the *fenestration*, and this is a very important element in the design of a building being second only in architectural importance to the overall form or mass of the building. Important factors in the fenestration pattern are the subdivision of the window, the proportion of the panes and the recessing or the projection of the window opening. It is important to remember that the lines of sight from windows which afford a good prospect or view should be unobstructed. There should also be clear lines of sight from standing or sitting positions unobstructed by transomes or mullions.

Weather resistance

A draft BS Code of Practice *Performance requirements for Windows* is under consideration which will attempt to define and measure in quantitative terms the functional requirements for windows in respect of resistance to water and air penetration. Methods of testing certain functional requirements for windows are given in BS 4315: Part 1: 1968 and BS 5368: Part 1: 1976. Provision of water checks is important and grooves in the frame and sash are necessary to prevent water being driven through the gap by difference of air pressure. Reference should be made to DD4: 1971 for recommendations for grading of windows relative to wind loads, air infiltration and water penetration, together with notes on window security. A consideration of the sections recommended by the British Woodworking Federation shows the careful thought that is required to produce a window section that will successfully resist water penetration. (This type of *double rebated* timber section is shown in figure 109, page 130. The

twin capillary groove between head and casement prevent water gaining access by capillary attraction and the groove and chamfer between the bottom rail of the casement and the sill is designed to prevent driving rain being blown into the room under the casement. The sill is throated

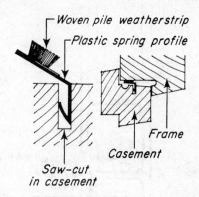

103   Details of woven pile weatherstrip to casements

to catch the water blown under the sill and to allow it to drip clear of the face of the building. The sill is also *weathered*, that is to say, the sloping surface is angled away from the building to take away the water which runs down the face of the glass. The opening casement is also protected by means of a drop mound which projects over the opening. The casement must be fixed so as to give an efficient tight fit against the edge of the rebates on the frame to prevent draughts. Metal window sections can be provided with effective seals in the form of compressible strips of synthetic rubber, or neoprene. With timber, spring strips of metal alloy can be used, but these are probably most effective in curing draughty old windows rather than for use in new windows. A further application of weather stripping by the use of a patented flexible plastic strip section with a tufted polypropylene pile is shown in figure 103.

This type of draught proofing, or *weather stripping* as it is called, helps to provide an even temperature and increase comfort conditions by reducing unwanted air infiltration (draughts). With timber windows, in particular after much use, gaps up to 3 mm may appear between the casement and frame and use of some form of flexible seal at these points is most useful. In respect of metal windows, the opening light may not fit perfectly evenly within its frame. The method of operation of an opening light has a bearing on the importance of including weather stripping. For instance, a reversible (pivot) window is more difficult to make accurately than a side hung casement and thus the

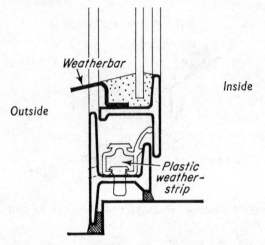

104 *Detail of inward opening casement at sill*

pivot window should always be weather stripped. The most difficult window to weatherseal is an inward opening casement, and an example of weather stripping technique using neoprene strip is shown used in conjunction with an inward opening metal casement in figure 104.

Thermal insulation

The need to conserve heat in buildings has resulted in careful consideration of the total amount of all the windows in a building (area of high heat loss) relative to the opaque part of the wall in which they are located. *The Building Regulations 1976 Part F* stipulates that the *average* thermal transmittance value of the external wall of dwellings (including opaque construction, doors and windows, etc) must not exceed 1.8W/m² °C. It also states that the value for single glazed windows should be taken as 5.7 and for double glazed windows as 2.8W/m² °C. The result is that only a limited proportion of a dwelling's external wall (expressed as a percentage) can be windows. In order to arrive at this percentage, detailed consideration must be taken of the thermal insulation value of the opaque wall (including lintol construction) and how much

of it is exposed to the external air, ie, whether forming a detached, semi-detached, or terraced dwelling. For example, the window area in a *detached* house with brick/block cavity walls ('U' value 1.00) is limited to 17 per cent if single glazed (5.7) or 44 per cent if double glazed (2.8) of the total *external* wall area in order that the average 'U' value for that wall does not exceed 1.8W/m² °C.

Part FF of the *Building Regulations 1976* (coming into force in June 1979) will also limit the areas of *single* glazed windows in buildings other than dwellings (houses, flats or maisonettes) to between 15 and 35 per cent according to the use of the building, ie whether office, factory, shop, warehouse, etc. Regulation FF4 states that the maximum 'U' valve for a wall must be either 0.6 or 0.7 W/m² °C according to the use of the building and the window is assumed to have a valve equivalent to the average 'U' valve of the wall. Apart from the 'U' valves given for single and double glazing above, reference is also made to a triple glazing 'U' valve of 2.0 W/m² °C.

Fire precautions

Another limitation set upon the amount of windows which can be placed in an external wall is that dictated by the need to ensure that fire will not readily spread from one building to another. In the *Building Regulations 1976*, both door and window openings are classified as *'unprotected areas'* when situated in an external wall and a fire within the building in which they are located could be spread rapidly through them to an adjoining property. Therefore, the permitted amount of 'unprotected areas' is again stipulated as a percentage of the remaining fire resisting external wall construstion and the precise amount is determined by its distance from the site boundary or a 'notional boundary' (imaginary boundary between buildings sharing common land). Generally, no windows are permitted within 1.00 M of a boundary, but an increasing percentage of window to fire resisting external wall is allowed the further a building is away from its site boundary.

Further information should be obtained from *Schecule 10* of the *Building Regulation 1976 Part E* and *MBS: Structure and Fabric, Part 2 Chapter 10* which also deals with the requirements of the GLC's London (Constructional) Byelaw 1972.

Sound insulation

A window may have to fulfil particular sound insulation requirements. In this case, special techniques such as various forms of double or treble glazing may be used. See page 185.

Maintenance and cleaning

Good watertight windows which are provided with ventilating openings are a complex piece of construction and need careful maintenance. It is important to consider this factor at the design stage

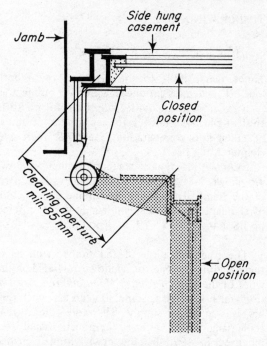

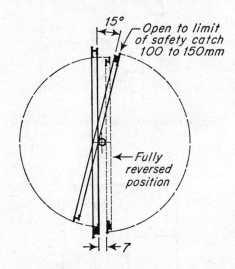

105 Reversible window-space requirements

and to bear in mind that a thoughtful building owner will usually be prepared to do more regular maintenance in return for increased comfort. Buildings which are likely to get rough usage and are impersonal in terms of maintenance should rely on simple detailing without too many refinements.

Cleaning is also a very important consideration: reference should be made to BSCP 153, Part 1: 1969 *Cleaning and Safety*, and CP 153, Part 1: 1970 Windows and Rooflights: Durability and Maintenance. In multi-storey buildings with large areas of glazing special cradles cantilevered from the face of the building may be necessary, but wherever possible, windows should be designed so that all parts can be cleaned from the inside. This will probably require special hinges or the choice of an inward opening type of window usually a pivot.

106 Extending (easy-clean) hinge.
Space requirements

In pivoted windows the design of the pivot hinge should allow the window to turn through 180°. This is illustrated in figure 105, and adequate space must be allowed in the design of the building where this type of window is used. The effect of fitting an extending hinge or *easy-clean* hinge is shown in figure 106. The space requirements for a standard top hung casement is shown in figure 107.

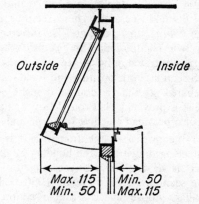

107 STANDARD TOP HUNG CASEMENT (B.S. 990) SPACE REQUIREMENTS

TIMBER WINDOWS

Standard timber windows

Timber lends itself to the manufacture of both 'one-off' and mass produced windows, but factors such as movement with variations in moisture content and the tendency for sapwood to rot, must be taken into consideration. See *MBS: Materials,* chapter 2.

Examples of typical standard timber windows are shown in figure 42 naming the various parts of the frame. The quality, design and construction of standard timber casement windows are covered in BS 644: Part I: 1951: *Wood Casement Windows.*

The standardization of the timber sections in these traditional types of windows are based on the work of the *English Joinery Manufacturers Association* which took place some 30 years ago when timber was in scarce supply. Therefore, the current trade name 'EJMA' refer to these sections and were inherited in 1976 by the newly formed *British Woodworking Federation* (an amalgamation of the former British Woodwork Manufacturers Association and the Joinery and Timber Construction Association). The BWF are concerned that these sections need revising in view of the present attitudes towards cost-in-use, weathering and energy conservation. For example, EJMA sections are not as cheap to manufacture as in the past because of imperial/metric dimensional conversion descrepancies, they cannot be effectively weatherstripped, and will not readily accept double glazing units.

Figure 108 shows a typical window manufactured from BS 644 sections. These sections are based on the *twin rebated* principle. The difference between the twin rebate section and a single rebate arrangement is illustrated in figure 109.

In the BS section, both opening and fixed members are rebated so that a double draught and weather check is provided. Half round anti-capillary grooves are also provided on edges of opening members and in the reveals of the frame. This is to prevent rain being drawn into the building by capillary attraction via a close fitting casement. The single rebate section, shown in figure 109(b), also has anti-capillary grooves and is a simple section to fabricate. Thus it is suitable for production of non-standard windows for small contracts. For comparison with the outward opening casement a timber inward opening casement section is shown in figure 110.

A selection from a range of modified BS windows prepared for double glazing is shown in figure 113. In respect of the production of a modular co-ordinated range of timber windows, the BWF

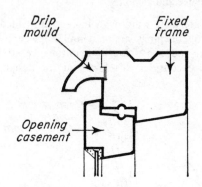

(a)   *Double rebated (lipped) casement*

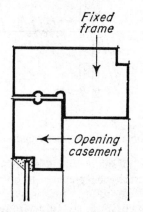

(b)   *Single rebated casement*
109   Window rebates

await the revision of the relevant British Standards. The British Standard windows shown, and windows made with sections, modified from the BS, are supplied from stock by approved manufacturers. These windows are highly competitive in price.

The lower members of wood windows frequently decay due to water entering via rebates and joints. The NBRC and the GLC now require window frames and sashes constructed from non-durable or perishable timbers must be treated with a preservative (see also page 35).

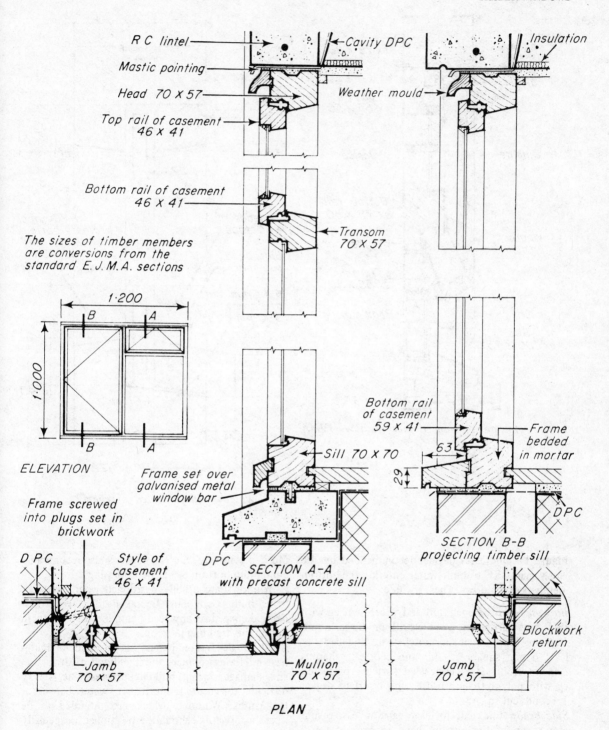

R C lintel

Mastic pointing

Head 70 X 57

Top rail of casement
46 X 41

Cavity DPC

Insulation

Weather mould

Bottom rail of casement
46 X 41

Transom
70 X 57

The sizes of timber members
are conversions from the
standard E.J.M.A. sections

1·200

B   A

1·000

B   A

ELEVATION

Frame screwed
into plugs set in
brickwork

DPC

Style of
casement
46 X 41

Frame set over
galvanised metal
window bar

Sill 70 X 70

DPC

SECTION A-A
with precast concrete sill

Bottom rail
of casement
59 X 41

Frame
bedded
in mortar

63

29

DPC

SECTION B-B
projecting timber sill

Jamb
70 X 57

Mullion
70 X 57

Jamb
70 X 57

Blockwork
return

PLAN

108   Standard casement windows (EJMA section)

131

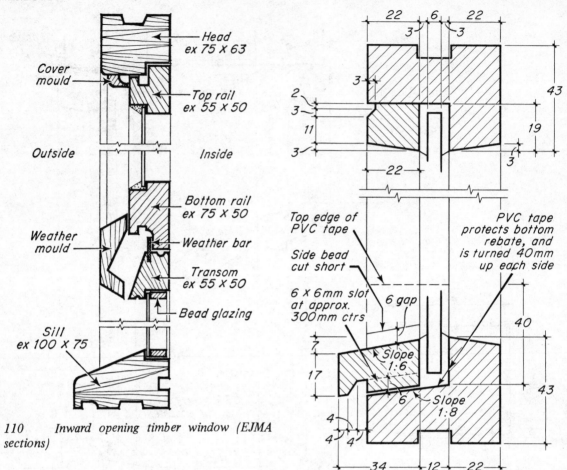

110   Inward opening timber window (EJMA sections)

111   Window with protected sill rebate

Figure 111 indicates devices recommended by the Norwegian BRE to limit water entering the bottom members of windows. These include:

Bottom rebate: sloped 1:8 and protected, eg with PVC tape carried up the sides 40 mm at each end.
Bottom bead: drainage notches in underside at least 6 mm square at 300 mm centres; generous drip to front edge; concealed surfaces protected eg with polyurethane varnish; upper surface sloped 1:6; ends cut square.
Side beads: Ends cut to leave gaps at least 6 mm above top of the bottom bead to prevent water entering the end grain.

More expensively, the Norwegian's also recommend aluminium bottom beads incorporating drips.

Windows are usually positioned when walls are being built. Care must be taken to prevent their being damaged or any load being imposed on them during the 'building in' process.

Although fixing joinery in formed openings (second fixing) reduces the likelihood of distortion and damage during building processes, it is very difficult to ensure an effective water barrier at the jambs. Windows which are intended to be 'fixed afterwards', should be positioned in specially designed rebated reveals — see figure 112.

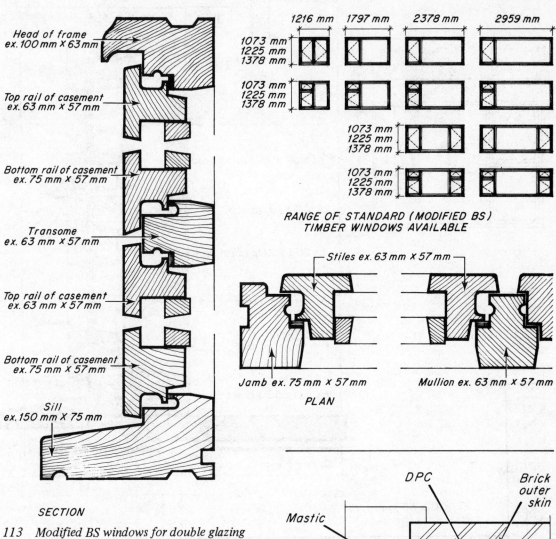

Head of frame
ex. 100 mm X 63 mm

Top rail of casement
ex. 63 mm X 57 mm

Bottom rail of casement
ex. 75 mm X 57 mm

Transome
ex. 63 mm X 57 mm

Top rail of casement
ex. 63 mm X 57 mm

Bottom rail of casement
ex. 75 mm X 57 mm

Sill
ex. 150 mm X 75 mm

SECTION

113   Modified BS windows for double glazing

	1216 mm	1797 mm	2378 mm	2959 mm

1073 mm
1225 mm
1378 mm

1073 mm
1225 mm
1378 mm

1073 mm
1225 mm
1378 mm

1073 mm
1225 mm
1378 mm

RANGE OF STANDARD (MODIFIED BS)
TIMBER WINDOWS AVAILABLE

Stiles ex. 63 mm X 57 mm

Jamb ex. 75 mm X 57 mm   Mullion ex. 63 mm X 57 mm

PLAN

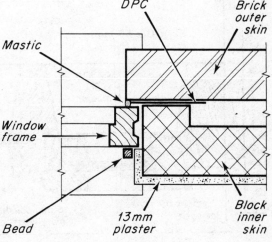

DPC

Brick outer skin

Mastic

Window frame

Bead

13mm plaster

Block inner skin

112   Rebated reveal

Double rebated casement

A non-standard window constructed on the double rebate, or lipped casement principle, is shown in figure 114. These sections must be carefully made to be a good fit on the comparatively small areas of timber that are in contact when the casement is

133

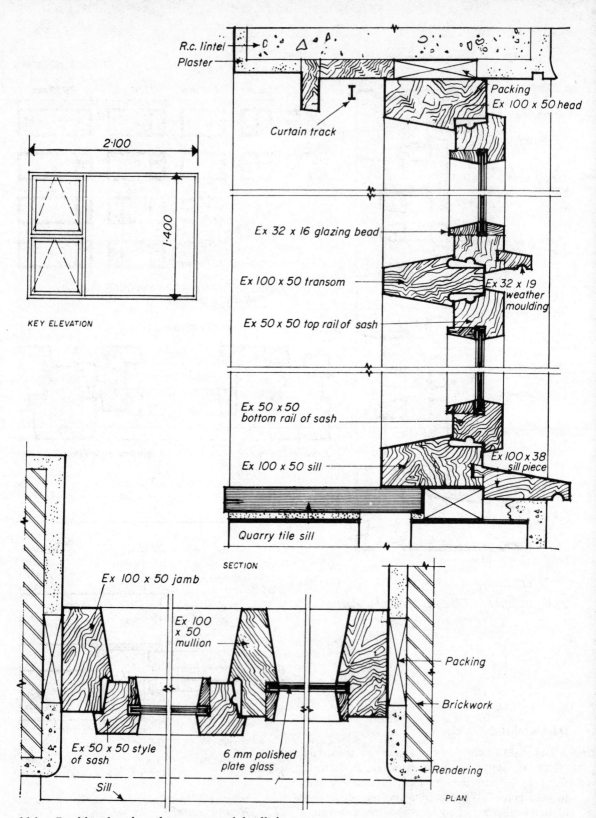

2·100

1·400

KEY ELEVATION

R.c. lintel

Plaster

Curtain track

Packing

Ex 100 x 50 head

Ex 32 x 16 glazing bead

Ex 100 x 50 transom

Ex 32 x 19 weather moulding

Ex 50 x 50 top rail of sash

Ex 50 x 50 bottom rail of sash

Ex 100 x 50 sill

Ex 100 x 38 sill piece

Quarry tile sill

SECTION

Ex 100 x 50 jamb

Ex 100 x 50 mullion

Packing

Brickwork

Ex 50 x 50 style of sash

6 mm polished plate glass

Rendering

Sill

PLAN

114   Double rebated top hung vents and deadlight

closed. Another point to note here, is that the two top hung opening lights are one above the other which means that the detail at the transom between the two openers must be very carefully considered. The additional weather moulding is very necessary at this point, otherwise the rain would run down the glass on the upper casement and be blown into the unprotected top rebate of the lower casement. Another point to notice is that the window is fixed (by screwing) to timber packing pieces plugged to the brickwork, which is a technique suitable where the window is part of the *second fixing* operations, being placed and secured in position after the opening is formed. The frame is set well forward in the opening and this leaves space for the formation of a *blind box* on the soffit, so that curtains may be hung within the window opening.

Inward opening casement

Figure 115 shows details of a lipped or double rebated casement window, inward opening and hung folding. This is to say, the two lock styles are rebated together and there is no centre mullion against which the casements would normally close. Inward opening is convenient for cleaning but inconvenient for conventional curtains. This type of window is much used on the continent and is meant to be either shut or fully open. The example is arranged on the inside of the wall thickness so that each casement can fold back, out of the way, against the wall. Note the zinc sheet covering dressed on a timber sill, also a continental detail which is quite satisfactory provided the ends are turned up against the brickwork and tucked in. The metal balustrade has a bottom rail so that the sill is not perforated by the fixing of the balusters. The sill details for an inward opening casement, always need special consideration because the rebate is reversed and rain will enter unless a waterbar or weather board is used. The channel waterbar shown gives double protection from driving rain and the outer flange is provided with draining holes at intervals.

Horizontal pivot windows

There is no British Standard for this type of window, but most manufacturers produce a 'standard' range for delivery from stock. Other types of timber windows not covered by BS, eg inward opening casements, casements for double glazing and double casements, are also made to manufacturers' standard ranges.

Figure 116 shows a horizontal pivot hung timber window – the word *horizontal* refers to the placing of the hinges, which are opposed horizontally. The hinges of a vertical pivot hung window would be one above the other in a vertical ine. The success of a pivot window depend upon the friction action of the hinge which should be strong enough to hold the window firmly in any open position. The pivot hung window is very much used because it gives a neat appearance to the facade of a building and provides good control of ventilation. There may be some difficulty in respect of hanging curtains or blinds on the inside of the window if the frame is set back into the window reveal. The example is shown fixed as far as possible towards the front of the brickwork opening and secured by rustproofed metal lugs. These lugs are screwed to the back of the frame and 'built in' as the brickwork is carried up when the opening is formed, as shown on the plan in figure 116. The opening casement is secured in this example by an espagnolette bolt which holds the casement to the frame at four points.

Double sash pivot window

The horizontally pivoted double sash has for a long time been developed by window specialists on the continent and is now produced by several manufacturers for use in this country. Details of such a window are shown in figure 117. The outer sash is secured to the inner sash and hinged so that the space between can be cleaned. The joint between the two sashes is not airtight, in fact the simple locking device is also a spacer to ensure that external air can circulate through the space. The air circulation should be enough to evaporate any condensation within the space but not sufficient to have any serious overall cooling effect. To separate the two sashes they have to be rotated through 180°. Accordian pleated, or venetian blinds can be fixed in the space and operated from the side with cords. These windows, being balanced, can be made to a large size, limiting factors being the distance the top swings into the room and the extra cost of plate glass. The window can be fastened with a mortice turn button into the sill, but larger windows need securing at all corners by an espag-

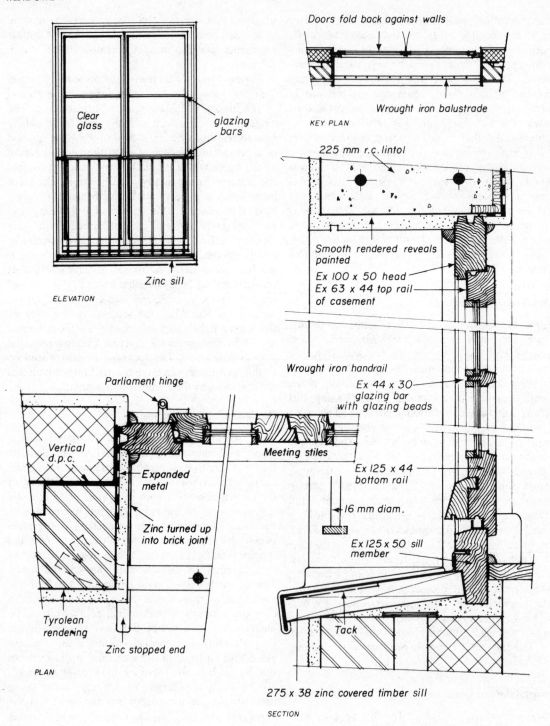

Clear glass

glazing bars

Zinc sill

ELEVATION

Doors fold back against walls

Wrought iron balustrade

KEY PLAN

225 mm r.c. lintol

Smooth rendered reveals painted

Ex 100 x 50 head

Ex 63 x 44 top rail of casement

Wrought iron handrail

Ex 44 x 30 glazing bar with glazing beads

Meeting stiles

Ex 125 x 44 bottom rail

16 mm diam.

Ex 125 x 50 sill member

Parliament hinge

Vertical d.p.c.

Expanded metal

Zinc turned up into brick joint

Tyrolean rendering

Zinc stopped end

PLAN

Tack

275 x 38 zinc covered timber sill

SECTION

115 *Inward opening casement*

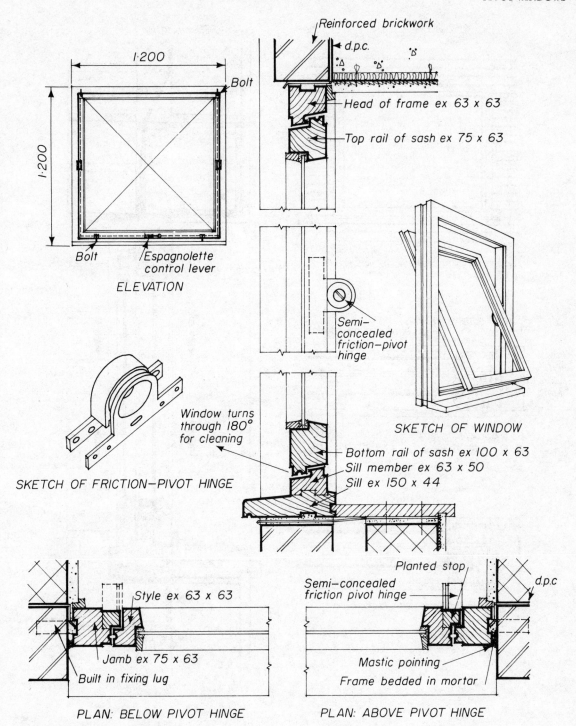

1.200

1.200

Bolt

Bolt

Espagnolette
control lever

ELEVATION

Reinforced brickwork

d.p.c.

Head of frame ex 63 x 63

Top rail of sash ex 75 x 63

Semi-
concealed
friction-pivot
hinge

SKETCH OF WINDOW

Window turns
through 180°
for cleaning

SKETCH OF FRICTION–PIVOT HINGE

Bottom rail of sash ex 100 x 63
Sill member ex 63 x 50
Sill ex 150 x 44

Style ex 63 x 63

Jamb ex 75 x 63

Built in fixing lug

PLAN: BELOW PIVOT HINGE

Planted stop

Semi-concealed
friction pivot hinge

d.p.c

Mastic pointing

Frame bedded in mortar

PLAN: ABOVE PIVOT HINGE

116   Horizontal pivot window – single sash

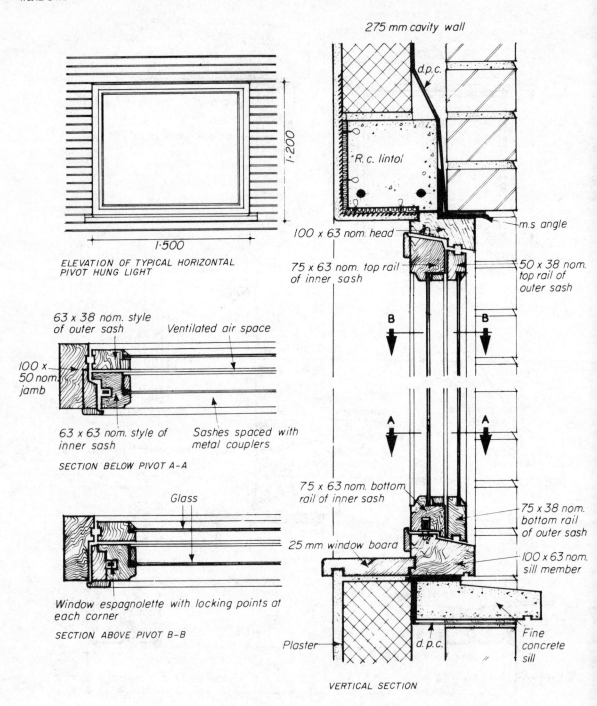

ELEVATION OF TYPICAL HORIZONTAL
PIVOT HUNG LIGHT

1·500

1·200

275 mm cavity wall

d.p.c.

R.c. lintol

m.s angle

100 x 63 nom. head

75 x 63 nom. top rail
of inner sash

50 x 38 nom.
top rail of
outer sash

B   B

A   A

75 x 63 nom. bottom
rail of inner sash

75 x 38 nom.
bottom rail
of outer sash

25 mm window board

100 x 63 nom.
sill member

Plaster

d.p.c.

Fine
concrete
sill

VERTICAL SECTION

63 x 38 nom. style
of outer sash

Ventilated air space

100 x
50 nom.
jamb

63 x 63 nom. style of
inner sash

Sashes spaced with
metal couplers

SECTION BELOW PIVOT A–A

Glass

Window espagnolette with locking points at
each corner

SECTION ABOVE PIVOT B–B

117 *Horizontal pivot window – double sash*

nolette bolt set in a groove on three sides and operated by one handle. The pivot mechanism holds the sash in any desired open position by friction. Note the traditional method of *weathering* the window opening, shown in figure 117, by means of a mild steel angle to support the outer leaf of brickwork and a sheet lead cavity *tray*. The lead must be carried over the metal angle to catch any water which may run down inside the cavity from a saturated outer leaf. This construction can now be effected using a specially fabricated all metal section which replaces the inner RC lintel, the cavity dpc and the mild steel angle.

Sliding and sliding-folding windows

In detailing sliding and sliding-folding windows bottom rollers are usually preferred to top track since the track is more difficult to conceal. Provision for draught exclusion is very important and this can be provided quite easily on the vertical edges. On the sill and head, however, there are many difficulties in particular with sliding windows. Where the window is sliding-folding however it is more easily draughtproofed as the final closing of the sash and shooting of the fixing bolts near the hinges can be ranged to clamp the sashes against the sill and at the head.

Horizontal sliding-folding window

Figure 118 shows details of a sliding-folding window. The sashes (nominal thickness 50 mm) are supported on bottom runners which incorporate the hinge and run on special hard brass or sherardized steel track screwed into the sill. There is ample provision for adjusting the rebate and sill and head as well as the jambs to ensure a close fit. Outward opening lights are most common as they do not interfere with curtaining and are easier to make weather-proof. The frame is shown nailed into fixing blocks built into the brickwork.

Horizontal sliding window

Straight sliding windows are more common and providing access to a terrace they should really be called sliding doors but the distinction is not important. Several alternative track arrangements are possible, the simplest is where single sliding windows are used, each sliding frame passes a fixed light of similar size. This reduces the amount of

track and the joints between the opening sashes. A typical example is shown in figure 119. In this case the timber posts or *mullions* support the lintel above. One large fixed light is fixed direct to the mullions in a rebate and the sliding window passes behind the mullion and fixed light. This simplifies the joint at the jambs and enables the top track to be fixed on a packing at the side of the lintel. The door is carried on rollers running on a track let into the floor. The larger sashes are nominal 63 mm thick with 150 mm styles and bottom rail and with 100 mm top rail. Cavity sealed double glazing is used in the example. The weight of these sashes is considerable so 8 rollers are used. For single glazing and smaller sashes 2 rollers should be sufficient. The precautions to exclude draught include at one side a phosphor-bronze weather strip against which the sash closes. At the other side a felt strip fixed to the mullion is pressed by a hardwood stop which can be scribed to fit close. At the top is another weather strip fixed to the head and which rubs against the top rail as it closes. As an alternative to the phosphor-bronze weathering shown, the detail could be draught and weather-proofed by the use of wool-pile or neoprene weather stripping in extruded aluminium sections. A metal water bar is fixed to the floor runner and a cover strip which can be scribed and fixed with cups and screws overlaps this.

Vertical sliding sash

The quality, design and construction of standard *double hung* sash windows is covered by BS 644: Part 2: 1958: *English Type* and Part 3: 1951: *Scottish Type.*

The frames were traditionally 'cased' with vertical boxes containing weights supported by cords carried over pulleys to counterbalance the sashes and hold them open in any required position. Today, sashes are supported by spiral balance springs. For smaller windows the springs are in grooves in the sashes and for larger windows in the frames.

Figure 120 shows typical arrangements for a domestic type window with cased and solid frames.

Fixing timber windows

Figure 12(a)-(e) illustrates various methods of locating timber windows in openings in the following types of construction

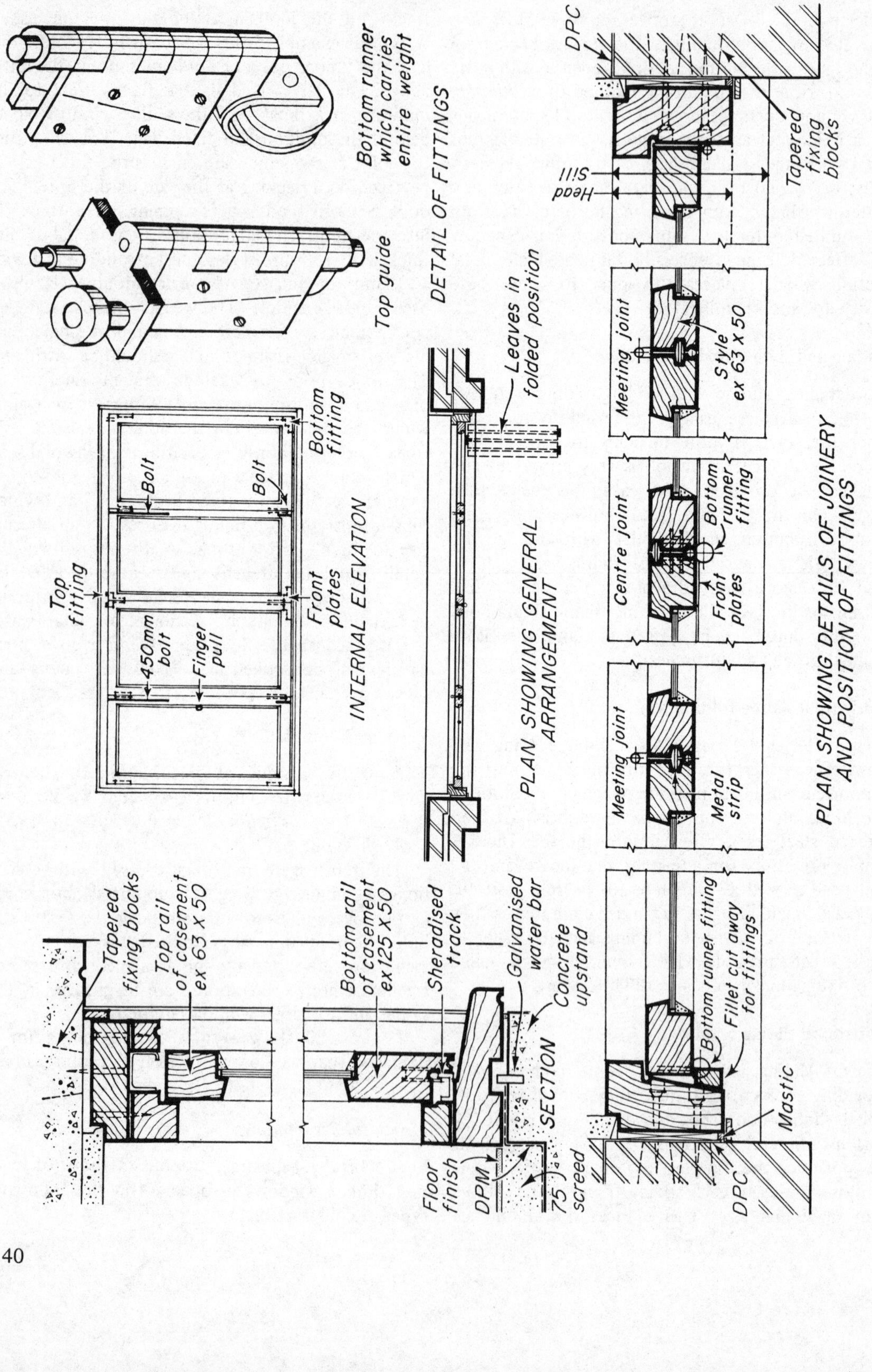

Bottom runner which carries entire weight

Top guide

DETAIL OF FITTINGS

Leaves in folded position

PLAN SHOWING GENERAL ARRANGEMENT

Top fitting

Bolt

Bolt

Bottom fitting

Front plates

450mm bolt

Finger pull

INTERNAL ELEVATION

DPC

Head

Sill

Tapered fixing blocks

Meeting joint

Style ex 63 x 50

Centre joint

Bottom runner fitting

Front plates

Meeting joint

Metal strip

PLAN SHOWING DETAILS OF JOINERY AND POSITION OF FITTINGS

Tapered fixing blocks

Top rail of casement ex 63 x 50

Bottom rail of casement ex 125 x 50

Sheradised track

Galvanised water bar

Concrete upstand

SECTION

Floor finish

DPM

75 screed

Bottom runner fitting

Fillet cut away for fittings

Mastic

DPC

118   Horizontal sliding-folding timber windows

140

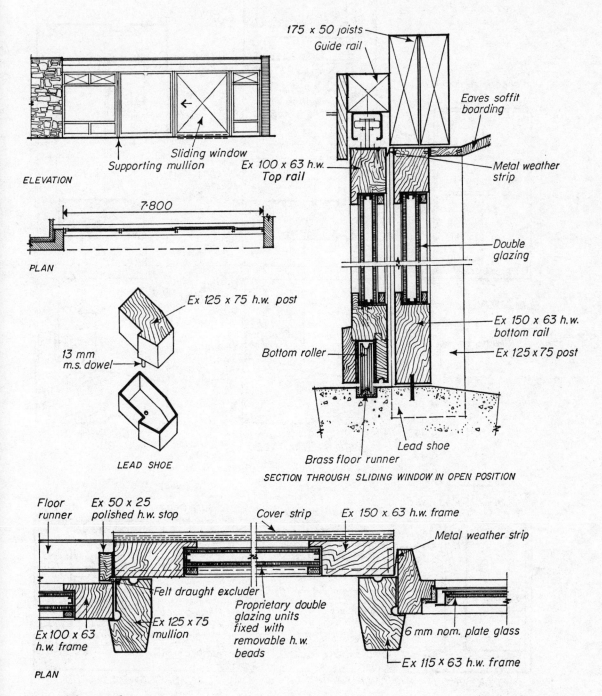

ELEVATION

Supporting mullion

Sliding window

PLAN

7·800

Ex 125 x 75 h.w. post

13 mm
m.s. dowel

LEAD SHOE

175 x 50 joists

Guide rail

Eaves soffit
boarding

Ex 100 x 63 h.w.
Top rail

Metal weather
strip

Double
glazing

Ex 150 x 63 h.w.
bottom rail

Bottom roller

Ex 125 x 75 post

Lead shoe

Brass floor runner

SECTION THROUGH SLIDING WINDOW IN OPEN POSITION

Floor
runner

Ex 50 x 25
polished h.w. stop

Cover strip

Ex 150 x 63 h.w. frame

Metal weather strip

Felt draught excluder

Ex 125 x 75
mullion

Proprietary double
glazing units
fixed with
removable h.w.
beads

6 mm nom. plate glass

Ex 100 x 63
h.w. frame

Ex 115 x 63 h.w. frame

PLAN

119   Sliding window

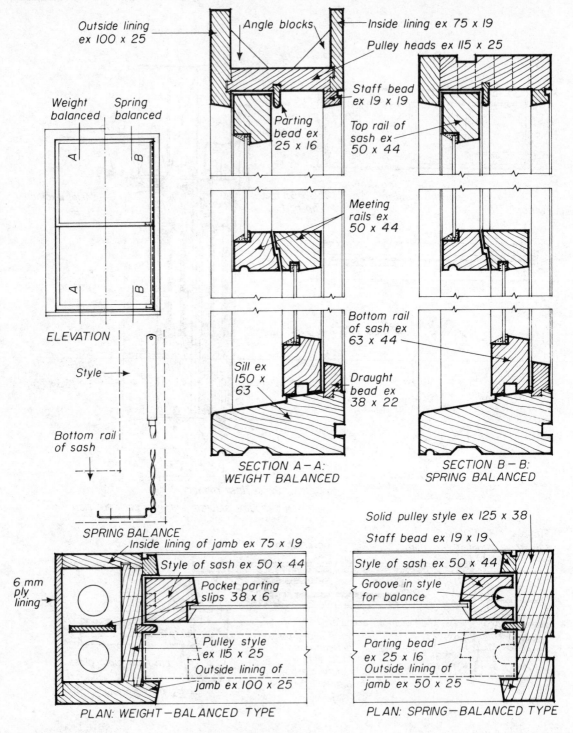

Outside lining ex 100 x 25

Angle blocks

Inside lining ex 75 x 19

Pulley heads ex 115 x 25

Staff bead ex 19 x 19

Parting bead ex 25 x 16

Top rail of sash ex 50 x 44

Weight balanced

Spring balanced

ELEVATION

Style

Bottom rail of sash

SPRING BALANCE

Meeting rails ex 50 x 44

Bottom rail of sash ex 63 x 44

Sill ex 150 x 63

Draught bead ex 38 x 22

SECTION A – A: WEIGHT BALANCED

SECTION B – B: SPRING BALANCED

Inside lining of jamb ex 75 x 19

Style of sash ex 50 x 44

Pocket parting slips 38 x 6

6 mm ply lining

Pulley style ex 115 x 25

Outside lining of jamb ex 100 x 25

PLAN: WEIGHT – BALANCED TYPE

Solid pulley style ex 125 x 38

Staff bead ex 19 x 19

Style of sash ex 50 x 44

Groove in style for balance

Parting bead ex 25 x 16

Outside lining of jamb ex 50 x 25

PLAN: SPRING – BALANCED TYPE

120 Standard timber vertically sliding sash windows

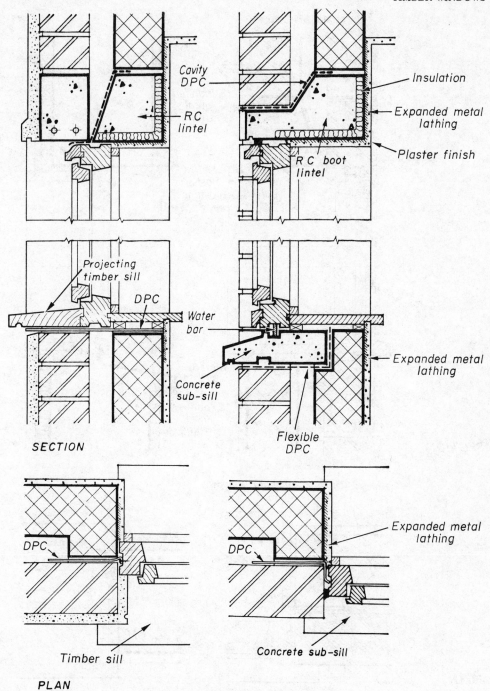

Cavity
DPC

RC
lintel

Insulation

Expanded metal
lathing

Plaster finish

RC boot
lintel

Projecting
timber sill

DPC

Water
bar

Expanded metal
lathing

Concrete
sub-sill

SECTION

Flexible
DPC

DPC

Expanded metal
lathing

DPC

Timber sill

Concrete sub-sill

PLAN

(a) *Cavity wall construction*

(b) *Cavity wall construction*

121   *Methods of locating timber windows*

143

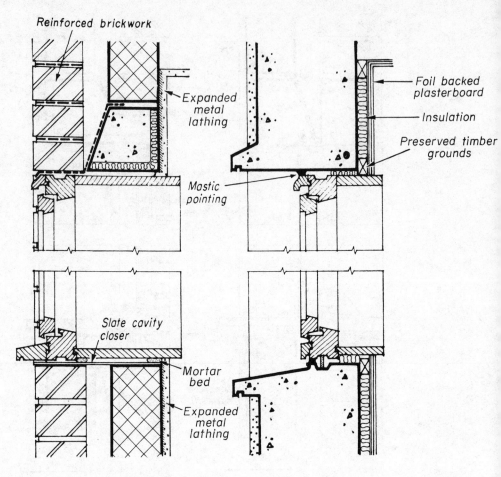

Reinforced brickwork

Expanded metal lathing

Mastic pointing

Foil backed plasterboard

Insulation

Preserved timber grounds

Slate cavity closer

Mortar bed

Expanded metal lathing

SECTION

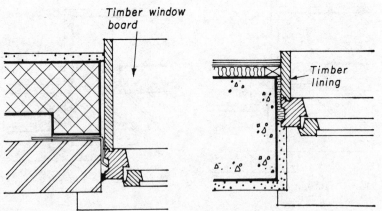

Timber window board

Timber lining

PLAN

(c) *Cavity wall construction*   (d) *Monolithic concrete construction*

121 Methods of locating timber windows

144

1 traditional load bearing cavity walling
2 monolithic concrete construction
3 timber framed construction.

The window frames should not be called upon to take any load from the structure; the opening being 'self-supporting'. It is not altogether easy to ensure that the frame is relieved of load if the frame is built into the opening as the main work of construction proceeds. On the other hand, this method ensures a good fit for the window. Where the window is placed in position after the opening is formed there may be difficulties in ensuring correct tolerances or a good connection with the jamb dpc, but there is likely to be less damage to the frame.

Wood windows should always be fixed to the dry leaf of cavity walling or otherwise be protected by a vertical damp proof course. There should always be a vertical dpc between the wet and the dry leaf in a cavity wall. The face of the gap between the woodwork and the brickwork should be sealed with a suitable strip of mastic. Rebates for glazing should be at least 9 mm deep. The glass is usually put in with putty formed to a triangular bead with a putty knife. For a higher class of work, weathered timber beads scribed or mitred at the corners can be pinned in with brass pins or screwed with brass screws. The glass in this case should have putty 'back and front' to allow for even support. For more detailed notes on glazing see chapter 5. The sill must be weathered at a sufficient slope to throw off the water and *throated* with a groove near the front on its underside so that the water will drip off and not run back to the bed of the sill. Sills are usually pointed in mastic and may have a water bar to act as an additional check against the penetration of moisture at this point, and to locate the sill horizontally.

In some cases, a sub-sill of tiles, stone, concrete, or metal on to which the timber window sill sits is specified. Again, the sub-sill must be provided with a *throating* or *drip* in order to shed water as far as practicable away from the wall face below.

Sills are very subject to defects caused by dampness. Either the weathering is not sufficiently steep to shed the water, or water can get back to the bed of the sill because the drip does not function, or because the slope of a concrete or stone sub-sill allows the water to run back instead of outwards. These are points to watch carefully. Paint cannot

be relied upon to protect timber at this critical point, and it will be noted that BS 1186 does not permit sapwood in timber sills.

The head is not so troublesome usually, but the dpc in a cavity above must catch water running down the inside surface of the outside skin and conduct it properly to the outside of the head.

Window frames should be secured to walls by means of metal lugs (see figure 72, page 95) or, alternatively, screwed in place into plastic or similar plugs cast or drilled into the surrounding masonry. The frames should be bedded in cement mortar with the external joint sealed by the application of the correct mastic.

Points to note about the various details shown are as follows:

(a) The head of the opening is supported by two reinforced concrete lintels, the inner one splayed to close the cavity over the frame. The exposed faces of the inner lintel have been lined with 12 mm polystyrene insulation to lessen the 'cold bridge' effect resulting in the differing thermal efficiency of concrete as compared with the *lightweight* concrete block it supports. In order to provide a good key to the subsequent plaster finish, this polystyrene skin is often lined with expanded metal lathing which may be extended to lap with the blockwork above to avoid the effects of differential cracking between the two materials (see also figure 117).

The *cavity tray* or *cavity flashing* can be of patented form consisting of a thin layer of metal (lead or copper) sandwiched both sides with bitumen impregnated felt.

The timber sill which should preferably be of hardwood is projected over the external rendering. This projection should be a minimum 35 mm and preferably 50 mm in order to shed water clear of the face of the building. The cavity wall should always be sealed with a dpc below the window sill and board to ensure that their undersides are protected from moist air within the cavity. This seal also counteracts possible damage to the wall below by water which may permeate around the sill's defences.

At the jamb the dpc is turned into the groove into the timber frame. The frame would be

145

set in mortar by 'buttering' the opening as the brickwork is built. The frame is built in as the work proceeds. Note that the dpc projects into the cavity by about 40 mm to avoid any 'short circuiting' of water at the brick/block junction.

At the jamb the cavity is closed by return of the inner leaf brickwork against a vertical dpc. This dpc will be the same material used as the horizontal damp proof course or asbestos based bituminous felt.

(b) Both leaves of the cavity wall are supported by a reinforced concrete *boot* lintel. This is a neat detail which allows a more satisfactory placing of the cavity flashing than in figure 121a. This detail shows a concrete sub-sill, whereby the bottom sill member of the timber window frame has a drip mould which guides the water on to the concrete sill which protects the main structure. This is more expensive but more satisfactory construction than in figure 121a which relies on the timber sill being of first class quality and being regularly maintained by painting. The window frame will be set in cement mortar at the jamb and head whilst the metal water bar which seals the gap between the timber frame and the concrete sill, will be set in mastic. The outer edges of the frame will also be pointed in mastic. The plaster is returned on the soffit of the concrete lintel at the head of window and is 'tucked in' behind the frame. The frame may alternatively be grooved to receive the plaster and a small cover strip would prevent a view of the crack which will develop between the frame and plaster.

(c) Here the inner leaf of the walling is supported by a splayed or reinforced concrete lintel whilst the outer brickwork is reinforced by expanded metal strips for 3 or 4 courses over the opening. The reinforcing (which could also be done by small diameter — say 6 mm mild steel rods — should extend a minimum of 225 mm beyond the opening on each side. The technique is suitable for small spans say up to 3.000 m and gives a very neat external appearance since the bonded brickwork carries on in an unbroken line over the opening. The window frame here is set towards the front of the

opening and the cavity gap is lined by timber. This saves the cost of plastering and provides fixings for curtains and blinds.

(d) The walling construction here is of reinforced concrete. The frame will be fitted into the opening afterwards and will be secured either by screwing through the frame into plastic or timber plugs cast into the concrete or by means of protected metal strips screwed to the back of the frame and into the concrete soffit and jambs. The frame will be set in mortar and pointed in mastic.

(e) A timber window is most easily screwed into timber framed construction as illustrated here.

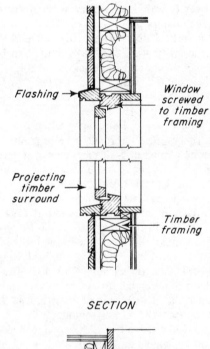

SECTION

PLAN

(e)   *Timber frame construction*

121   *Timber windows – continued*

The weatherboarding will be backed by a building paper lining and a metal flashing over the projecting window head would be an advantage.

In general, timber windows will be screwed or nailed to plugs or secured by means of metal fixing lugs, at the jambs only. Large windows will also be secured at the head but the sill will almost always be used to locate but not to secure the window. The minimum number of fixing points will be 4 for a window say 600 mm square up to 8 for a window say 1800 mm square.

Figure 122a and b shows the location of timber windows with projecting surrounds set in a tile hung opening.

For details of dormer windows and skylights in pitch roof see Chapter 6 pages 198-201.

METAL WINDOWS

Steel and aluminium are the most common metals used in the manufacture of window sections. Where cost, in terms of permanency and freedom from maintenance, can be justified bronze is a material which can be used as an alternative. Stain-less steel is a material which is eminently suitable for use for window frames and its rapid development as a building material for more general use may make it the window material of the future.

Steel windows

Galvanized hot rolled steel provides a material from which an economical range of windows with reasonable maitenance costs can be produced. White hot steel ingots are passed through rollers to form a billet of steel some 50 mm square 1200 mm long. The billet is then re-heated and 're-rolled' through a further series of rollers under very heavy pressure which produces the correct section profile from which the window frame is welded up. Sections are then normally galvanized by dipping in molten zinc. Regular painting is nevertheless essential.

Standard steel windows

The relevant main British Standards for metal windows are as follows:

BS 990: 1972: *Steel windows generally for domestic and similar buildings*

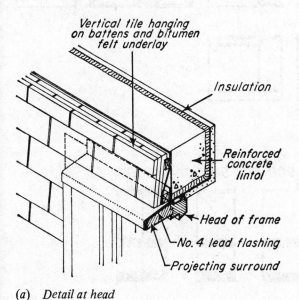

(a) *Detail at head*

122 *Projecting timber window surround*

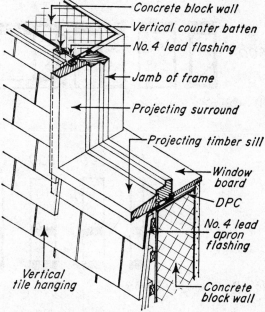

(b) *Detail at sill and jamb*

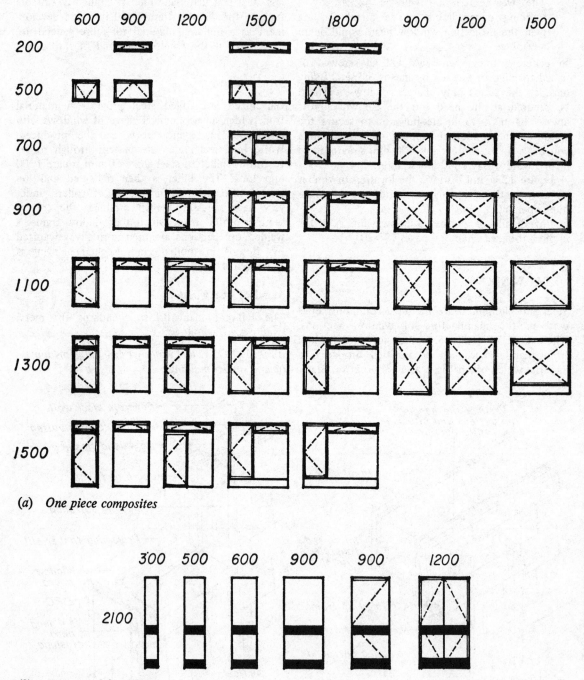

(a) *One piece composites*

(b) *Doors and fixed lights*

123 *Selection of module 100 steel windows*

BS 1787: 1957: *Steel Windows for Industrial Buildings*

BS 2503: 1954: *Steel Windows for Agricultural Use*

BS 1285: 1963: *Wood Surrounds for Steel Windows and Doors.*

'Module 4' windows

Module 4 sizes based on BS 990 are not dimensionally co-ordinated. The window sizes are based on multiples of 102 mm, the vertical increments being basically 203 mm and the horizontal increments 305 mm. Top hung casements are normally 203 mm high.

size, and also the relationship of the metal frames in timber surrounds to the modular size.

The *Modular 100* metric range is the *standard* window and the *Module 4* is a *special* window available to order.

Typical details illustrating the standard steel sections and coupling arrangements used to form composite windows are shown in figure 126. The standard range includes fixed lights, side hung casements opening outwards, horizontally pivoted reversible casements and top hung casements opening outwards, with a selection of casement *doors* opening outwards. Windows and *doors* may be coupled together by the use of vertical coupling

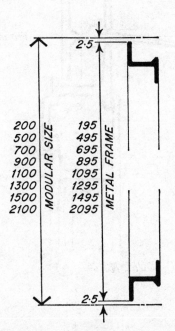

124   *Relationship of metal frames to modular sizes*

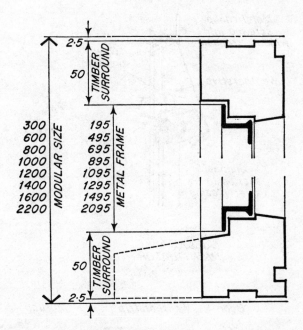

125   *Relationship of metal frames in timber surrounds to modular sizes*

'Module 100' standard windows

This is the dimensionally co-ordinated range of standard steel windows. A range of basic spaces for the windows are shown in figure 7, page 25. Single or multi-pane window units will fit into these spaces. A selection of windows from this range is shown in figure 123. Figures 124 and 125 show the relationship of the metal frames to the modular

bars (*mullions*) and horizontal bars (*transoms*), and by the use of filler panels to form composite assemblies. There are limits to the sizes to which composites may be made, both in respect of the difficulties associated with the manufacturing tolerances and by reference to designated wind loadings. Advice should thus be obtained from the window manufacturers when these questions

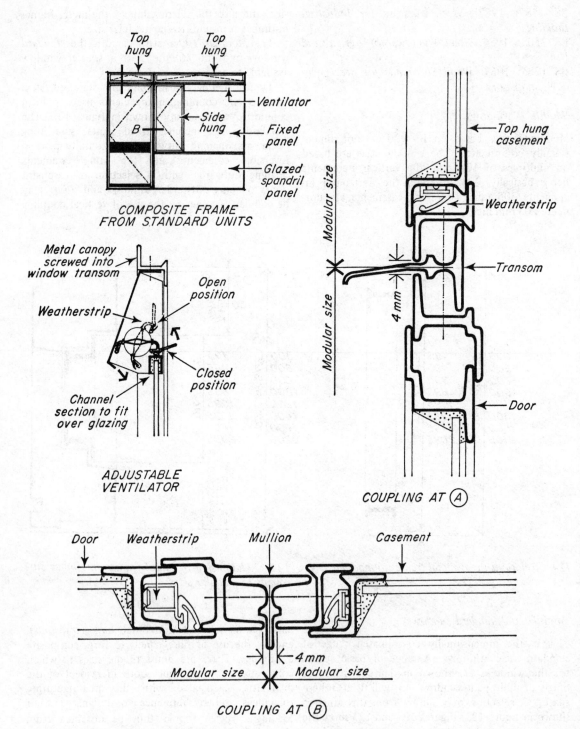

COMPOSITE FRAME
FROM STANDARD UNITS

ADJUSTABLE
VENTILATOR

COUPLING AT Ⓐ

COUPLING AT Ⓑ

126 *Coupling of standard steel sections*

arise. The windows are manufactured from *test guaranteed* steel. The main frames of the windows are constructed from bars, cut to length and mitred, with all corners welded solid. Intermediate bars are tenoned and riveted to the outer frames, and to each other. The windows are hot-dip galvanized after manufacture. A tolerance of 2 mm above or below (±) the standard dimensions is allowable and a fitting allowance of 2.5 mm all round the window is allowed between the outside window size and the basic dimensions of the openings to receive the window units.

Side hung casements are hung on projecting friction hinges without a stay. They are made of steel and are welded or riveted to the frames. The hinge pins are either rust proofed steel or aluminium alloy. The friction hinge is adjusted by the manufacturer at his works to require a given pressure on the handle to move the casement, and the hinge can be adjusted in-situ. When the casement is open to 90° the projecting arm gives a clear distance between the frame and casement of not less than 85 mm as shown in figure 106, page 129. This will allow both sides of the glass to be cleaned from inside the window which is an important factor in reducing maintenance costs where the window is used in multi-storey buildings. If so ordered side hung casements can alternatively be supplied with non-friction hinges and peg stays. The side hung casement will also be provided with a lever handle providing limited or *crack* ventilation by means of a notch, engaging on a striking plate which is bevelled. Side hung (and top hung) casements are not weather stripped as standard, but if ordered specially the weather stripping is carried out in a suitable plastic, ie PVC.

The horizontally pivoted casements are fully reversible and are weather stripped by synthetic rubber. This type of window also permits cleaning of the outside face of the glass from the inside of the building and also the cleaning of all the adjoining glass areas within arm's reach. Thus with careful design the whole of the glazing to a multi-storey building can be cleaned with safety from the inside, with considerable savings in maintenance costs. The glass in a reversible window can also be replaced from inside the building. The hinges for reversible casements are of the friction type, so adjusted as to hold the casement in any position. Automatic safety devices (releasable by hand)

limit the initial opening of the casement to approximately 15°, which, depending on the height of the window, will mean that the window projects into the room from 100 mm to 150 mm. When the safety device is released, the window can be reversed, pivoted through 180°. There is then a further safety catch which can be operated to hold the window firmly in the reversed position whilst maintenance or cleaning take place. This is shown in figure 105, page 129.

For the standard range of windows, handles are made in the following alternative finishes; hot pressed brass; nickel chromium plated on brass, or on zinc based alloy; and various aluminium alloys. Handles are detachable and can be replaced without disturbing the glass.

The whole range of windows to this BS is manufactured from only 12 basic steel sections, thus by standardization, and the application of industrial techniques of large scale manufacture, an acceptable and comparatively inexpensive range of windows giving a choice over a wide range of types and sizes can be produced.

Standard steel windows for agricultural buildings

In order to provide an inexpensive window, for an inexpensive building types, a limited standard range of windows is produced, covered by BS 2503. Three standard sizes are made with small panes of glass, each type incorporating an inward opening bottom hung hopper ventilator. The rolled steel sections used are similar to those specified in BS 990.

Standard steel windows for industrial buildings

BS 1787: 1951 with amendments August 1966, which is due for revision, covers this type of window. A point to bear in mind is that there are other forms of sidewall glazing in metal frames which have an industrial application.

Purpose made steel window sections

A range of weather stripped *universal* steel sections is produced known as *W20* from which purpose made windows can be manufactured. The rolled section is heavier than that used for the BS 990 window and the maximum permissible sizes for the basic type of window made from these sections is given in table 17

Method of opening	Size of Section	Height plus width	Height	Width
Side hung	Normal	2600	1900	700
	Heavy	3300	2600	900
Folding	Normal	3200	1900	1300
	Heavy	3900	2400	1800
Vertically	Normal	2900	1900	1100
Pivoted	Heavy	3900	2600	1400
Folding vertically	Normal	3600	1800	1800
Pivoted	Heavy	4700	2400	2300
Top hung	Normal	2600	1500	1500
	Heavy	3200	1800	1800
Horizontally	Normal	2600	1500	1500
Centre hung	Heavy	3200	1800	1800
Bottom hung	Normal	2600	1500	1500
	Heavy	3200	1800	1800

Table 17 *Extreme sizes of ventilators made of steel W20 Universal Section* (*dimensions in mm*)

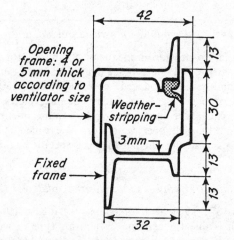

127 *W20 steel section for purpose made windows*

A detail of the section is shown in figure 127. Basic units of purpose made windows are coupled together by mullions and transomes, to form composite units in the same way as a standard window, but it is usual to employ a specialist sub-contractor to fix purpose made windows. Purpose made windows are usually fitted with good quality handles and other furniture, possibly of bronze.

The basic spaces for purpose made steel windows are shown in figure 128 from which the preferred range of *W20* windows will be manufactured for use in dimensionally co-ordinated buildings.

Fixing steel windows

The windows are fixed by means of counter-sunk screws accommodated in pre-drilled holes in the web of the sections. The position of the fixings for standard windows are indicated in BS 990 and vary from 2 to 12 points of fixing per window depending on the size of the frame. The types of fixings are as follows:

1 Wood screws, not less than (3.25 mm) 10 gauge for fixing into proprietary plastic or fibre plugs in pre-drilled holes in precast concrete surround or in-situ concrete openings.
2 Short counter-sunk screw and nut for securing the frame − before building in − to steel lugs set in the joints of brick or masonry openings. The lug has elongated slots to allow adjustment to accommodate variation in joint positions.
3 Self tapping screw for fixing to pressed metal sub-frames.

Where fixed direct into the opening, the metal windows are set in a waterproof cement fillet, which is *buttered* to the jambs of the opening before the window is offered into position. The space between the frame and the opening is then pointed in a suitable mastic, and the inside reveal usually plastered.

Typical fixing details are shown in figure 129. Three examples of the arrangement of a metal frame within a surround are shown in figure 130.

(a) shows the use of a pressed steel combined lintel and cavity flashing at the head, and a pressed metal surround. This type of surround is described in BS 1422: 1956: *Steel Sub-frames, Sills and Window Boards for Metal Windows.*
(b) shows a purpose made slate surround into which is fixed small cross section hardwood fillets to receive the steel window. The surround serves as sill, head and window board.
(c) is an alternative to this where the slate is expressed only in the external face of the building.

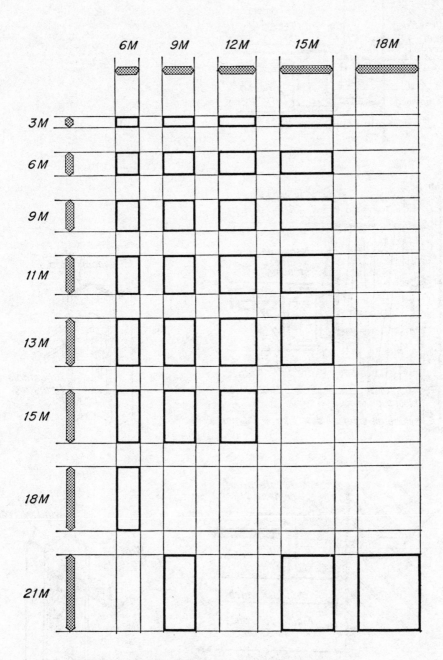

M = 1 module of 100 mm and refers to the size
of opening into which the window fits

128   *Basic spaces for purpose-made steel windows*

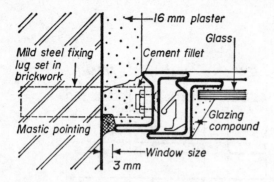

16 mm plaster

Glass

Mild steel fixing
lug set in
brickwork

Cement fillet

Mastic pointing

Glazing
compound

Window size
3 mm

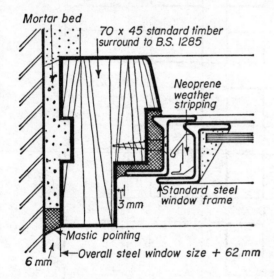

Mortar bed

70 x 45 standard timber
surround to B.S. 1285

Neoprene
weather
stripping

Standard steel
window frame

3 mm

Mastic pointing

Overall steel window size + 62 mm

6 mm

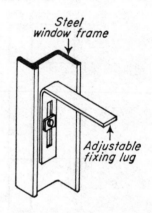

Steel
window frame

Adjustable
fixing lug

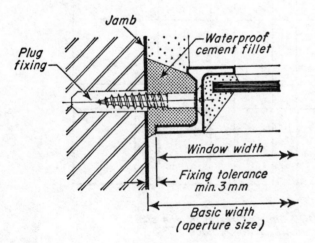

Jamb

Waterproof
cement fillet

Plug
fixing

Window width

Fixing tolerance
min. 3 mm

Basic width
(aperture size)

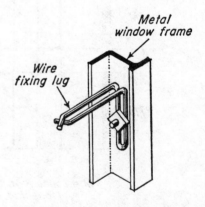

Metal
window frame

Wire
fixing lug

129 *Typical metal window fixing details*

Alternative types of adjustable fixing lug

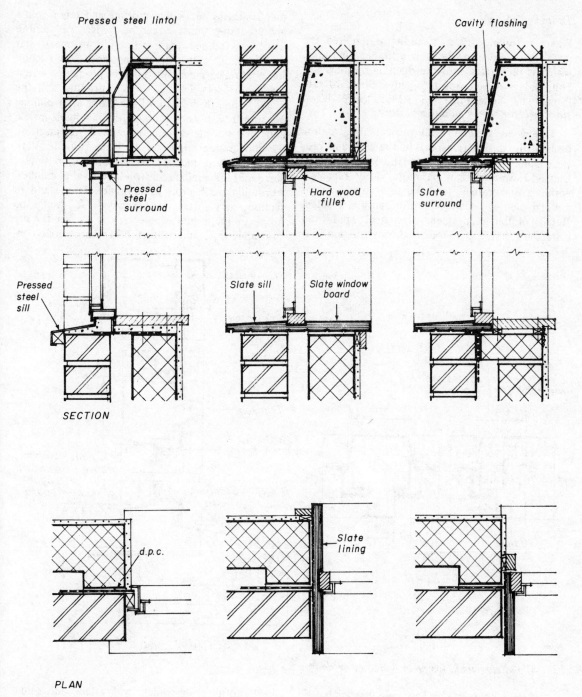

130 *Metal window in brick/block openings*

Timber surrounds

Where a superior type of fixing is required the metal window can be set into a timber sub-frame, which is then fixed into the opening by means of built-in lugs or screwing into plugs. Standard sub-frames are detailed in BS 1285: 1963: *Wood surrounds for steel windows and doors.*

The wood surround will protect the window particularly during transport to the site, and provides a more satisfactory bed for the mastic sealants. Damaged windows can be more easily replaced, within a timber frame and the thin appearance of a metal window set direct into masonry is avoided. Details of the arrangement of a steel window in a standard timber surround are shown in figure 131.

metal star dowel. Where mortice and tenon joints are used they must either be wedged or – more usually – pinned with a non-ferrous metal star dowel. Both combed joints and mortice and tenon joints are also glued. In order to produce a water-tight joint between the timber surround and the metal frame, the rebates of the frame after pinning are spread with a continuous strip of suitable mastic and then the metal frame is screwed into position, 32 mm counter-sunk screws, being suitable. Very often standard metal windows are set in timber surrounds of similar construction to the standard surround described but using timber of non-standard section, very often in hardwood. It should be borne in mind that where teak is chosen for the surround, this, and certain other hardwoods con-

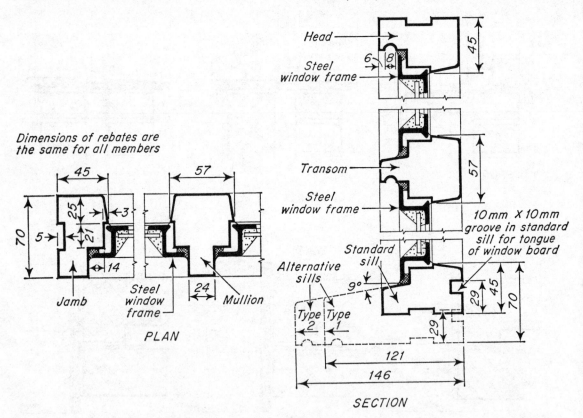

131 *Wood surrounds for steel windows or doors: BS 1285*

The joint between the head and the jamb, and the sill and the jamb in the timber surround will either be a mortice and tenon, or a combed joint. Combed joints will be pinned with a non-ferrous

tain harmful acids which will attack untreated steel. It is therefore particularly important that the protective coating should be made good, where damaged, before the window is screwed into the

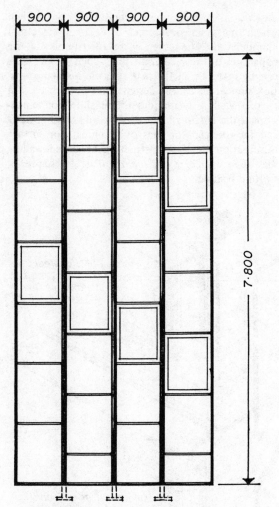

900 | 900 | 900 | 900

7·800

150 x 150 mm m.s. base plates welded on to mullions

KEY ELEVATION

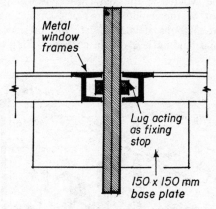

2 no. 175 x 10 m.s. flat section, drilled, tapped and secured by countersunk screws

Metal window frames

Lug acting as fixing stop

150 x 150 mm base plate

DETAIL OF MULLION: CONCEALED FIXING STOPS

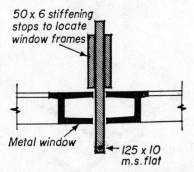

50 x 6 stiffening stops to locate window frames

Metal window

125 x 10 m.s. flat

PLAN OF BUILT—UP MULLION, EXPOSED FIXING STOPS

132 Large metal windows

frame. Brass or stainless steel screws should be used for fixing.

Purpose made steel windows

Where floor to ceiling glazing is required and purpose-made metal windows are indicated the mullions are usually the primary structural members. Figure 132 shows such a window detailed to have substantial mullions. Each mullion is 175 mm deep with a total height of 7.800 m. The problems of jointing mullions of this kind can be solved in several ways. In the example the stops are concealed so that the mullion is built up of two lines of 9 mm thick steel flats lapping each other and screwed together. This facilitates erection and reduces the

157

parts to a convenient length for galvanizing. In the example shown the feet and tops of the mullions are cast into an in-situ concrete sill and head. This is a simple technique for the window fixer and for the contractor but it is not easy to get a good finish on the in-situ concrete sill. Precast sills with joints on the mullion lines are an alternative technique but moisture penetration must be avoided at the joints where it will attack the foot of the mullion. It is, of course, possible to joint mullions at intermediate supports such as floor and landing levels as in curtain walling tech-

Expansion in large metal windows is a problem which must be overcome. The larger structural members are the chief cause of trouble as the expansion of the smaller members such as the sashes can be taken up in the many mastic bedded joints. Box stanchions can be designed such as are used in curtain walling techniques which allow for expansion in the length of the window and sliding fixing can be arranged for tops of mullions. For further information on the construction of glazed walling see *MBS: Structure and Fabric,* Part 1, chapter 5, Curtain Walling.

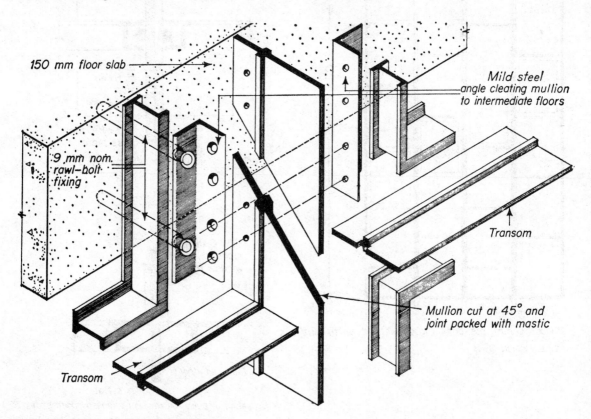

133   Coupling of large metal windows

niques. The fixing plate is shown on the detail in figure 133. The splayed cut gives a neat water tight joint which must be well sealed with mastic. In erecting large windows of this kind sashes may be coupled together with transoms if they are not structural, and built from the sill up, fixing to one side. The first mullion is placed and the next vertical range of sashes and so on across the total width.

Pressed metal frames

Metal pressings first came into the building industry in the use of standard door frames, which proved strong, quick to erect, and clean in outline.

Skirtings, stair treads, risers, window frames and shelving have been made of pressed sheet metal for some time. Now doors, particularly lift doors, large window frames, and many other elements are produced.

Mild steel sheet is used mostly in a range of gauges, 26 gauge for angle bead, 20 gauge for door frames, 12, 14 and 17 gauge for window frames and sometimes 10 gauge, approximately 3 mm thick, where greater strength and rigidity is required. Sheets up to 3.000 m x 1.300 m are used, depending on the size of the press or folder the manufacturer has.

Typical profiles of pressed steel sections are shown in figure 134. Folds can be made through any angle up to 105°, that is forming an angle of not less than 75°, but a stiffened edge can be made by pressing a fold down flat. This is called a *bar fold*. Surfaces of the member must be flat planes: Sharp angles cannot be obtained, the minimum outside radius being usually 2 mm for 16 gauge and 5 mm for 10 gauge. Minimum width of any face is from 12 mm for 16 gauge sheet to 20 mm for 10 gauge. Sections are usually open for most of one side, this being necessary for connections, fixing stiffening cross-members, etc. If a member is to be formed with the fourth side mostly closed, it is necessary to form it with a false fold as shown.

Cutting is done by mechanical saws or by grinding wheels, or by burning. Sheet metal is also cut by knife in a guillotine. Burning is now precise enough to be used for cutting square mortices for a square member to pass through. Holes, including small mortices, are of course formed by drilling or punching. The latter may cause some deformation of the metal member which, if there are many holes, may accumulate to measurable increase in length and width. Running joints are made with sleeves, bedded in mastic and tapped and screwed with counter-sunk screws, as shown in the diagram. Junctions between members are formed by scribing the end of the stopping member to the profile of the continuing member, filling it with a shaped cleat and screwing it to the continuing member, with a good supply of mastic packed in the joint. It will be seen how the use of a simple rectangular profile simplifies the junction. Complicated profiles call for a complicated cleat and may present difficulties in screwing up. Similarly, the scribing can only be done against flat planes; but, most important of all, the stopping members should be smaller than the continuing member so that it is quite clear of the slightly rounded angles of the continuing member. This is shown in the same diagram. The joint of mullion to sill is made in the same way, the end of the mullion being filled with a cleat and being well filled with mastic before screwing up. It is essential that the cleat be solid behind the front edge of the mullion, so that the mastic is squeezed between the two metal faces and there is no cavity to hold moisture. In some cases it may be more convenient to make a joint in the sill at each mullion; the latter will then continue down with the sill scribed to it. Figure 135 shows typical sill and million sections. If the front or back face of a frame of pressed-steel members is to be in one plane, it is necessary to form the angles by mitring and welding, and forming site joints with sleeves in the lengths of the members as shown in figure 135.

Large members can be built up out of several pressings. This is satisfactory if the joints can be masked by the sashes, or hidden on internal angles.

Where long members are used — tall mullion or a long sill — it is important to ensure that the arris is dead straight and the planes are ture. What may look satisfactory in elevation may look very bad when seen from directly below or from one side, where it is easy to get 'an eye along the edge'. To get this trueness it is essential that the metal be thick enough to keep its folded shape and that it is carefully fixed. The architect can get the latter put right, but if the metal is too thin any remedy is rather expensive.

Aluminium windows

The use of aluminium windows has increased very much over the past few years. Aluminium alloy is an attractive and adaptable material, which produces windows to a very high degree of accuracy and with a high standard of finish. Because of its lightness it is particularly suitable for use in the manufacture of both horizontal and vertical sliding windows; frames which are to receive double glazing; and reversible pivot windows. Aluminium sections can be very easily weather stripped, and where this is carefully designed, a remarkable degree of sound insulation is obtained as a bonus to the draught and weatherproofing.

Aluminium window sections are extruded by forcing under extreme pressure, a heated billet of aluminium through a die of the desired profile.

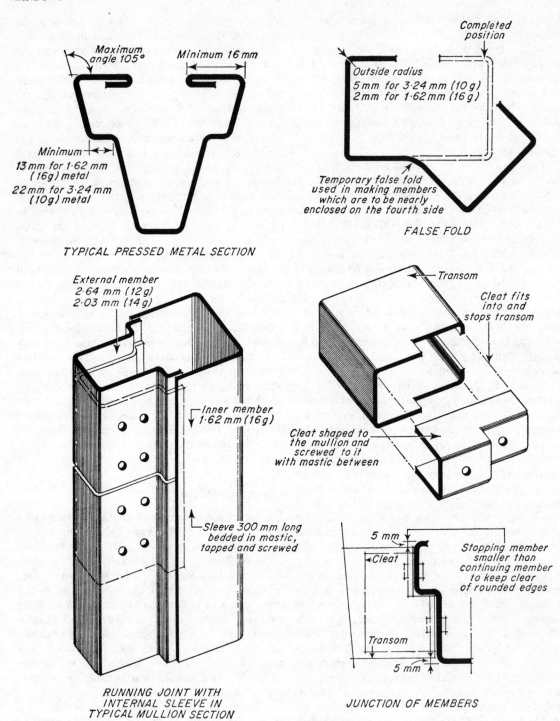

Maximum angle 105°

Minimum 16 mm

Minimum
13 mm for 1·62 mm (16g) metal
22 mm for 3·24 mm (10g) metal

TYPICAL PRESSED METAL SECTION

Completed position

Outside radius
5 mm for 3·24 mm (10g)
2 mm for 1·62 mm (16g)

Temporary false fold used in making members which are to be nearly enclosed on the fourth side

FALSE FOLD

External member
2·64 mm (12g)
2·03 mm (14g)

Inner member
1·62 mm (16g)

Sleeve 300 mm long bedded in mastic, tapped and screwed

RUNNING JOINT WITH INTERNAL SLEEVE IN TYPICAL MULLION SECTION

Transom

Cleat fits into and stops transom

Cleat shaped to the mullion and screwed to it with mastic between

5 mm

Cleat

Stopping member smaller than continuing member to keep clear of rounded edges

Transom

5 mm

JUNCTION OF MEMBERS

134 *Pressed metal frames (1)*

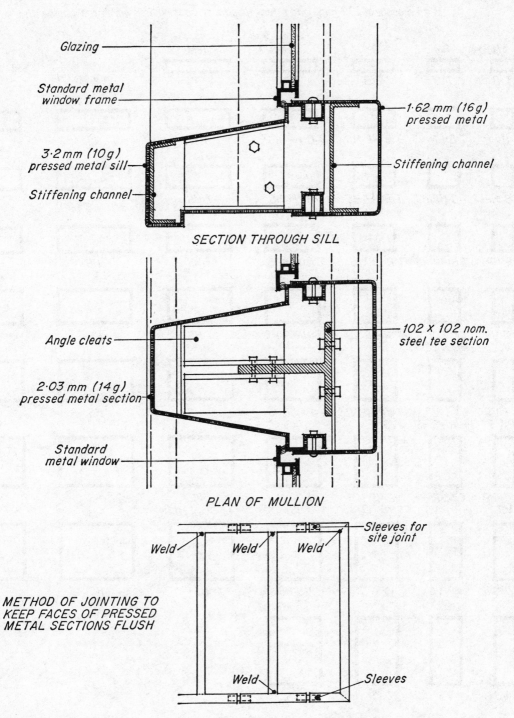

Glazing

Standard metal
window frame

1·62 mm (16 g)
pressed metal

3·2 mm (10 g)
pressed metal sill

Stiffening channel

Stiffening channel

SECTION THROUGH SILL

Angle cleats

102 × 102 nom.
steel tee section

2·03 mm (14 g)
pressed metal section

Standard
metal window

PLAN OF MULLION

Weld   Weld   Weld   Sleeves for
site joint

METHOD OF JOINTING TO
KEEP FACES OF PRESSED
METAL SECTIONS FLUSH

Weld   Sleeves

135   *Pressed metal frames (2)*

M = 1 module of 100 mm, and refers to size of opening into which the window fits

	6M	9M	12M	15M	18M	21M	24 M
3M	T:B	T:B	T:B	T:B	T		
5M	T:B:HP	T:B:HP:HS	T:B:HP:HS	T:B:HP:HS	T:HS	HS	HS
6M	T:B:HP	T:B:HP:HS	T:B:HP:HS	T:B:HP:HS	T:HS	HS	HS
7M	T:B:HP	T:B:HP:HS	T:B:HP:HS	T:B:HP:HS	T:HS	HS	HS
9M	C:T:HP VS	C*:T:VP HP/R:VS:HS	T:HP/R:VS HS	T:HP/R:HS	T:HS	HS	HS
11M	C:T:VP HP:VS	C*:T:VP HP/R:VS:HS	T:VP:HP/R VS:HS	T:HP/R:HS	T:HS	HS	HS
13M	C:VP:HP VS	C*:VP HP/R:VS	VP:HP/R VS:HS	HP/R:VS HS	·HS	HS	HS
15M	C:VP:VS	VP:VS	VP:VS	VS:HS	HS	HS	HS
18M	C:VS	VS	VS	VS			

136   *Basic spaces and ranges of aluminium windows*

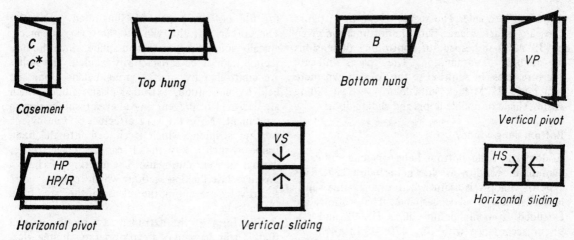

136   Basic spaces and ranges of aluminium windows – continued

With this technique it is a simple matter to incorporate grooves in the section during extrusion to accommodate efficient weather stripping material. Aluminium windows are either supplied *mill*, that is, natural finish, or anodized. The *mill* finish should be allowed to weather naturally and provided the atmosphere is not industrially corrosive then this will be satisfactory. Natural finish aluminium can of course be painted provided that a zinc chromate primer is used, though a painted finish on aluminium seems to be a contradiction in economic terms.

If it is desired to enhance the appearance of the window, then anodizing should be specified to be carried out in accordance with BS 3987: 1974: *Anodic oxide coatings on wrought aluminium for external architectural applications.* See also *MBS: Materials,* chapter 9.

Anodizing, although expensive, produces a beautiful finish on polished aluminium. Certain colours will not remain *light-fast*. In order to retain its attractiveness, anodized aluminium requires regular cleaning — with soap and water.

Mill finish windows will normally be despatched from the factory unprotected and must be cleaned down by the Contractor just before the scaffolding is dismantled. Where windows are anodized they should be coated by a film of wax and then protected by strong self-adhesive tape on all the visible and exposed surfaces. The Contractor can then easily remove the tape and polish the wax away to give a finished surface. This should not of course be done until there is no risk of damage by following trades.

The manufacture of the frames and opening sashes follows the methods generally used for steel windows, the corner jamb being electrically welded and using mechanical mortice and tenon joints for glazing bars and intermediate members and riveting or screwing for the fixing of the fittings. The maximum sizes for primary ventilators will depend upon the cross-sectional strength of the extruded sections.

Allowances for expansion of aluminium members are made roughly the same as for steel windows. One factor which should not be overlooked when aluminium windows are used is the necessity for great care in handling and treatment on site. Members are not so strong as steel and will not support scaffold poles or boards etc., and aluminium will show ill-effects at once. Preferably they should not be fixed until all the structural work and wet finishes are completed and should be protectively wrapped before dispatch and carefully stored on the site. They should be kept very clean during the progress of the work as cement or plaster will adhere to the surface and will leave a mark on bright aluminium.

Basic spaces

The Aluminium Window Association have produced a chart of the basic spaces and ranges in which dimensionally co-ordinated aluminium windows will be made. The spaces – shown in figure 136, are in accordance with the information given in BS 4330 in respect of controlling dimensions in modular co-ordination. The spaces indicate aperture sizes. In addition to the sizes shown there is a range 21 M high suitable for vertical sliding sashes, single or double doors and sliding doors.

Bottom hung window

A domestic scale bottom hung opening indwards aluminium window is shown in figure 137. This type of window is useful where draught-free ventilation at low level is desirable. The sections are extruded from aluminium alloys HE 9P and HV 9P in accordance with BS 1470: 1972: *Wrought Aluminium and Aluminium Alloys* for general engineering purposes – plate, sheet and strip. Note the dovetailed grooves to receive the neoprene insert to act as weather stripping. The lengths of weather stripping *clip in* and can be removed for replacement if they become damaged or worn over the life of the window. The hinges have nylon bushed stainless steel pins and the opening casement is returned on hinged side arms which can be released to allow the window to fall back for cleaning and maintenance.

The figure shows examples of both single and double glazing. The glass which is put into the frame from the inside is bedded in suitable glazing compound and in the case of the single glazing the inner glazing bead which is extruded aluminium section, is clipped over, and retained by a nylon stud fixed to the frame. The alternative is an extruded aluminium section bead screwed to the frame. Note the mastic pointing at the head and the sill and the weather bar which protects the vulnerable joint at the base of the inward opening casement.

It is interesting to compare the profile of the extruded aluminium sections used in this window with the mild steel rolled sections used in the standard steel window illustrated in figure 126, page 150.

Vertical sliding sash

A fully framed purpose-made aluminium double-hung sash window of sophisticated design is shown in figure 138.

The alloy used is the same as for the extrusions for the bottom hung sash illustrated previously. The corners for this window, however, are mechanically jointed by screw and spline, since the box section cannot be satisfactorily welded. The sashes are controlled by special spring balances and are held by continuous extruded plastic guides which are designed to prevent any uneven response during movement. Note the very effective polypropylene weather stripping which is clipped into the fixed frame in such a way that it can be replaced after damage or wear during use. The meeting rails have a positive interlocking action which ensures good security by preventing the release of the catch from the outside.

The form of the extruded sash section is such that it will accommodate proprietary double glazing units up to 14 mm overall thickness. The glazing is *internal*, that is to say the glass is fixed from inside the building which is an important factor in cost and ease of maintenance. The front edges of the glass are bedded in polysulphide glazing compound; each sheet being located by small spacing blocks within the frame, to give the correct balance all round. The glass is secured by an extruded aluminium *clip-on* bead with a *push-in* vinyl glazing trim complete the glazing procedure.

Two very neat design points incorporated in the extruded sections are the gap left to receive a window pole, and the continuous neat recess on the lower rail of the outer sash to act as a sash pull.

A window of this type could be made up to a maximum height of 2.440 m and a maximum width of 1.525 m with the limitation that the perimeter measurement must not exceed 7.625 m, which means that the maximum width and height cannot be used in the same window. The basic spaces relative to this type (VS) of window are shown in figure 136, page 162.

The following points should also be noted. The rain screen principle of design has been used to prevent water being blown under the bottom sash. The pressure created within the hollow inverted U section of the bottom rail in conditions of high wind and rain, has a screening effect which helps to prevent rain penetration – the higher the pressure, the more positive the screening effect. The sashes are factory glazed so that the helical spring balances can be adjusted to the correct tension by taking into account the variations in weight of

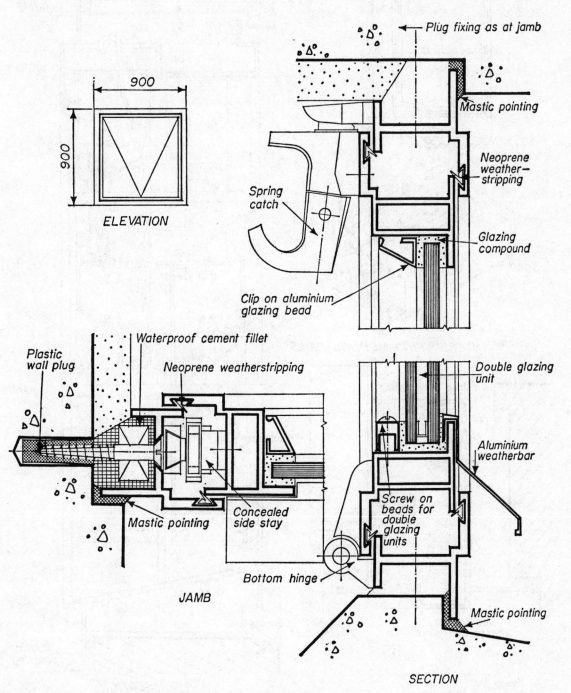

900

900

ELEVATION

Plug fixing as at jamb

Mastic pointing

Neoprene weather-stripping

Glazing compound

Spring catch

Clip on aluminium glazing bead

Waterproof cement fillet

Neoprene weatherstripping

Plastic wall plug

Double glazing unit

Aluminium weatherbar

Screw on beads for double glazing units

Mastic pointing

Concealed side stay

Bottom hinge

JAMB

Mastic pointing

SECTION

137 *Aluminium window: bottom hung, opening inwards*

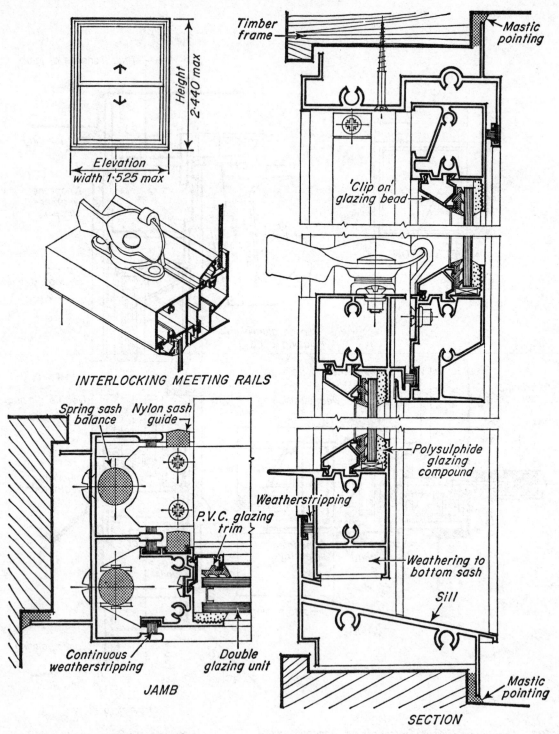

Height 2·440 max

Elevation
width 1·525 max

INTERLOCKING MEETING RAILS

Spring sash balance

Nylon sash guide

Timber frame

Mastic pointing

'Clip on' glazing bead

Polysulphide glazing compound

P.V.C. glazing trim

Weatherstripping

Weathering to bottom sash

Sill

Continuous weatherstripping

Double glazing unit

JAMB

Mastic pointing

SECTION

138   *Aluminium sliding sash window*

glass. The nylon sash guides are to prevent crab-bing — or sideways motion of the sash during opening. This is a fault which occurs with loosely fitted sashes and causes the sash to become jammed. The U-shaped tube outline seen on the sections is part of the continuous extrusion and receives long self tapping screws which connect the horizontal and vertical members of the frame. The timber frame is built into the opening and the complete factory glazed window fixed later.

Horizontal sliding window

Figure 139 shows a purpose made horizontal sliding window in aluminium which is made in a range of sizes to comply with the basic space recommendations for aluminium windows shown in figure 136, pages 162 and 163. The horizontal sliding window is a type much-used in commercial buildings, schools, and hospitals, being particularly suitable for high rise development. The window is detailed so that both sashes can be cleaned from the inside without removal, and a feature to note is the nylon skids upon which the sashes run. In large windows using say 6 mm glass, or heavier, or in double glazed windows nylon rollers would be used as an alternative, as shown. The windows are fixed into the opening by the use of purpose made brackets which *twist lock* into position in the frame and are then screwed or shot fired into the concrete or brickwork. The tracks are fixed into the opening first and then the pre-assembled window at a later date. Alternatively the window can be set in a timber surround. A point to remember in respect of fixing aluminium is that ordinary steel or brass screws should not be used otherwise bi-metallic corrosion will be set up. This window has a security bolt which locks the window in the partially open position, and this is a point that must be watched with all horizontal sliding windows.

The window will be factory glazed, the glass being sealed into the frames by reusable neoprene gaskets.

The problem of weather resistance is difficult to overcome with a horizontal sliding type of opening light and much careful thought has been given to this problem in the example shown, which is designed to conform with the forthcoming British Standard on resistance to wind and water penetration. Woven pile double weather stripping is incorporated at the head, sill, and meeting style of the window panes and the PVC jamb sections ensure a good weather seal. Note also the use of the PVC channels which isolate the weather stripping and nylon skids from the aluminium frame. This use of PVC reduces friction and resists the deteriorating action due to accumulation of dust and grit.

Horizontal sliding window in timber surround

Figure 140 gives an example of a standard aluminium horizontal sliding window in a timber surround which is competitive in price with a standard timber window. The timber surround provides the basic construction with the opening part of the window in aluminium. This window is made in the standard metric range of sizes to fit the openings shown in figure 136. The figure illustrates a 1300 mm high window inserted over a deep middle rail to give a 2100 mm composite unit. Note that the actual frame size of the window will be 5 mm less than the aperture size subject to a manufacturing tolerance of ±3mm. The metric sizes are in multiples of a basic module of 100 mm and are derived from the preferred dimensions in Appendix A of BS 4330: *Recommendations for the Co-ordination of Controlling Dimensions in Building.* The timber frames, which should be vacuum treated with preservative, and afterwards primed, will be built into the opening in the usual way. Then when all the wet trades are completed the head and sill of the aluminium component are set in mastic and screwed in position. The sashes are factory glazed with 3 mm or 4 mm glass according to overall size.

'Built up' aluminium window

The detail of a large window in aluminium is shown in figure 141. The dimensions here necessitate substantial structural members which in the form of transoms span the full width of the opening to avoid obstruction to the windows below. Steel sections are used for the main members and built up to give an arrangement which also supports the pressed aluminium casings. The heavier lower transom also supports a heater. This is a good example of a large but relatively simple profile in pressed aluminium. The external exposed members are in hardwood.

167

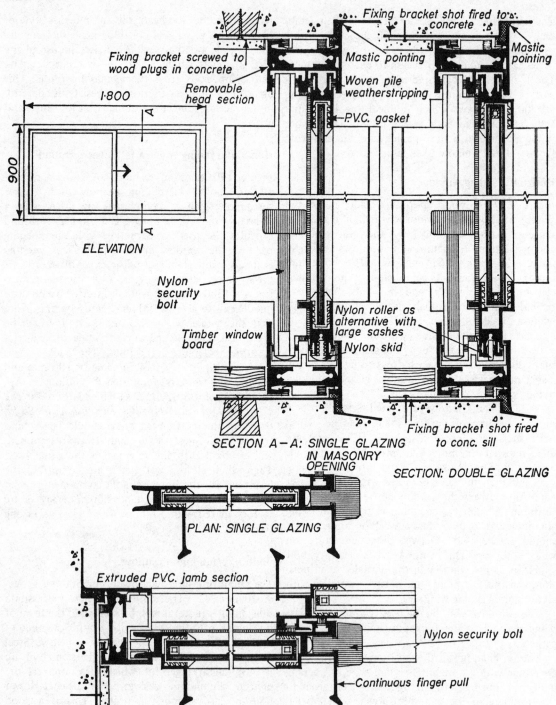

Fixing bracket screwed to wood plugs in concrete

Removable head section

Fixing bracket shot fired to concrete

Mastic pointing

Mastic pointing

Woven pile weatherstripping

P.V.C. gasket

1·800

900

ELEVATION

Nylon security bolt

Timber window board

Nylon roller as alternative with large sashes

Nylon skid

SECTION A—A: SINGLE GLAZING IN MASONRY OPENING

Fixing bracket shot fired to conc. sill

SECTION: DOUBLE GLAZING

PLAN: SINGLE GLAZING

Extruded P.V.C. jamb section

Nylon security bolt

Continuous finger pull

PLAN AT JAMB AND INTERLOCKING MEETING STYLE: DOUBLE GLAZING

139 *Purpose-made aluminium horizontal sliding window*

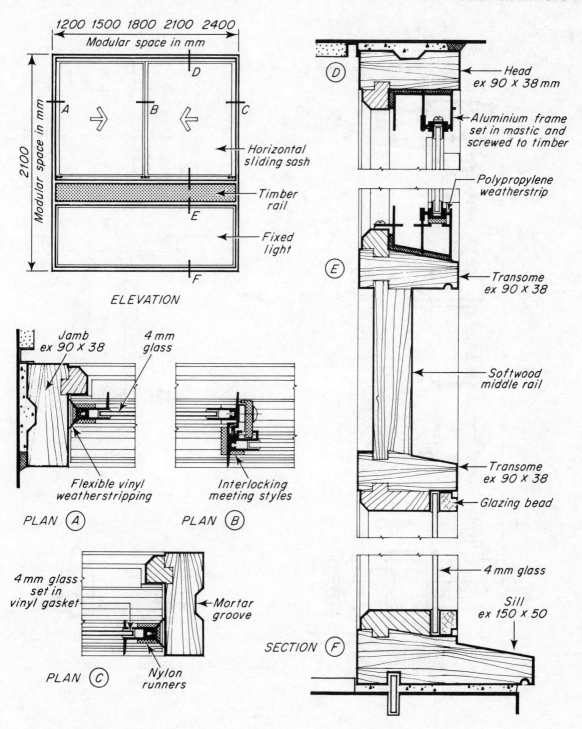

ELEVATION

1200 1500 1800 2100 2400
Modular space in mm

Modular space in mm

2100

Horizontal sliding sash

Timber rail

Fixed light

Jamb ex 90 × 38

4 mm glass

Flexible vinyl weatherstripping

PLAN (A)

Interlocking meeting styles

PLAN (B)

4 mm glass set in vinyl gasket

Mortar groove

Nylon runners

PLAN (C)

Head ex 90 × 38 mm

Aluminium frame set in mastic and screwed to timber

Polypropylene weatherstrip

Transome ex 90 × 38

Softwood middle rail

Transome ex 90 × 38

Glazing bead

4 mm glass

Sill ex 150 × 50

SECTION (F)

140   *Aluminium sliding window in timber surround*

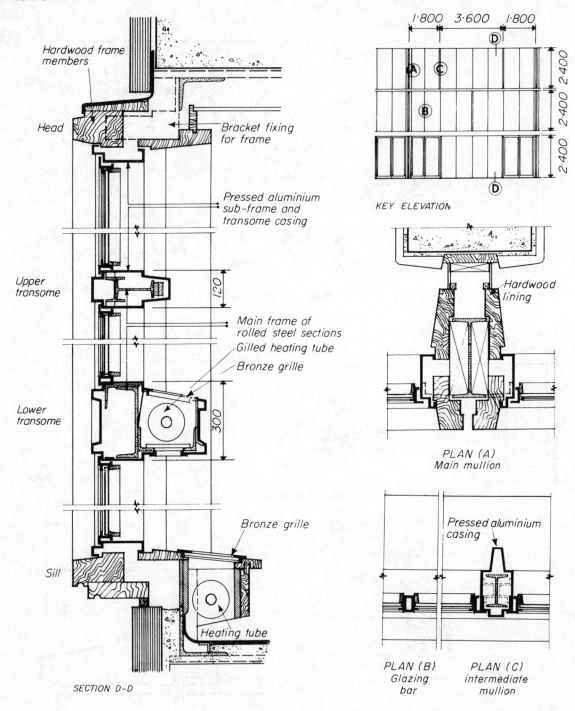

Hardwood frame members

Head

Bracket fixing for frame

Pressed aluminium sub-frame and transome casing

Upper transome

120

Main frame of rolled steel sections

Gilled heating tube

Bronze grille

Lower transome

300

Bronze grille

Sill

Heating tube

SECTION D-D

1·800 3·600 1·800

2·400 2·400

2·400

KEY ELEVATION

Hardwood lining

PLAN (A)
Main mullion

Pressed aluminium casing

PLAN (B)
Glazing bar

PLAN (C)
intermediate mullion

141   Large aluminium window

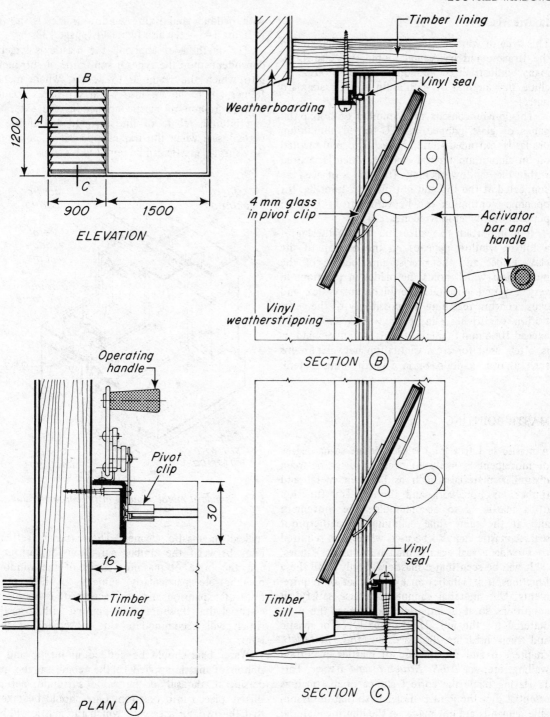

ELEVATION

SECTION B

PLAN A

SECTION C

142 *Louvre window*

Louvre windows

This type of window (see figure 142), originated in the tropics, and has gained popularity elsewhere. Many industrialized Building Systems also include this method of ventilation in their standard range.

The louvre consists of a number of horizontal panes of glass gripped in a U-shaped aluminium or plastics extruded section at each end, and pivoted on an aluminium vertical channel which is secured within the window opening. The blades of glass are connected at the top and bottom to a lever bar for opening. Ventilation can be varied from 1 to 95 per cent of the net louvred area.

It is important to realize that the weathering of a louvre window depends on the overlap of the glass blades and the precise interlocking of the mechanism which holds the blades in position. In very exposed positions the blades may flex and cause concern regarding the possibility of the penetration of driving rain, clear widths should not exceed 1066 mm to minimize this. A louvre window is often used for cross ventilation between rooms such as over a door, or in a partitioning system.

MASTIC JOINTING

A mastic seal to a joint is used where some degree of movement is likely to occur, usually between dissimilar materials, such as between metal and timber, or brickwork and timber. The function of a mastic is to accommodate the movement and at the same time maintain a weatherproof seal. A mastic can also be used where it is required to provide a seal against draughts, dust or fumes.

It will be seen that a mastic will only fulfil these functions if it satisfies an exacting set of requirements. One material cannot of course satisfy all conditions so it is important to choose the right material for the job. The various types of mastic and their uses are discussed in *MBS: Materials*, chapter 16 and for the use of mastics in curtain walling, etc, see *MBS: Structure and Fabric*, Part 1. Having made the correct choice of mastic it is essential that the joint is designed so that unreasonable demands are not made on the jointing material in its effort to accommodate the movement. The practical application of mastic seals in connection

with bedding and fixing window frames is shown in figure 143 – see also figure 113, page 133.

The method of applying the mastic is largely dependent upon the type of sub-frame or surround into which the frame is to be set. Where metal frames are to be set into wood surrounds a continuous ribbon of mastic applied in the external and internal rebate of the surround will ensure a perfect seal when the frame is placed in position. Any surplus mastic can be removed by a rag

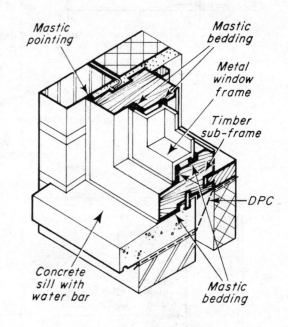

143   *Standard metal window in timber sub-frame*

soaked in mastic cleaner. The external vertical joint between the timber sub-frame or surround and the brick or masonry jambs of the window opening are particularly subject to differential rates of expansion and contraction. It is therefore essential that these joints be pointed with a mastic which will accommodate this movement of the joint.

Water bars should be bedded in mastic and a ribbon of mastic applied to the rebate on the underside of the sill of the wood surround, before this is placed into position. Care should be taken that the two surfaces with which the mastic will be in contact are dry and free from dust. The vertical joints between sub-frame and window opening should be grouted in a weak cement mix, raked out to a depth of not less than 12 mm and, when dry, pointed with mastic. With old property where a mastic joint has not been used a deep, wide cavity may exist; in this case the joint should either be packed with hemp to within 12 mm of surface before pointing with mastic, or grouted with a weak cement, raked out and pointed.

Figure 144 shows the use of mastic for the joints between frames and loose mullions (or transom rails) in metal windows.

With composite windows a certain amount of movement is inevitable at the junction of the fixed frames and the mullions and transoms. It is therefore essential, and is indeed now common practice, to seal these joints with mastic. It is recommended that a ribbon of mastic for the internal and external joint be applied either to the fixed frame or to the mullion or transom as convenient during assembly.

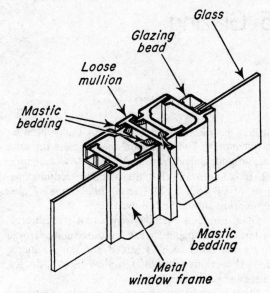

144 Metal window with loose mullion

5 Glazing

Glazing is the fixing of glass, and today plastics, in *surrounds*. The fixing of opaque glass on solid backgrounds is dealt with in *MBS: Materials,* chapter 12. It is important that the detailed recommendations of CP 152: 1972 *Glazing and fixing of glass for building* should be followed.

Glass products include transparent, translucent, patterned and opaque, 'clear', coloured and mirrored sheets and units such as leaded and copper lights, channel sections (*Profilit*[1]), hollow blocks, domes, lenses and pavement lights.

Plastics products for glazing include sheets and domes, and plastics are also used as interlayers in laminated glass products. Plastics for glazing, such as polycarbonate and polymethylmethacrylate are dealt with in *MBS: Materials,* chapter 13. They are less hard than glass, have high thermal movement, tend to develop electro-static charges, may suffer loss of transparency and ductility with age, and they are combustible — although flame-retardant grades are available. However, plastics are being used increasingly for vandal-resistant and 'safety' glazing.

Glass

Unless stated to the contrary glass is referred to in this chapter. It is dealt with in *MBS: Materials,* chapter 12. Glass is extremely durable in ordinary circumstances, and easily cleaned. *Annealed* glass, including wired glass, is easily broken in the thicknesses which are commonly used and the fragments are very dangerous, although wire in glass holds fragments in position and fragments of laminated glass are held in position by plastics interlayers. *Toughened* glass is much stronger than annealed glass and the fragments are relatively harmless. Glass cracks and melts in building fires.

Glass is required to fulfil one or more of the functions, which are listed below, together with sources of information:

[1] Registered trade name.

Functions	*References*
Generally	1 BS 952: 1964 *Classification of glass for glazing and terminology for work on glass* 2 CP 152: 1972 *Glazing and fixing of glass for building* 3 CP 153: Part 1-4 *Windows and rooflights* 4 Publications of glass manufacturers and merchants
Wind resistance	CP 3: *Code of basic data for the design of buildings,* chapter V *Loading:* Part 2: 1972 *Wind loads;* 42
Rain, air, dust and odour exclusion	
Sound and thermal insulation	CP 153: Part 3: 1972 *Sound insulation* BRE Digest 140 *Double glazing and double windows*
Solar heat control	BRE Digest 68
Fire resistance	CP 153: Part 4: *Fire hazards associated with glazing in buildings*
Resistance to accidental breakage	2 and 4
Prevention of injury	2
Resistance to deliberate breakage by bandits, bullets and blast	BS 5051: *Security glazing* Part 1: 1973: *Bullet resisting glazing for interior use* BS 5357: 1976 *Installation of security glazing*
Radiation shielding	
Light transmission — true vision — obscuration — 'one-way'	4
Opacity	
Light reflection	

Decoration/
information

Safe cleaning	CP 153: Part 1: 1969
	Cleaning and safety
Durability and	CP 153: Part 2: 1970
maintenance	*Durability and maintenance*

Wind resistance

Glass must be sufficiently thick to resist stresses due to wind, which vary with the severity of exposure, the type of glass and the method of fixing.
Design wind speeds are found by applying a *topography factor* (usually 1.0), an S2 factor (0.56 – 1.27) for *ground roughness*, building size and height above ground, and a *life factor* (usually 1.0) to the *basic wind speeds* (38 – 56 m/s) for various parts of the UK as given in CP 3: chapter V: Part 2. *Maximum wind loadings* on glass are given in CP 152 for stated design wind speeds.

Figures 145 and 146 show minimum safe thicknesses for wind loadings for the more common types of glass, glazed vertically and supported at four edges in panes of stated areas. The thick lines are for square panes and the extremities of the shaded bands are for length:width ratios of 3 to 1 and more. Proportional positions on the bands should be read for ratios between 1 to 1 and 3 to 1. Thicknesses of single laminated glass and of clear glass in double glazing are given in figures 43 and 44 in *MBS: Materials*. The Technical advisory service of Pilkington Bros. Ltd., should be consulted where glass is not vertical, not fixed on four edges, and wherever conditions are not straightforward.

Fire precautions

Ordinary glazing fails rapidly in fires, but limited areas and thicknesses of certain glasses properly fixed in fire resisting frames, can survive BS 476: Part 8 tests, other than that for insulation, for up to one hour. Although radiation from the side of the glass away from a fire reduces with an increase in glass thickness, it may ignite combustible glazing beads. CP 153: Part 4 *Fire hazards associated with glazing in buildings* gives minimum distances from fire resisting glazing for combustible parts of buildings, including floors, and for storing combustible materials, in buildings with 'high fire load' and for 'lower intensity fires', respectively. To ensure that persons using fire escape routes during the 'early stages of fires' are not exposed unbearably to radiation a nomogram in CP 153: Part 4 relates fire load, length and height of glazed screens, widths of fire escape corridors and speed of walking.

Fire research technical paper 5 deals with *Heat radiation from fires and building separation,* Margaret Law, JFRO, HMSO.

The external surfaces of rooflights are restricted by regulations in respect of radiation, penetration by burning brands, spread of flame, in number, area and disposition. They are not required to resist internal fire. In fact, venting of fires can be beneficial in fire fighting – see *Fire venting in single-storey buildings,* G.J. Langdon-Thomas and P.L. Hinkley, *Fire note* 5, 1965 FOCJ, FRO.

Annealed glass cracks in fires, but wired glass and plastics interlayers in laminated glass hold broken particles for a time. Toughened glass withstands uneven temperatures up to 250°C, but all glasses soften at high temperatures. Double glazing offers no significant advantage.

All plastics are combustible and polymethylmethacrylate (acrylic) materials are not self extinguishing. UPVC has inherent self-extinguishing properties and fire retardants in GRP materials may render them self-extinguishing, if with some loss of durability. CP 153: Part 4 includes the following examples of fire resistance performances, which with the exception of the first example are for resistance to both collapse and passage of flame:

Wood frames

½ hour resistance to collapse and 20 minutes resistance to passage of flame
Frame members and dividing bars not less than 56 mm deep x 44 mm wide with rebates worked from the solid material at least 13 mm deep. Beads, both sides of the glass, to have a melting point not less than 650°C.
½ hour resistance
Frame members and dividing bars as above, but beads on both sides must not melt or disintegrate in any way at temperatures up to 900°C. Wood beads must be 13 mm wide and protected with intumescent paint, or more permanently, with a metal capping.

1 hour resistance
Subject to testing of individual designs, the code

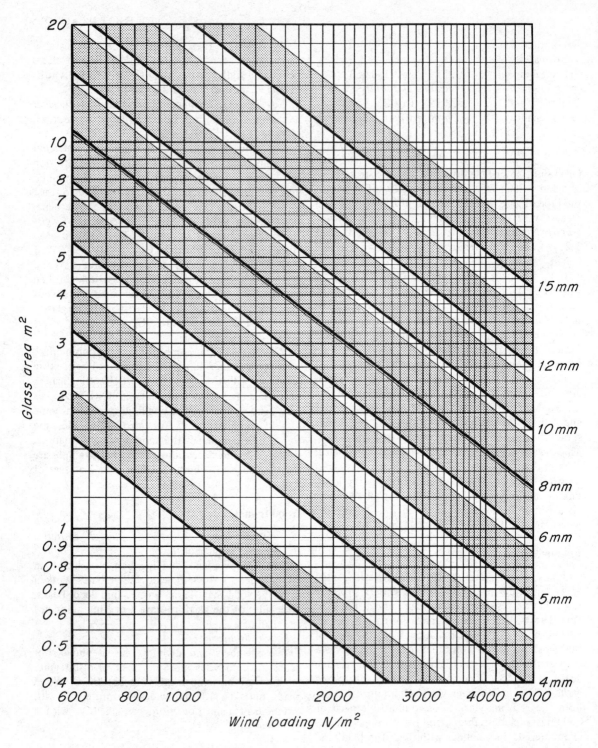

145 *Minimum thicknesses of Clear glasses (except laminated) subject to 3 second mean wind loadings (Glass held vertically and at 4 edges)*

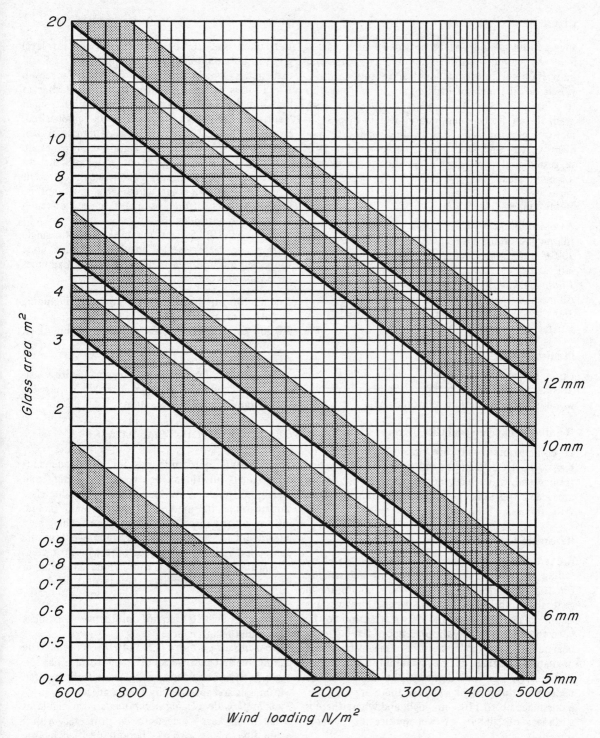

146 Minimum thicknesses of wired, rough cast and patterned glasses subject to 3 second mean wind loadings (Glass held vertically and at 4 edges)
Graphs reproduced by courtesy fo Pilkington Bros Ltd

177

suggests this period will be provided where glass is held by non-combustible, preferably non-metal inserts (metal inserts conduct heat too readily), which do not melt or disintegrate in any way up to 980°C. Compositions such as *Marinite*[1] are available. A frame construction which gave satisfactory performance had dividing bars 90 mm deep x 105 mm wide with 20 mm rebates. It is suggested that wired glass panes should not exceed 0.5 m² in area.

Metal frames

½ hour resistance
All members must have a melting point not less than 900°C and fixing methods must be proved to be satisfactory.
1 hour resistance
All members must have a melting point not less than 980°C and fixing methods must be proved to be satisfactory.

Plastics frames

Unreinforced plastics frames cannot achieve fire resistance, but this may be possible with certain wood, steel or aluminium reinforcement.

Reinforced concrete and GRC frames

If combustible beads are not used 1 hour fire resistance can be achieved with reinforced concrete frames and wired glass not more than 1.2 m² in area, and the same period may be possible with GRC frames.

Resistance to impact

Broken glass may cause injury by cutting and by failing to prevent persons penetrating balustrades. CP 152 (amended 1976) cites doors which are in general use for access to rooms and passageways as the 'major risk area' and draws attention to the need to indicate visually the presence of fixed glazing near doors. The code classifies as 'special risks', unguarded glazing up to 800 mm from floors, particularly: in non-domestic buildings, where pedestrian traffic is high, where there are children, balustrades up to 1100 mm high, and where there is a danger of slipping on wet surfaces, eg shower screens.

The code recommends the use of laminated or toughened glass for bathing screens and low-level glazing in non-domestic buildings, and for all balustrades which protect a difference in level. Wired glass is approved for low-level glazing in non-domestic buildings and for high level glazing in 'specialist' buildings. It must be emphasised, however, that although wire in glass retains broken particles it reduces its strength, and even if panes are correctly fixed, wired glass has poor resistance to impact and penetration. Experience and recent research[2] confirms that wired glass must not be used to protect differences in level in positions such as balcony balustrades.

Table 9 in CP 152 gives maximum areas for single glazing and factory-sealed insulating glazing units supported on four edges in 'risk areas'. Examples for 6 mm glasses are:

2.5 m² for wired and ordinary annealed, including patterned, glasses.
3.0 m² for laminated glass with a 0.38 mm thick interlayer
4.0 m² for toughened glass.

Where both resistance to impact and fire resistance are required it may be necessary to provide barrier rails or similar protection.

GLAZING COMPOUNDS AND GASKETS

The selection of compounds for glazing depends upon their functions for securing, bedding and sealing, differential movement between the glass and surround, the material of the surround (including any preservatives or water repellents which may be present – see CP 98) and upon whether the compound is to be painted or otherwise protected.

Glazing compounds are described in detail in CP 152, table 1. Briefly, the classifications are:

Group 1
Compounds which require protective treatment and regular maintenance:
Type a linseed oil putty (BS 544: 1969) needs to be painted within two weeks after the surface has set.
Type b metal casement putty needs to be painted within a period specified by the manufacturer.
Type c flexible glazing compounds – available as strips or in kegs – need to be protected with a compatible paint within a period specified by the manufacturer.

[1] Trade name
[2] Edinburgh University – see Architects' Journal 25 October 1978

Group 2

The Code suggests that although these compounds do not require protective treatment they require regular inspection and occasional maintenance:

Type d non-setting compounds for knife or strip application These flexible compounds are usually mainly based on synthetic rubbers. Strip can act as continuous distance pieces but must resist wind loads.

Type e sealants for gun application. These specialised products are usually based on elastomeric polymers such as polysulphides. They are very flexible, adhere tenaciously to suitable surfaces and are very durable.

Type f solid or cellular (closed cell) synthetic rubber strips. These are for use between bead, rebate and glass, held under pressure by the bead. They can perform as continuous load-bearing distance pieces and fillers, with glazing compounds or sealants used as cappings.

Type g gaskets of solid or cellular (closed cell) synthetic rubber – see *MBS: Materials* chapter 16.

GLAZING TECHNIQUES

References

CP 152: 1972 *Glazing and fixing of glass for buildings,* BS 5357: 1976 *Installation of security glazing, MBS: Materials* Chapter 12 for fixing of opaque glass to solid backgrounds, hollow glass block and *Profilit* glazing.

The terms used in measuring glass for surrounds are illustrated in figure 162, page 186.

Tolerances

It is always necessary to fix glass with at least 2 mm gaps between its edges and the surrounds, to allow for differential movements. More generous clearances are needed, of 5 mm or more all round where the larger glass dimension exceeds 750 mm, and for clear, and particularly wired glasses, which have dark backgrounds, for solar control glasses and for double glazing units where any of them are exposed to sunlight. Such glasses can reach 90°C in temperate climates and as little as possible of their surfaces should be shaded by beads which cause stresses in glass by keeping the edges cooler than the exposed parts.

Edges of glass

Where the thermal stresses referred to above occur, it is important that the edges of glass should be cut cleanly and not be weakened by being nipped or damaged.

Rebate sizes

The minimum *width*, ie dimension back front, of a rebate in wood or metal surrounds should be the thickness of the back putty, which should not be less than 2 mm for linseed oil and metal casement putties and 3 mm for non-setting compounds, plus the thickness of the glass and the width of the front putty.

The minimum *depth* of a rebate in wood or metal surrounds should be 6 mm for glass areas up to 0.42 m² internally and 0.1 m² externally, and 8 mm for larger panes glazed with putties. Where non-setting compounds are used the depth of rebates should be at least 10 mm and preferably 12 mm. Even greater depths are needed for larger panes, for panes that butt together for exposed conditions and for bottom edges of shop front plates – see CP 152. Manufacturers' instructions should be followed for double glazing units.

Rebates for glass and leaded lights in stone, brick and similar surrounds should be at least 10 mm deep, and widths must total at least 3 mm for a mortar bed, the thickness of leaded lights plus at least 12 mm for a mortar fillet.

Sizes of grooves for leaded lights

The width of grooves in stone, concrete, etc. should be at least the thickness of the leaded light plus 3 mm each side for mortar. Depths should be 20 mm at the top and on one side, and 12 mm at the bottom and the other side. Where there is a rebate at the bottom of an opening a 20 mm deep groove is needed on one side only.

We now consider the main methods of glazing under these headings:

1   Putty glazing
2   Bead glazing
3   Gasket glazing
4   Gasket and glazing compound
5   Direct into the structure
6   All-glass construction
7   Suspended glazing

8   Double glazing
9   Patent glazing
10   Roof lights – see chapter 6

1   Putty glazing

This, the most commonly used method of fixing glass illustrated in figures 108 and 129, is associated with ordinary quality painted joinery or painted metals in smaller pane sizes, but rarely for internal glazing, it being difficult to ensure a very neat appearance. Also putty embrittles with age – it must be painted and it is difficult to remove it without damaging wood sashes or frames. Putty is too rigid to accommodate large differential movements and for wind loadings up to 1900 and 2300 N/m², the combined lengths and heights of panes should not exceed 2700 and 2300 mm, respectively.

Putty glazing in wood frames

Linseed oil putty to BS 544 sets partly by absorption of the oil in wood surrounds, and partly by oxidation. Thus, to prevent excessive and premature absorption of oil into absorbent woods, it is necessary to prime the rebates and beads. The primer should be one coat to conform with BS 2521: 1966 *Lead-based priming paints*, or be a non-leafing aluminium-based wood primer.

Setting blocks are placed in position for the glass and the rebates are puttied with bedding putty. The glass is then pressed into position and secured with glaziers' sprigs spaced at about 450 mm apart around the perimeter of the frame. On pressing in the glass, the remaining *back putty* should be not less than 2 mm thick between the glass and the rebate. Some putty will be squeezed out and this should be stripped inside at an angle, to prevent shrinkage causing a groove in which condensation and dirt would accumulate.

The glass is then *front puttied* and formed with a putty knife at about 45° to throw off water at this vulnerable point. The putty should be stopped about 2 mm from the sight line of the rebate so that when paint is applied it is carried over the glass up to the sight line and so seals the edge of the putty to the glass. The putty must be protected with paint as soon after the initial hardening of the surface, to prevent long-term shrinkage and cracking.

As an alternative to linseed oil putty, flexible glazing compounds in strip form can be used. This type also needs protection by paint after initial setting.

Putty glazing in metal frames

Rebates in galvanized steel windows, unless suitably treated or painted 'at works', should be primed with calcium plumbate or self-etching primers. Aluminium surrounds should be primed with zinc chromate, or an etch primer where Group 1 glazing materials are used – see page 178.

This method is similar to that described for wood frames, but, as no absorption of the oil in the putty can take place, a special type of glazing compound is used containing a hardening agent. The glazing compound should be left for about 14 days in order to harden before painting commences. A wire clip, used to retain the glass before the front putty is applied, is shown in figure 147.

Single glazing and a small double glazing unit in metal frames are shown in figures 148 and 149.

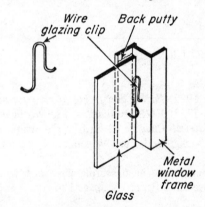

147   Wire glazing clip

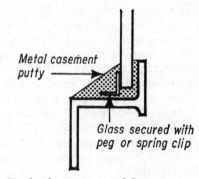

148   Single glazing in metal frames

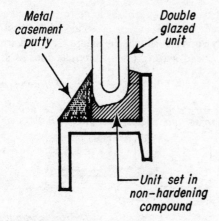

Metal casement putty — Double glazed unit — Unit set in non-hardening compound

149 Double glazing in metal frames

2 Bead glazing

Beads are neater than putty fillets, more easily removed, and they are necessary to retain large

panes. However, as replacement beads cannot be guaranteed to be waterproof, and the possibility of unauthorised removal must be considered, beads are better fixed inside windows.

Panes over, say 0.2 m² in area, should always be on small *setting blocks* of resilient material such as lead, sealed hardwood or rigid nylon. Unplasticized PVC is suitable only for light single panes of clear glass. They should be thicker than the single or double glazing, and generally from 25 mm to 75 mm long. The exception is a vertical pivotted window, in which case blocks should not be less than 150 mm long. *Location blocks*, which are used at the sides and top of the window to ensure correct edge tolerances, are usually about 25 mm long. The positions of setting and location blocks are shown in figure 150.

In addition to setting and location blocks, where non-setting compounds may be displaced by wind pressure, *distance pieces* should be placed between

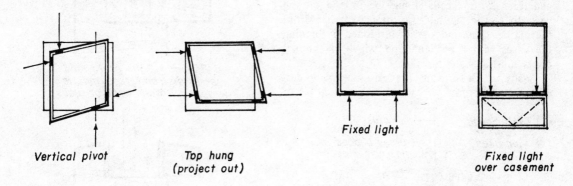

Vertical pivot   Top hung (project out)   Fixed light   Fixed light over casement

(min. 75 mm from corner of frame)

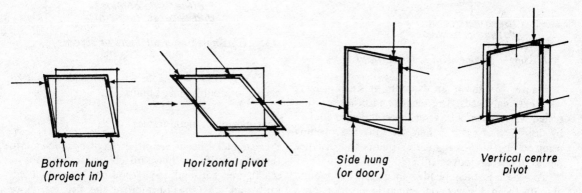

Bottom hung (project in)   Horizontal pivot   Side hung (or door)   Vertical centre pivot

150 Positions of setting and location blocks

the back edge of glass and the rebate — as shown in figure 155, page 184 — in this case for a double glazing unit. Distance pieces are usually 25 mm long and of a depth to give a 3 mm cover of mastic. They should be under slight compression when beads are fixed. Distance pieces must not coincide with setting or location blocks.

Location blocks and distance pieces should be softer than setting blocks, and they are usually plasticized PVC.

Bead glazing in wood frames

For cheaper work which is painted, softwood beads are often fixed by panel pins, with some risk to their being damaged if they have to be removed later. For better quality work in particular, clear finished hardwood beads are fixed with screws, preferably in cups. In windows, both the glass and beads are set in mastic which must be of good quality, and be applied generously so water will not penetrate. Wood beads should be primed on the back to prevent initial absorption of binder from the mastic. Glass indoors, is cushioned by binding the edges with a resilient tape, which in external doors, must be water resistant.

Beads which provide fire-resistance were described on page 175.

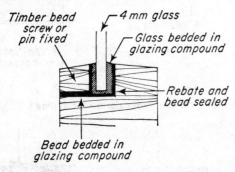

151 Single glazing with external bead

Figure 151 shows an example of single glazing with external beads. The rebate and beads are first sealed with a proprietary sealing compound applied by brush, the glass is then set into the opening using setting blocks at quarter points and distance pieces to restrain movement.

The glass is then bedded in glazing compound and the bead screwed or pinned in position on a fillet of sealant, usually applied by gun. For in-

ternal bead glazing, the bedding for the bead can be omitted. The fixing of a solid infill panel such as plywood is shown in figure 152. Figure 153 shows bead glazing for an internal door or screen.

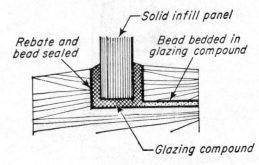

152 Fixing a solid infill panel

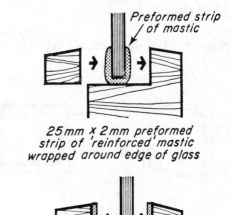

153 Glazing to internal doors or screens

Figures 154 and 155 show examples of bead glazing of double glazed units.

Bead glazing in metal frames

Pressed metal beads are either fixed by screws into threaded holes or they are clipped over studs — see figures 156 and 157. Wood beads can be used, but solid steel beads improve the fire resistance of metal frames. A group 2 glazing compound is

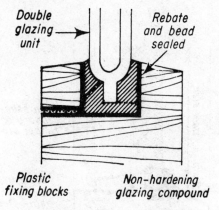

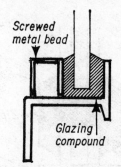

154 Internal bead glazing of double glazed units

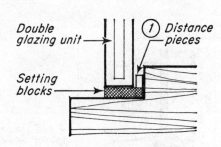

156 Metal beads fixed by screws

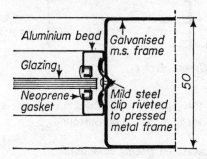

157 Metal beads fixed by clipping over protruding studs

used in conjunction with bead glazing in metal frames. A typical technique is illustrated in figures 147 and 148, page 180.

3 Gasket glazing – see figures 158 and 159 and *MBS: Materials,* chapter 16.

Gasket sections extruded in materials such as neoprene, permit movement and hold glass and other sheets in compression to effect a weather seal. After the sheet has been inserted in the gasket pressure on the seal may be further increased by a 'zipper' strip being inserted into a groove in the gasket with a special tool. These strips can be easily removed for reglazing.

Being resilient, corners can be curved as is appropriate for surrounds such as GRP. For angles injection moulded corners can be welded in to provide a jointless periphery.

Although specialized and more costly than putty or bead glazing, gasket glazing is quick and neat and particularly suitable for factory assembled units.

In figure 158 the lower groove of a gasket is snapped over a metal subframe. A double glazing

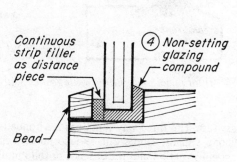

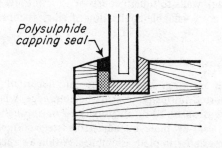

155 External bead glazing of a double glazed unit

unit is then placed in the upper groove with a spatula and 'zipper' strips are inserted to increase pressure on the seal.

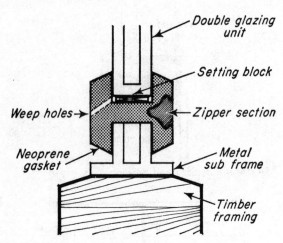

158   Gasket glazing

Figure 159 shows a type of gasket used with a solid panel with glass in a timber surround.

4   Gasket and glazing compound

In this technique, glass set in a glazing compound is secured by a PVC or elastomeric glazing strip.

5   Glazing direct into structures

Glass can be glazed in rebates or grooves in stone, concrete and similar surrounds. Manufacturers of glazing compounds should be consulted as to the need for alkali resistant priming, and compatability of their products. Non-setting compounds need not be painted, but setting blocks and distance pieces should be used. CP 152 suggests mortars for leaded lights consisting of: 2 Portland cement: 1 slaked lime: 6 stone dust, and 1 Portland cement: 2 slaked lime: 8 sand.

Glass block walls are considered in *MBS: Materials*, chapter 12. Glass lenses and pavement lights, with thermal movement similar to that of concrete, are cast directly into concrete.

6   All-glass construction

Single height plates of annealed glass can be butted at their vertical edges and stiffened by full height

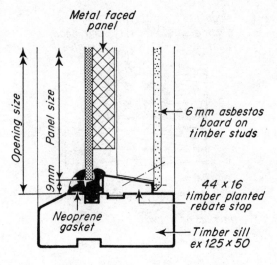

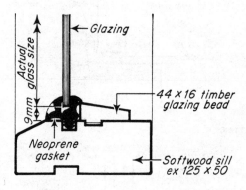

159   Infill panel and glazing with gasket seal

glass fins. The three way junctions are bonded with silicone sealant. Doors can be incorporated in all-glass construction and the absence of solid mullions is an advantage for showcases.

Back walls to squash courts of 12 mm toughened glass are a valuable application of all-glass construction.

7   Suspended glazing

There are strict limits to the safe height of glass supported normally, ie at its bottom edge, whereas a height up to 20 m of (usually 12 mm) toughened glass can be hung by adjustable steel suspension clamps and grip plate assemblies. Within a structural opening there is clearance at the bottom edge, and the glass plates are joined at their corners by bolts passed through holes in metal patch plates, and through the glass with resilient bushes which avoid metal to glass contact and allow thermal movement. 19 mm stabilizing fins at the back, which resist wind loads are fixed similarly. Glass – glass joints are normally sealed with silicone or by extruded plastics or rubber H sections. Cover plates which allow major movements are available.

8   Double glazing

Double glazing reduces thermal transmission, but not solar gain. In vertical glazing a cavity width of about 20 mm halves the heat lost by a single pane of glass, but a 3 mm gap provides about 70 per cent of this optimum. The thickness of glass has no practical effect on thermal insulation. Widths of cavities for sound insulation must be much wider – see *2 Double windows*.

Double glazing requires rebates wide enough to accommodate the additional thickness of the units, and sashes must be sufficiently strong to support the doubled weight of glass.

1 Double glazing units
These factory made, hermetically sealed, units are of two types:

(a) A unit in which dry air is sealed between two panes of glass separated at the edges by a metal spacer, which is protected by a metal tape. The spacer may be a tube which contains a dessicant to absorb any moisture between the panes. Units are purpose made, but the following glass thickness – air space – areas of unit relationships are typical:

glass mm	air space mm	approximate maximum size mm
3	3	750 x 750
3	5	
4		6 and 12
6	6 and 12	3000 x 6000
9		12
10		12

Maximum sizes vary also, according to exposures – see page 175 – and the type of glass. Different types of glass are sometimes possible on the two sides of the unit.

Figure 161 shows a unit glazed in a wood surround and figure 162 shows the terms used.

(b) This all-glass unit shown in figures 149 and 154 is not available at present.

The handling and fixing of double glazed units calls for considerable care and skill. Figures 154 and 155 show examples of fixing of double glazed units. The fixing of a stepped unit in a small rebate is shown in figure 46 in *MBS: Materials.*

As site and exposure conditions vary widely it is important that the glazing compounds should be carefully chosen. Two or more bedding or weathering materials may have to be used in the fixing of a unit. More detailed information should be sought from the manufacturers, and their recommendations should always be followed.

Information can also be obtained from the Insulation Glazing Association, 6 Mount Row, London W1.

Whichever method of glazing is used, the edges of the units must not be in continuous contact with trapped water, or there is a danger that the seal will be damaged.

2 Double windows

These comprise two single glazed surrounds, fitted separately into window openings as shown in figure 160. This construction is suitable where sound insulation is the main consideration and for

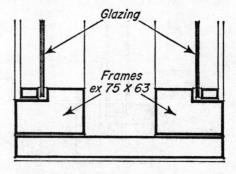

160   Double window

this the space between panes should be at least 100 mm and preferably 200 mm, and the surrounds should be separated. The glass should be as thick as possible, and sound insulation is further improved by lining the reveals with a sound absorbent material. The surrounds should be sealed at their edges as tightly as possible, but one of them should be hung to give access for occasional cleaning within the cavity.

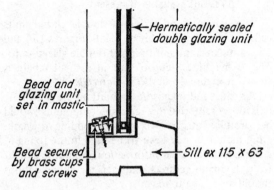

161 Double glazed sealed fixed unit

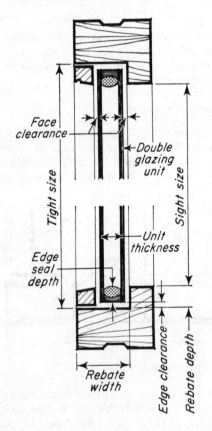

Glazing size (actual size) = tight size − clearance

162 Terms used in glazing

The edge seal depth varies with width of the air space and the area of the unit, from 11 mm with a unit having a 5 mm air space to 29 mm for units having a 12 mm air space.

Clearances and rebate depths for bead fixing have been discussed under those headings. Front 'puttying' is possible for units up to 2.3 m² and not exceeding 11 mm thick, but a polysulphide sealant must be used − *not* linseed oil putty.

3   Coupled windows

These have two surrounds which normally open together as one unit.

The secondary is either hinged, or completely removable for cleaning. This principle is illustrated in figure 163.

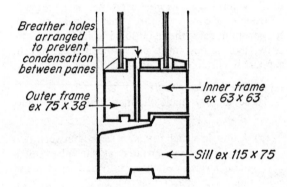

163 Coupled surrounds separately glazed

4   Dual glazing

Figure 164 shows two panes of glass fixed in one

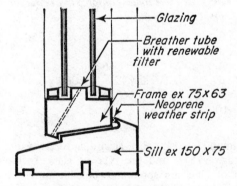

164 Single frame double glazed

sash. The air space between the panes should be allowed to 'breathe' to the outside to prevent condensation, since a complete seal is a practical impossibility. In addition to this precaution, one sheet of glass should be removable for periodic cleaning.

5 Converted single glazing

There are many proprietary systems which convert existing windows to 'double glazing'. Most of them attach a second pane of glass in aluminium alloy or plastics channels, by clips and/or screws, to the original surround.

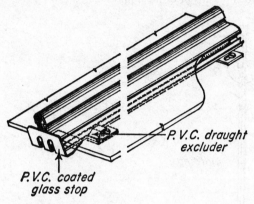

(a)   Support for glass

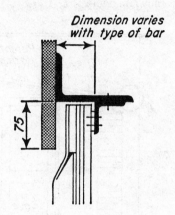

(b)   Fixing detail

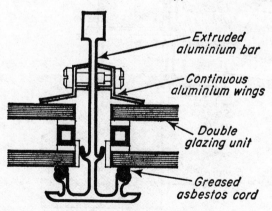

(c)   PVC covered glazing bar

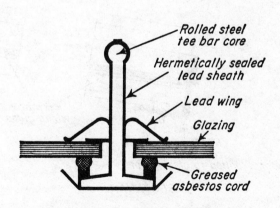

(d)   Aluminium glazing bar

(e)   Lead covered glazing bar

165 **Patent glazing**

9 Patent glazing

This form of 'puttyless' glazing is an economic and flexible system, (once patented!), which requires very little maintenance. BS 5516: 1977 is a *Code of practice for patent glazing.* It can be used to form a glazed roof as shown in figure 166 or for vertical glazing as shown in figure 167.

Bars are made for single and double glazing in steel and in aluminium alloy – see figure 165(a)-(e) Steel must be galvanized and protected by a jointless lead or PVC sheath. The inverted T section supports the glass on greased resilient cords. Bars are made in different depths for varying spans between purlins or other supports.

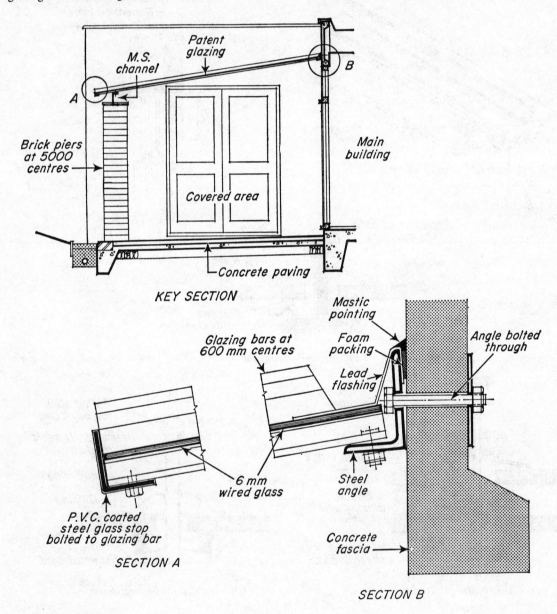

166 *Glazed covered area*

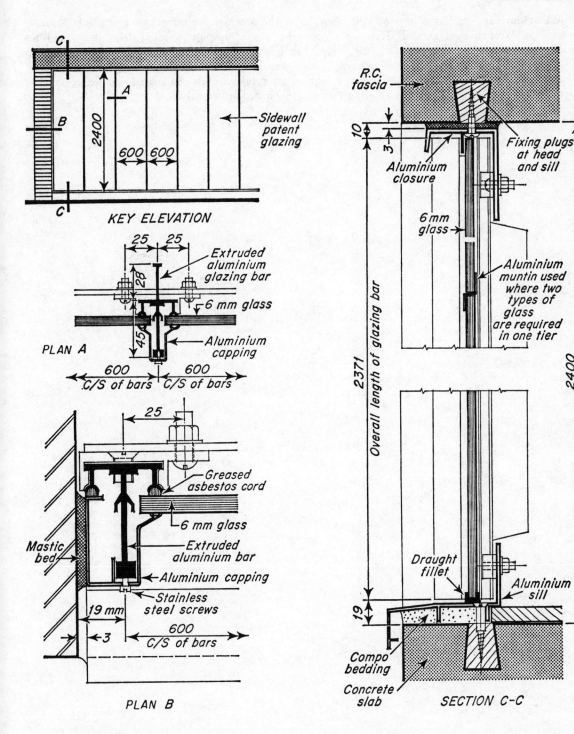

KEY ELEVATION

2400

600 600

C

C

A

B

Sidewall patent glazing

PLAN A

25 25

28

45

Extruded aluminium glazing bar

6 mm glass

Aluminium capping

600
C/S of bars

600
C/S of bars

PLAN B

25

Mastic bed

Greased asbestos cord

6 mm glass

Extruded aluminium bar

Aluminium capping

Stainless steel screws

19 mm

3

600
C/S of bars

R.C. fascia

10

3

Aluminium closure

6 mm glass

Overall length of glazing bar

2371

19

Fixing plugs at head and sill

Aluminium muntin used where two types of glass are required in one tier

2400

Draught fillet

Aluminium sill

Compo bedding

Concrete slab

SECTION C-C

167   *Vertical patent glazing*

189

Aluminium caps, or aluminium or lead 'wings' provide an external weather seal. The profile has grooves for water which may penetrate the 'wings', and also for condensation from the underside of the glass. A shoe fixed to the structure at the foot of each bar prevents the glass from sliding downwards — see figure 165(a) page 187.

The spacing of glazing bars is the 'safe' span of the glass (typically 6 mm wired glass), and by handling conditions — 600 mm can normally be taken as a 'safe' maximum spacing for bars. In roof glazing glass must be wired, or exceptionally, toughened or laminated.

The provision of natural lighting units for roofs, usually by dry glazing techniques in the form of dome lights, monitors, skylights and lantern lights, has become a specialist matter. Since the roof light is situated on the most vulnerable and exposed part of a building, formidable problems of weather resistance have to be overcome. A system of roof lights must, in addition to being completely weatherproof, be burglar proof and strong enough to withstand roof deal loads, provide for the escape of condensation and smoke in the event of fire, be easy to replace and inexpensive to maintain.

As for windows (see page 128), roof lights can also be a major source of heat loss from a building. For this reason, they should be double glazed which will also reduce the risk of condensation and the irritation of dripping water into the building. *The Building Regulations 1976, Part F* requires the roof construction and any associated roof space and ceiling to have a 'U' valve not exceeding 0.6 W/m^2 °C for dwellings. There is no requirement that the area of rooflights should be limited to keep heat losses to a minimum to correspond with the limitation of window areas in external walls. However, *Part FF* of the same Regulations (coming into force in June 1979) will limit the areas of roof lights for *buildings other than dwellings* to 20% of the total roof area, and the *maximum* 'U' valve will be either 0.6 or 0.7 W/m^2 °C according to the purpose group of the building (see Regulation FF4, Tables 1 and 2). Under this regulation a roof light must have a 'U' valve equivalent to the *average* 'U' valve of the roof construction.

METAL FRAMED ROOF LIGHT

Figure 168 shows a form of roof light constructed from a rolled steel, hot-dip galvanized frame into which is set wired glass in non-hardening glazing compound using setting blocks to allow thermal movement. The roof light is either fixed or openable. The latter is illustrated, having a pressed steel

hood to protect the opening. It is always difficult to guarantee that rain will not be blown into a building when an open type roof light is used and for this reason the opening end of the light should always be placed with its back to the direction of the prevailing wind.

Many manufacturers have a detail which incorporates a louvre flap or 'hit and miss' ventilator in the upstand, which means that the top of the roof light can remain fixed, whilst ventilation can be obtained from the side. This is a slightly easier weathering problem. Some manufacturers also incorporate a temperature operated catch on the opening section which provides an automatic vent in case of fire.

DOME LIGHTS

These are made in glass or plastics. The glass domes are usually either circular or rectangular on plan and have wired glass in most cases secured by means of special clips. Upstand curbs are of concrete or wood, galvanized steel or aluminium.

Dome lights in various plastics are now popular. They are available in clear and opaque acrylic (PMMA) and glass fibre reinforced polyester resin (GRP). The glass fibre tested in accordance with BS 476: Part 3 must give an 'External FAA' designation. Solar energy transmittance and glare control can be achieved by the use of special bronze tinted acrylic. Care must be taken to ascertain the fire risks in respect of the use of acrylics. Figure 169 illustrates a selection from a range of dome lights made in a number of very pleasing forms, on a dimensionally co-ordinated 300 mm module.

Also in figure 169 a dome light is shown fixed to a pre-formed GRP base. The foam strip and clamp fixing detail provides a good weather seal and allows thermal movement to take place without damaging the dome light or surrounding struc-

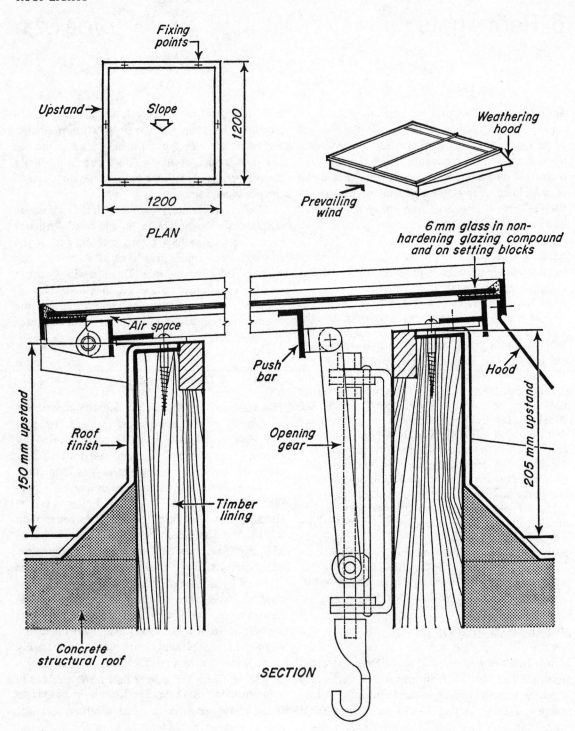

Fixing points

Upstand →

Slope

1200

1200

PLAN

Weathering hood

Prevailing wind

6 mm glass in non-hardening glazing compound and on setting blocks

Air space

Push bar

Hood

150 mm upstand

205 mm upstand

Roof finish

Opening gear

Timber lining

Concrete structural roof

SECTION

168   *Galvanised steel roof light*

ture. Condensation falls into the gutter formed by the upstand and the moisture then drains away through the plastic edge strip. Insulation can be improved by the placing of the roof lights one over the other to make a double skin construction.

Insurance companies are now demanding very high standards of security for construction and

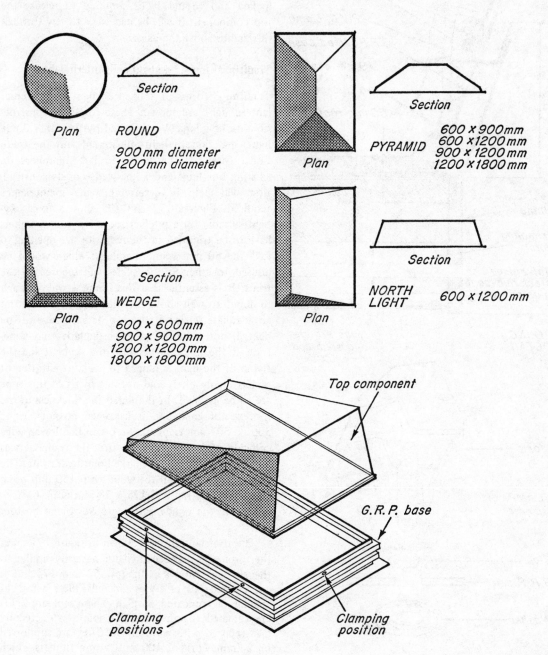

169   Plastics dome lights (1)

193

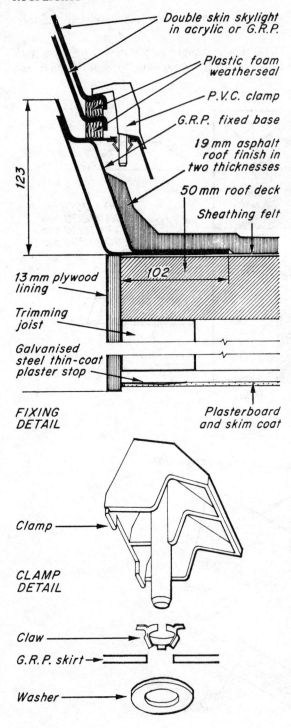

Double skin skylight in acrylic or G.R.P.

Plastic foam weatherseal

P.V.C. clamp

G.R.P. fixed base

19 mm asphalt roof finish in two thicknesses

50 mm roof deck

Sheathing felt

123

102

13 mm plywood lining

Trimming joist

Galvanised steel thin-coat plaster stop

FIXING DETAIL

Plasterboard and skim coat

Clamp

CLAMP DETAIL

Claw

G.R.P. skirt

Washer

170   *Plastics dome lights (2)*

manufacturers are aware of this and provide security fixings for their products. Figure 170 gives an example of this. The L clamps shown are easily fixed but once in position they are permanently locked and should it be required to release the top component it will be necessary to saw through the clamps above the base.

Traditional timber skylight and lantern light

Traditional forms of a fixed skylight and a timber lantern light are shown. These forms of construction are now largely superseded by the other dome lights and lantern lights illustrated, but the traditional form will be found in large numbers on existing buildings and a knowledge of its construction will help in determining the maintenance required. Figures 172 and 173 show a fixed skylight suitable for a pitched roof. The roof members have to be trimmed to the requisite size opening to take the 50 mm frame members, which would be housed together at the angles and secured to the trims. It is essential that this frame is wide enough to stand up well above the roof finish and to form an adequate gutter at the top or back edge of the light. If not, water or snow, particularly, may penetrate at the junction between the skylight and the frame. If the light is hinged to open, penetration of rain is highly likely and opening lights of this type are to be avoided. In the detail the thickness of the roof is not great and it has been possible, using 300 x 50 mm framing, to make the lower edge coincide with the ceiling so that the frame acts as a lining as well; it is so marked on the drawing. The light itself is 50 mm softwood with 150 mm nom. styles and top rail and 175 x 38 mm nom. bottom rail. Note the condensation groove to the bottom rail.

The roof lantern light shown in figure 171 takes the form of 4 inclined skylights basically similar to the skylight shown in figures 172 and 173 but is constructed out of styles and rails, these being cut angular or truncated on plan. These separate lights are tongued together and the joints protected by lead secured with a wood roll. They are supported on a framework of 100 x 100 mm timbers which themselves form the heads and corner posts with

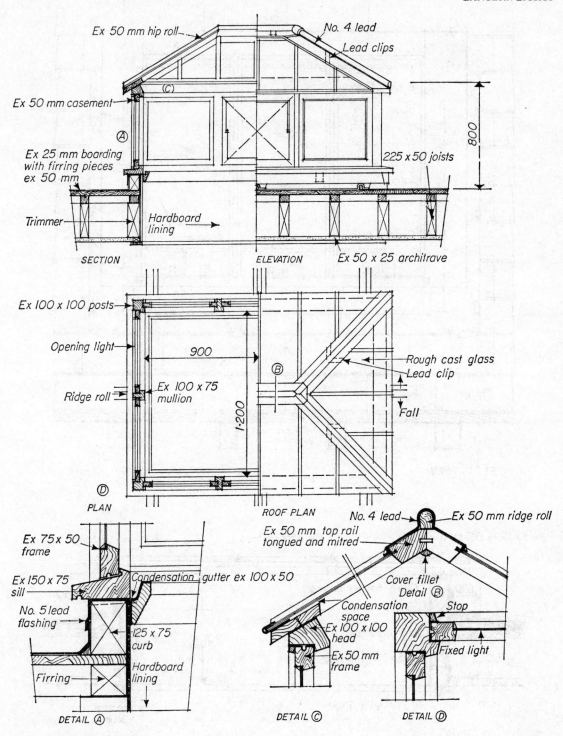

Ex 50 mm hip roll
No. 4 lead
Lead clips
Ex 50 mm casement
800
225 x 50 joists
Ex 25 mm boarding with firring pieces ex 50 mm
Trimmer
Hardboard lining
SECTION
ELEVATION
Ex 50 x 25 architrave

Ex 100 x 100 posts
Opening light
900
Rough cast glass
Lead clip
Ridge roll
Ex 100 x 75 mullion
1·200
Fall
PLAN
ROOF PLAN

Ex 75 x 50 frame
Ex 150 x 75 sill
Condensation gutter ex 100 x 50
No. 5 lead flashing
125 x 75 curb
Firring
Hardboard lining
DETAIL A

No. 4 lead
Ex 50 mm ridge roll
Ex 50 mm top rail tongued and mitred
Cover fillet Detail B
Condensation space
Stop
Ex 100 x 100 head
Ex 50 mm frame
Fixed light
DETAIL C
DETAIL D

171 Timber lantern light

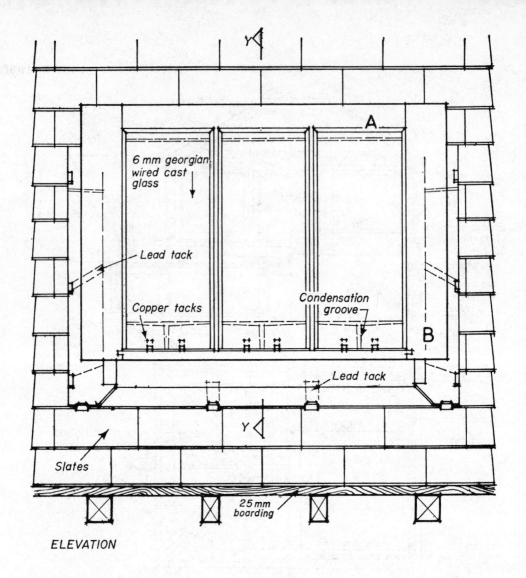

6 mm georgian
wired cast
glass

Lead tack

Copper tacks

Condensation
groove

A

B

Lead tack

Slates

Y

25 mm
boarding

ELEVATION

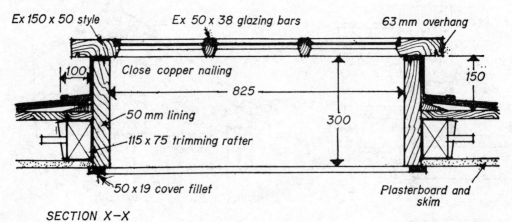

Ex 150 x 50 style

Ex 50 x 38 glazing bars

63 mm overhang

100

Close copper nailing

825

150

50 mm lining

300

115 x 75 trimming rafter

50 x 19 cover fillet

Plasterboard and
skim

SECTION X–X

172   *Skylight (1)*

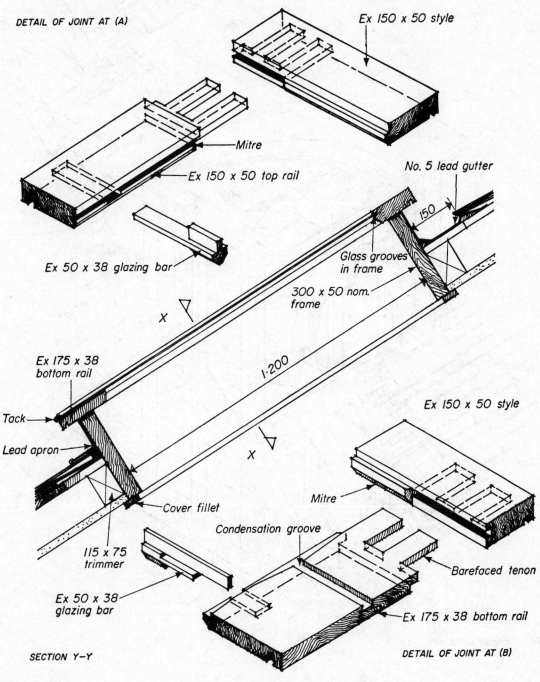

DETAIL OF JOINT AT (A)

Ex 150 x 50 style

Mitre

Ex 150 x 50 top rail

No. 5 lead gutter

150

Ex 50 x 38 glazing bar

Glass grooves
in frame

300 x 50 nom.
frame

X

1·200

Ex 175 x 38
bottom rail

Tack

Ex 150 x 50 style

Lead apron

X

Cover fillet

Mitre

Condensation groove

Barefaced tenon

115 x 75
trimmer

Ex 50 x 38
glazing bar

Ex 175 x 38 bottom rail

SECTION Y—Y

DETAIL OF JOINT AT (B)

173   Skylight (2)

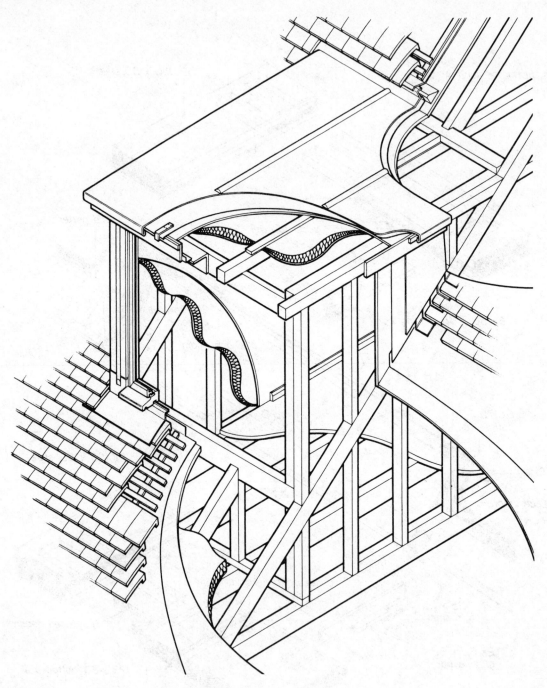

174   Dormer window

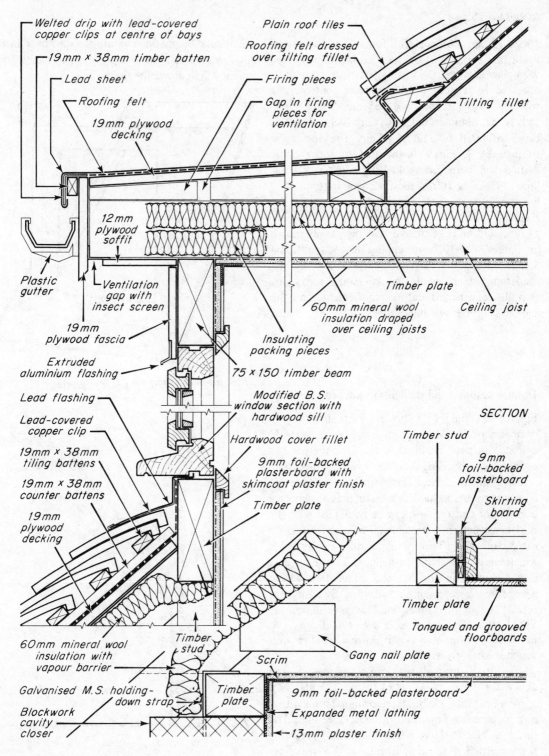

Welted drip with lead-covered copper clips at centre of bays

19mm × 38mm timber batten

Lead sheet

Roofing felt

19mm plywood decking

Plain roof tiles

Roofing felt dressed over tilting fillet

Firing pieces

Gap in firing pieces for ventilation

Tilting fillet

12mm plywood soffit

Plastic gutter

Ventilation gap with insect screen

19mm plywood fascia

Extruded aluminium flashing

Lead flashing

Lead-covered copper clip

19mm × 38mm tiling battens

19mm × 38mm counter battens

19mm plywood decking

Insulating packing pieces

75 × 150 timber beam

Modified B.S. window section with hardwood sill

Hardwood cover fillet

9mm foil-backed plasterboard with skimcoat plaster finish

Timber plate

Timber plate

60mm mineral wool insulation draped over ceiling joists

Ceiling joist

SECTION

Timber stud

9mm foil-backed plasterboard

Skirting board

Timber plate

Tongued and grooved floorboards

Timber stud

60mm mineral wool insulation with vapour barrier

Galvanised M.S. holding-down strap

Blockwork cavity closer

Timber plate

Scrim

Gang nail plate

9mm foil-backed plasterboard

Expanded metal lathing

13mm plaster finish

175 Typical section through dormer window

100 x 75 mm mullions. This frames a set of vertical casements, some fixed and some horizontally pivoted with planted stops. The opening casements would be operated by cords or other remote control. The whole skylight stands on a 125 mm timber curb. This is the minimum height of curb to avoid the sill being saturated by rain splashing. The opening is trimmed by 75 mm wide trimmer and this and the firrings and curb are masked by a lining of hardboard. There is 100 x 20 mm condensation gutter lined with lead formed around the base of the glazing.

It should be remembered that the details shown in figures 170-172 are applicable to traditional design criteria and do not indicate the thermal insulation which would be necessary today for compliance with mandatory requirements and the need to conserve heat in buildings.

Dormer windows and skylights in pitched roofs

Figures 174 and 175 indicate typical details for a dormer window. Although their use is not currently common in new dwellings in the UK, the need to economise on building costs and space heating could result in their increased adoption. By making the roof space a usable habitable space, the conventional upper floor construction can be combined with the roof construction – particularly now that prefabricated trussed rafter configurations are available which easily allow this to happen. The practice of providing the upper floor accommodation within a roof space is common today in Sweden. For further details of dormer window construction see *SF(1) MBS: Chapter 7 pages 193-196*. Figure 176 indicates a proprietary GRP dormer window unit which is currently available.

An alternative to the *dormer window* is the *skylight* which is indicated in figures 177 and 178.

When providing habitable accommodation within a roof space it is important that reference should be made to *The Building Regulations 1976* regarding the permitted headroom. Regulation K8 stipulates that the statutory height for habitable rooms of

2.3 m must be provided within the roof over an area not less than half the area of the room measured on a plane 1.5 m above the floor.

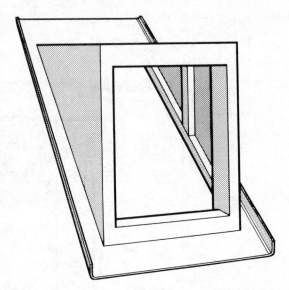

176 Preformed GRP dormer window

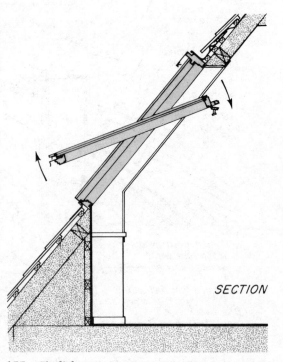

SECTION

177 Skylight

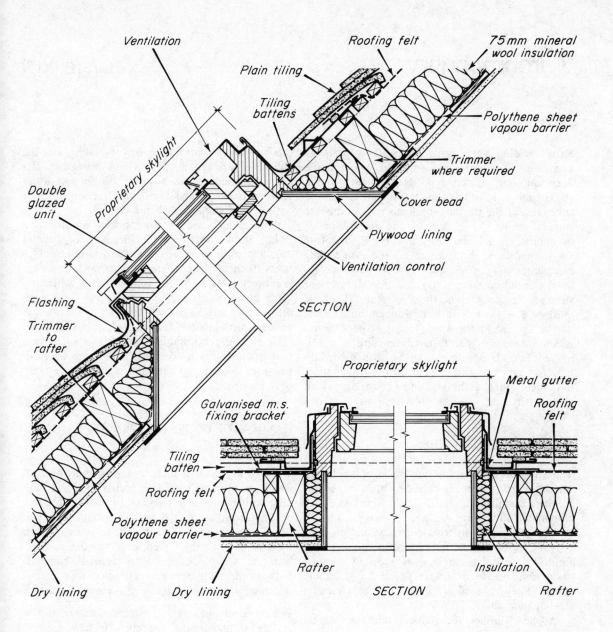

Ventilation

Roofing felt

75 mm mineral wool insulation

Plain tiling

Tiling battens

Proprietary skylight

Polythene sheet vapour barrier

Double glazed unit

Trimmer where required

Cover bead

Plywood lining

Ventilation control

SECTION

Flashing

Trimmer to rafter

Proprietary skylight

Metal gutter

Roofing felt

Galvanised m.s. fixing bracket

Tiling batten

Roofing felt

Polythene sheet vapour barrier

Rafter

Insulation

Rafter

Dry lining

Dry lining

SECTION

178   Skylight

Many building components are 'working parts' of a building, ie doors and windows, which must open and shut. However good the quality of the workmanship, it will fail in its function and cause annoyance if the working mechanism is not durable and efficient. The choice of the right type of ironmongery, and the right quality, is therefore very important. For instance, the self-closing mechanism of a door into a shop may operate hundreds of times every day and in a department store perhaps a million times a year. The door must be easy for a child to push open, but it must not be opened by the wind. Thus the specification which ironmongery is required to fulfil is a formidable one. Ironmongery can be divided broadly into two types of fittings: (1) fittings which allow movement, such as hinges, and (2) fittings which give security, such as locks, bolts and bars.

MATERIALS AND FINISHES

The strongest lock fittings are made of steel with wearing parts of special bronzes. Brass is used as the base metal for a plated finish. The less costly aluminium alloys are also widely used because of their relative freedom from corrosion and pleasant appearance. It must be remembered that an applied finish will not last so long as regularly cleaned *matt finish, satin* or *bright* polishes on durable metals like nickel-silver, brass, bronze, stainless steel or aluminium.

Applied finishes such as chromium or nickel plating can be electro-deposited, or the finish can be an enamel or a lacquer. A black japanned lacquer finish is common for inexpensive ironmongery. Real BMA (*Bronze Metal Antique*) is a finish for bronze and gunmetal produced by heating after polishing to give an iridescent finish. This is an expensive process and is sometimes imitated by other means, but imitation BMA is visually inferior to the real thing. Aluminium alloy ironmongery can be anodized. This is an electrical process by which an anti-corrosive film is produced. The metal

can be stained with colour before sealing, but the colours available are not always attractive. Uncoloured anodizing is a 'silver' finish and looks very well. Metals and finishes on metals are dealt with in *MBS: Materials,* chapter 9.

Plastics are used in ironmongery mostly as a finish on a metal base, ie plastic door handles moulded onto a metal core. Items not subject to stress, such as finger plates, can be made from unreinforced plastic sheet. Some fittings which receive much wear, such as sliding stays for casements and some hinges, are made in nylon. Plastics are dealt with in *MBS: Materials,* chapter 13.

It is vital for durability, as well as appearance that ironmongery is fixed with the correct screws, wherever possible, of the same metal as the body of the fitting.

HANGING OF DOORS AND WINDOW FITTINGS

Many fittings such as locks and handles are handed, which means that they are specifically for a door hung either on the left side or the right side of an opening, so it is essential to have a standard way of describing on which side the door is hung. It is usual to describe the direction of opening as clockwide or anti-clockwise when viewed from the outward opening position. The clockwise part is self-evident, but the 'outside' is generally agreed as:

1 For external doors – the corridor side of a room
2 For external doors – the 'open air' side
3 For cupboards – the room side.

Then, describing locks, view the door from the outside and a lock on the left side will be a left-hand lock.

HINGES

The *butt hinge* is the most common hinge screwed to the edge of a door. Butt hinges are recessed into the frame and into the door. Normally one pair of 75 mm or 100 mm butts suits a standard internal door; external and other heavier doors might well have 1½ pairs, ie three 100 mm butts. Butt hinges are made in steel, brass with steel pins, brass with brass pins, or in nylon. Rising butts lift the door as it opens so as to clear the carpet, and this type of hinge is in some degree self-closing. Rising butts must be 'handed'. A falling butt hinge is also available which will keep a door in the open position.

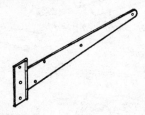

179   *Butt hinge and rising butt*

Tee hinges of cross-garnets are used for heavy doors of the ledged type.

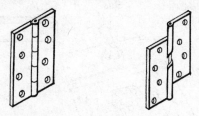

180   *Tee hinge*

With lift-off butts or pin hinges the door can be taken down without unscrewing the hinge and this type of hinge is therefore always used for doors that are pre-hung and assembled in the factory.

Back-flap hinges are for screwing on the face of the work where the timber is too thin to screw into the edge, or where appearance is not important. They make a strong job when used on internal joinery fittings.

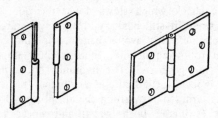

181   *Lift-off hinge and back-flap hinge*

The parliament hinge is used to enable a door to fold back. It projects from the face of the timber. The centre hinge is used where it can be fixed to the top or to the side of a fitting.

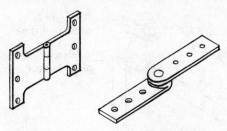

182   *Parliament hinge and centre hinge*

The cranked hinge is necessary for lipped or rebated casements and is usually made with the two halves separate so that a pin fixing can be used in assembling the casements in factory production of windows.

The offset or *Easy-clean* hinge is used to allow the outside of windows to be cleaned when open at 90°.

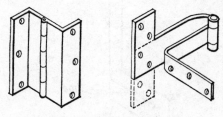

183   *Cranked hinge and offset hinge (easy-clean)*

The counter flap hinge is set in flush with the face of the work — its name being indicative of its use. The strap hinge is similarly used but has a projecting knuckle.

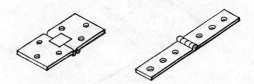

184   *Counter flap and strap hinge*

DOOR SPRINGS

For the control of swing doors, pivoted floor springs are the best, but they are expensive. The component consists of a strong spring contained in a metal box; a *shoe* which is attached to the base of the door; and a top pivot. The assembly is shown in figure 185. The box is fitted into the floor

thickness so that the cover plate is flush with the finished floor level. For this reason the use of a floor spring is somewhat restricted, since many types of floor and threshold construction do not permit easy cutting away to receive the box. The adjustable pivot plate or top centre is fixed to the head of the frame and top of the door, and is adjusted up and down by a screw. The lower pivot is connected to the shoe, which is in turn firmly fixed

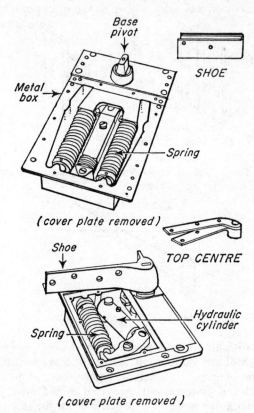

185 Double and single action floor springs

to the bottom of the door and to the side of the door at the base. The spring should have an hydraulic check which slows down the door at a point where it still has, say, 150 mm to travel before closing. This avoids banging or injury to a person following behind. Floor springs are illustrated in figure 185. The hydraulic check mechanism is seen in the figure as a cylinder attached by a lever arm to the strong metal springs. Double action (swinging both ways) and single action (swinging one way only) floor springs are shown.

185 Typical installation of floor spring

The cover plates which are available in a variety of finishes to match the general ironmongery specification, have been omitted for clarity. To ensure the smooth working of a double swing door in conjunction with a floor spring, it is important that both the closing and fixed edges of the door are profiled to the correct radius. The recommended dimensions are given in figure 187.

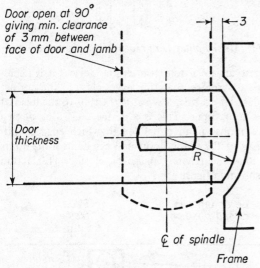

Door heels and their radii for standard applications

Door thickness	40	44	50	64
Heel radius R	32	35	38	48

187   Door heels and their radii

DOOR CLOSERS

There are several alternative methods for checking and controlling the opening and closing of doors. For swing doors there are various types of spring hinges. Figure 188 illustrates a patented type of hinge controlled by a small but powerful horizontal spring held in a metal cylinder at the back of the face plate. The cylinder or cylinders have to be housed into mortices cut into the frame and are covered by the face plate. The moving part of the hinge clips round both sides of the door in a shallow housing and is screwed firmly into position so that there are no projecting knuckles or plates. Both double and single action hinges are illus-

trated, the former controlled by two springs, the latter by one. This type of hinge is not made with a check action.

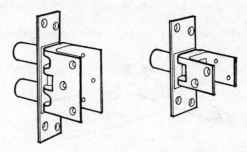

188   Single and double barrel, double action Hawgood spring hinges

Another type of spring hinge is illustrated in figure 189. This is similar in form to a butt hinge but has a large knuckel, the hinges are obtainable with double action or single action as shown. The spring, which is contained in the vertical metal cylinder, is adjustable by means of a *Tommy* bar in the hole at the top of the cylinder. This adjustment controls the momentum of the closing action. Spring hinges of this type can be obtained in matching pairs, the top hinge acting as the spring, the bottom hinge being made to provide a check action.

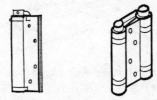

189   Single and double action spring hinges

The closing action of doors hung on ordinary butt hinges can be controlled by the fixing of check mechanisms on the top of the face of the door and the door frame head. There is a very wide range of this type of overhead door closer which provides a combined closing and check action control. This type of closer is adjustable to balance the weight of the door and is much less expensive than the pivot floor spring control. The overhead closer is available in double and single action patterns; handed and reversible. Three alternative methods of fixing are shown. Figure 190 shows an

205

example of a closer in a pleasantly designed case, for surface fixing to the opening face of the door. Figure 191 shows the same spring, but for fixing to the closing face of the door, and figure 192 shows a closer which fits into the thickness of the door at the top and is thus concealed with the exception of the projecting arm.

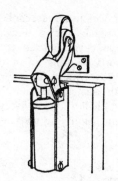

193 Door holder (to prevent door slamming)

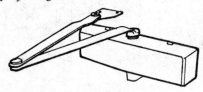

190 Hydraulic check, single action door check, surface fixing to opening face

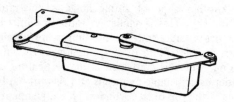

191 Hydraulic check, single action door check, surface fixing to closing face

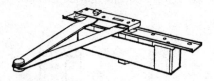

192 Concealed fixing door check (fits into thickness of door)

DOOR CHECKS

The door closer fittings so far described control the whole of the movement of the door, but perhaps a more universal requirement is to prevent the slamming of the door. Figure 193 shows such a device which by engaging a wheel attached to a cantilevered arm, causes the movement of the door to be checked. This type of check would be used in conjunction with a spring hinge which works in conjunction with the check to achieve final and positive closing.

Where pairs of doors which have rebated meet-

ing styles are fitted with closing devices it is necessary to arrange that the leaves close in the correct order. To do this, a *selector* is fitted to the head of the door frame. This is a device consisting of two leve rarms of an equal length which engage both leaves of the swing doors and can control the doors so that the rebates engage on closing. This action is shown in figure 194.

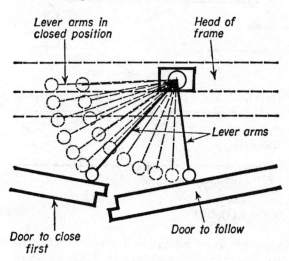

194 Door selector

LOCKS AND LATCHES

Locking gear contains complex mechanism and very great care must be exercised in the specification of the appropriate quality. The specifier must be quite clear as to the precise requirements since in general terms cost is proportionate to security. It is important to realize that, apart from the convenience of the user, the insurance company required to cover the contents of the building will be concerned with security whilst the local authority will be concerned with providing easy means of escape in case of fire. These two conditions are not always easy to reconcile.

There are four basic types of lock and latch. All others are variations of these.

1 *Dead lock* The dead lock illustrated in figure 195 has a single bolt which is pushed out and drawn back by operation of a key only; it is used for store rooms and other places where simple security is required. For additional security a dead lock is used with another type of fastening, such as a latch.

195 Mortice dead lock

2 *Latch* The latch illustrated in figure 195 has a bolt held in the extended position by a spring and which is drawn back to allow the door to open by the turning of a handle only. This keeps a door in the shut position without providing security.

196 Upright mortice latch

3 *Two bolt lock set* The two bolt lock illustrated in figure 197 combines the previous two types of fastening in one lock case, and is probably the best lock for general use. The spring latch operated by a handle serves for all general purposes; the dead bolt operated by a key from either

side permits the door to be locked when needed. A fortice lock of this type is preferred for security by insurance companies because of the separate dead bolt. It is such a common type of lock that it is not necessary in specifying to use the term *two bolt*. Reference to a lock set implies two bolts.

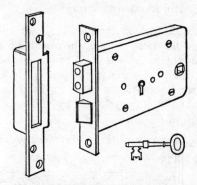

197 Horizontal mortice lock

4 *Night latch* A rim night latch, illustrated in figure 198, has a spring bolt operated by a handle on the inside and a key on the outside. When going out the door can be 'pulled to' behind the user, but a key is necessary for re-entering the premises. This gives a sense of security, but ordinary night latches do not provide a great deal of security, since by cutting a hole in the glass or wood panel of a door the

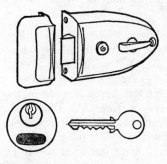

198 Cylinder rim latch

inside handle can be turned. This can be done in a few seconds by an expert. Also the spring bolt or latch in ordinary latches can be pushed back by a knife. On the other hand, cylinder latches are small and easily fitted and take a small key

207

which adds to their convenience in use and many special kinds of cylinder latches have been developed to overcome the defects referred to. A knob or thumb slide, operated from the inside, will hold the bolt open or shut when needed and the key will then not operate. When fitted with these devices the cylinder lock is a most useful additional security.

A lock, with latch mechanism, is shown in figure 199. This illustrates most of the essential features. A measure of security is given by the number and complexity of the wards. If the cuts on the key bit do not correspond to the wards the key cannot be turned. The bolt is released by tumblers, or a

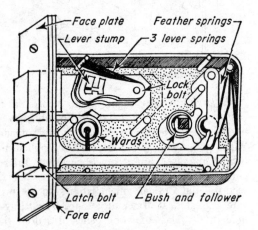

199 Horizontal mortice lock showing component parts

system of levers. When the key turns, the levers have to be lifted to a certain position before the bolt will pass and so a larger number of levers gives greater security. The tumber mechanism (pin tumblers) is applied in the normal cylinder lock as shown in figure 200. The V-cuts on the key have to lift the pins the exact amount so that their tops become flush with the surface of the rotable plug to enable the latter to be turned and the latch to operate. There are many thousands of combinations of pin positions, which gives many thousands of 'differs' or locks requiring different keys. It is important when writing the specification for the locks to be clear as to what differs are needed. In a house there is usually no point in having different room locks; in fact it is convenient, in the event of a room key being lost, to be able to

use another from an adjoining room. However, on the other hand, in a building such as an hotel all room keys must differ. For this type of building locks which differ can be opened by a master key, or a number of locks, perhaps all on one floor, can be opened by a sub-master key. There is a large range of mastering 'possibles' to suit all requirements and the technique of arranging the mastering of the keys in the most convenient way is known as *suiteing*. Each group of keys being called a *suite*.

There are two methods of fixing for locks in general use. The four types of lock described are, in most cases, manufactured to be suitable for either method of fixing. The choice is whether to fix the lock on the face of the door or whether to set the lock into the thickness of the door. Where the lock is screwed to the inside face of the door it is referred to as a rim lock or rim latch. Where a lock is set into a mortice within the thickness of the door it is known as a mortice lock or mortice latch. Obviously the rim fixing is cheaper, but less secure and less neat. On the other hand, mortice fixing is not suitable for very thin doors. 13 mm thick locks will suit 35 mm finished thickness doors. 16 mm locks suit 40 mm doors, which is the recommended thickness. Many modifications of the four types of lock described can be studied in merchants' showrooms and in manufacturers' catalogues, so it is only necessary here to make special mention of one or two types which may need clarification. Dead bolts are sometimes designed to have *double throw*. This means that the bolt goes further into the staple when the key is turned a second time; this gives added security.

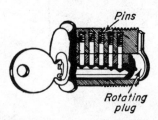

200 Cylinder lock showing pin tumbler mechanism

A dead bolt for a sliding door requires a claw or hook bolt as illustrated in figure 201.

Where pairs of doors with rebated meeting stiles are used, it is necessary to fit a rebated mortice lock as illustrated in figure 202. Here the fore-

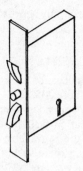

201   *Double hook bolt for sliding doors*

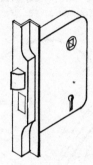

202   *Rebated mortice lock*

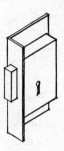

203   *Cupboard lock*

bined lock-latch set which needs only two holes to be drilled has been produced. This type of lock, which is now in common use, has the locking mechanism in the knob, and is usually referred to as a *knob set*. A typical example is shown in figure 204.

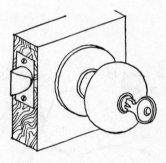

204   *Knob set*

Ball catches and roller catches are used for cupboards and because they are inexpensive they have also been used for the doors to living rooms in place of a latch. They are, however, very noisy and tend to give trouble in adjustment unless the projection can be easily altered to suit any change in the gap between door and frame.

LEVER HANDLES AND KNOBS

Knobs should not be used where the backset of the lock is less than, say, 60 mm. The backset is the distance from the outer face of the fore-end of the lock to the centre of the key hole. The reason for this is if a knob-set is fixed too near the door frame the user will suffer damaged knuckles when operating the knob. The question of the fixing of the

end of the lock case is cranked to fit the rebate on the stiles.

The normal mortice lock is made 'horizontal', ie suitable for a deep mortice into the middle rail of the door, and this type of lock is illustrated in figure 199. Where a lock must fit into a narrow style it is made 'upright'. This type of lock, which is illustrated in figure 196, has a comparatively narrow case. In a lock (lock and latch) set, the keyhole and spindle mortice are in line vertically in a vertical mortice lock, and the keyhole and spindle mortice are in line horizontally in a horizontal mortice lock. The horizontal set is usually used in conjunction with knob furniture, and the vertical set with lever handle furniture. Drawer and cupboard locks are usually for a flush fixing. This means that they are let into the inside face of the work, so that the outside of the lock is flush with the inside face of the timber. The cover plate is usually extended round the side to give a neat finish. Figure 203 shows a typical cupboard lock. Simplification of the fixing is an attractive proposition as mortice cutting takes a long time. A com-

knob in relation to the spindle and rose requires some special consideration.

There are many methods of fixing knob furniture, several of which were patented. The two basic variants are

1 A spindle which is 'fixed' to the knob by a grub screw or patented fixing so that the pull of the knob is resisted directly by the spindle. This is a strong and most satisfactory method but requires exact and careful fitting.
2 'Floating' or free spindle which slides on to the knob and which relies for its fixing by screwing the rose to the face of the door. This type is easily fitted but a disadvantage is that when used

with mortice locks only short screws can be used to secure the rose because of the thickness of the lock case. These screws may work loose even in the best quality doors.

An 'exploded' drawing of a knob and spindle fixing is shown in figure 205.

Knob furniture provides a neat, unobtrusive and strong specification well suited to resist rough usage. Knob furniture is available in various alloys. Bronze is the most expensive but most hard wearing, but aluminium, because of its pleasant appearance and relatively low cost, is very popular.

Lever furniture must be well designed and strongly constructed since the lever arm produces

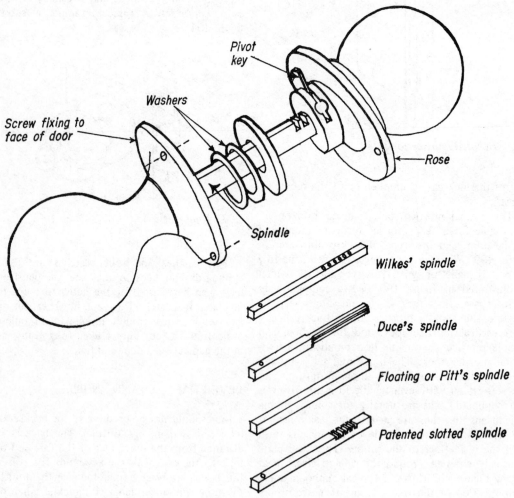

205 *Knob furniture*

considerable strain on the lock or latch mechanism.

Where upright mortice locks are specified, lever furniture is essential because the distance of the spindle from the edge of the door is small. Most British lever furniture is of the floating spindle type in which the handles take the pull of the door through the handle plates or roses. Lever handles sometimes have, in place of a rose, a handle plate which allows the screws to be fixed beyond the mortice and so ensures that the fixing screws will not foul the lock case. This, of course, makes a stronger fixing. British lever handles often embody a spring to counterbalance the weight of the handle as British locks do not normally have strong springs on the latch. Continental locks have a strong latch spring and so their handles also operate on this. This point should be borne in mind when considering using continental lever handles on British locks. In a vertical mortice lock the spindle for the lever handle or knob is vertically above the key hole. This means that a specifier can choose between lever furniture which has a long handle plate incorporating a key hole and a lever handle with a small handle plate and a separate key escutcheon plate. The key escutcheon plate is used as a cover plate for the key hole. In order to hide the large number of screws which are necessary for fixing door furniture of this kind, several different types of cover plate have been produced. The cover plate will either clip over or be screwed over the fixing plates. The screw type are usually better but can only be used where circular roses are specified since the clip on types tend to give trouble

in use unless very well designed. A drawing of a lever handle showing the fixing is given in figure 206.

Lever furniture is available in a very wide range of materials. The choice of stainless steel, bronze, aluminium alloy, plastic covered metal, or nylon, will depend on considerations of first cost, appearance, type of use and subsequent maintenance costs.

DOOR SCHEDULE

A schedule of all the items of door furniture is usually prepared for each job. A typical schedule is illustrated in chapter 11, figure 249, page 261.

BURGLAR PROTECTION

BS 3621: 1963: *Specification for Thief Resistant Locks for Hinged Doors,* was prepared at the request of the police and the insurance companies to ensure a minimum degree of security against professional intrusion. However, it must be borne in mind that locks must be properly fitted for them to be acceptable and the Burglary Surveyors employed by the insurance companies may require a higher degree of security than offered by BS 3621. For situations of high security risk the specifier would be wise to contact the insurance company's surveyor for advice.

WINDOW FASTENINGS

Window fastenings, such as casement turns, sash fasteners and stays, are illustrated with the window details where appropriate in chapter 4. Typical examples of these are shown in figure 207 and need no further reference. The use of pegs and stays to regulate the opening of side hung casements is now being largely superseded by the use of fiction hinges. The cam opener illustrated in figure 208 is now largely used to top hung steel window casements. Other forms of casement stay are shown in figure 209. Of particular note is the roller stay for use on bottom hung casements which open inwards; and on horizontal centre pivot hung windows to control the projection of the top part of the window into the room.

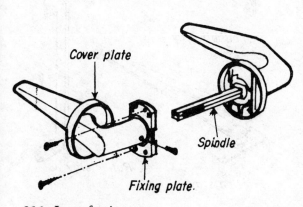

206 Lever furniture

Cover plate

Spindle

Fixing plate.

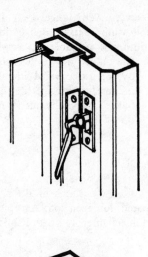

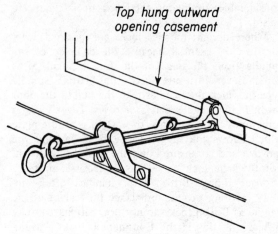

Top hung outward opening casement

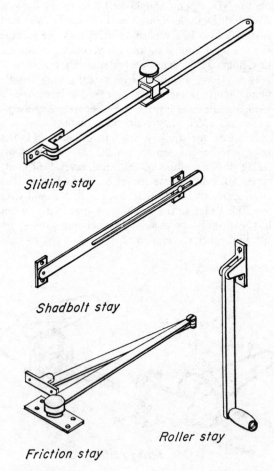

208 Window cam opener

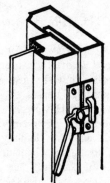

Sliding stay

Shadbolt stay

Roller stay

Friction stay

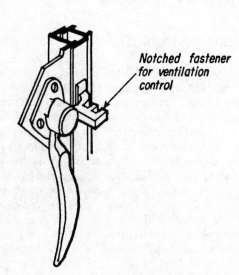

Notched fastener for ventilation control

207 Casement turns or fasteners

209 Casement stays

Bolts

Bolts are used as well as locks in additional security for doors and windows. They are usually fixed at the top and bottom of doors and should always have a socket to receive the shoot of the bolt. This is particularly important at the threshold. The diameter of the sheet, the type of metal used and the method of fixing of the bolt are an indication of its strength. The most common type of bolt is the barrel bolt, which has a round or *barrel*-like shoot on a back plate for surface fixing, as shown in figure 210. The shoot runs in a guide

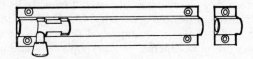

210   Barrel bolt

and is slid home into a metal keep. This type of bolt is inexpensive and easy to fix. For better class work a flush lever bolt is used, as shown in figure 211. This is more expensive and takes more time to fix. It is recessed into a shallow housing

211   Lever bolt

in the door until the face plate is flush with the surface of the timber. It is operated by a thumb slide or a lever action. A particular type of bolt which is used for minimizing the twisting of a door or window is the cremorne bolt, as shown in figure 212. This bolt extends the full height of the door or window so that when the handle is turned the top bolt slides upwards and the bottom bolt slides

downwards to give top and bottom fixing. A variation of a cremorne bolt is an espagnolette. This type of bolt provides centre fixing as well as

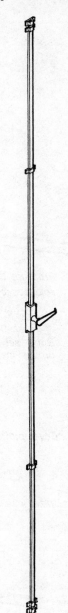

212   Cremorne bolt

fixing at the top and bottom. The centre fixing is commonly a lock. Espagnolettes may be surface or flush fitting as required. See figure 116, page 137.

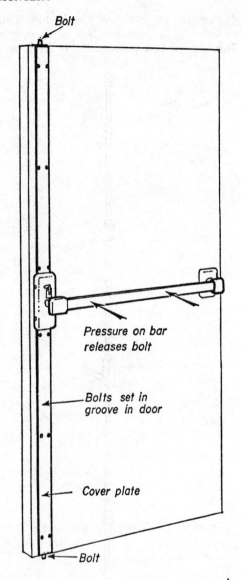

Bolt

Pressure on bar
releases bolt

Bolts set in
groove in door

Cover plate

Bolt

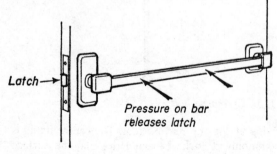

Latch →

Pressure on bar
releases latch

213   Mortice panic bolt

Fire regulations for public buildings do not permit the use of ordinary locks on doors which are classified as means of escape in case of fire. To overcome this difficulty a panic latch or bolt is used. A panic latch is used on single doors and consists of a cross bar which is pushed against a latch to release it. A locking knob is often fixed to the outside of the door to enable two-way traffic to operate. A banic bolt will have a striking plate at the top and bottom of the door so that the door is held in three places, and thus gives a greater degree of security than a panic latch. A mortice panic bolt which is let into the face of the door for neatness is shown in figure 213. There are various designs of panic latches and panic bolts to suit different degrees of security. The height of the bar of the panic bolt is important since in an emergency it must operate when people fall against it. A generally acceptable height for the bar above the floor is 1050 mm.

CUPBOARD CATCHES

There are very many designs and types of cupboard catches as reference to the manufacturers' catalogues will indicate. The specifier must decide on the exact requirements before choosing the most suitable catch, depending for instance, on

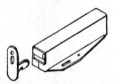

214   Cupboard catch

whether or not the catch is used in conjunction with some form of handle. Catches should be arranged, if possible, both at the top and bottom of a cupboard door since they will then act as a form of restraint to prevent the door warping. A cupboard interior catch which eliminates the need for door furniture is illustrated in figure 214. When the door is pressed it springs open and when the door is pushed closed it clicks shut.

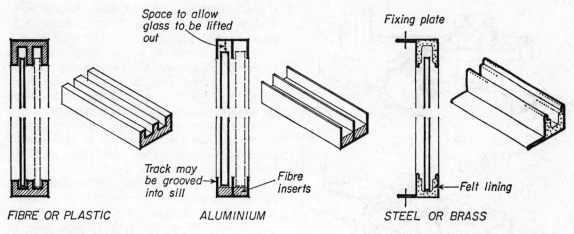

FIBRE OR PLASTIC   ALUMINIUM   STEEL OR BRASS

215 Track for glass

SLIDING GEAR

Sliding gear for doors and windows has been described separately with the fittings illustrated in
the appropriate chapter. Sliding gear for cupboard
doors is available in a very wide range. Small cupboard or bookcase fronts of plate glass with
polished edges can be fitted directly into the channels of fibre, metal or plastic made in single, double
or triple section. Thin plastic-faced sheet, or plywood, can also run in most of these tracks. Typical
sections of this type of track are shown in figure
215. For larger plate glass doors a metal section
track is provided in aluminium or brass which
incorporates small wheels or ball bearings that run
on a bottom track to take the extra weight of glass.

For larger plywood or blockboard, or framed
cupboard doors, a fibre track with sliders is manufactured. The track is grooved into the sill, the
sliders being morticed into the under edge of the
door. This type of track is also made in nylon and
an example is illustrated in figure 216. As an alternative to this there are a number of small ball-bearing
roller fittings, for running on a bottom track, which
are illustrated in figure 217. These run easily and
so are used where the door is tall in proportion to
its width and which might jam in a simple channel
track.

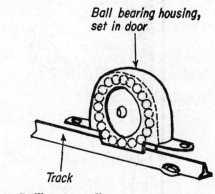

217 Ballbearing roller

WINDOW OPENING GEAR

The rod and worm gear type of control has been
traditional for large and heavy windows – it is
suitable where cost is the main consideration and

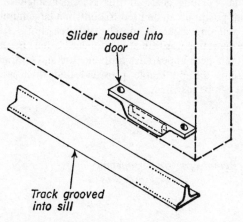

216 Sliders and track

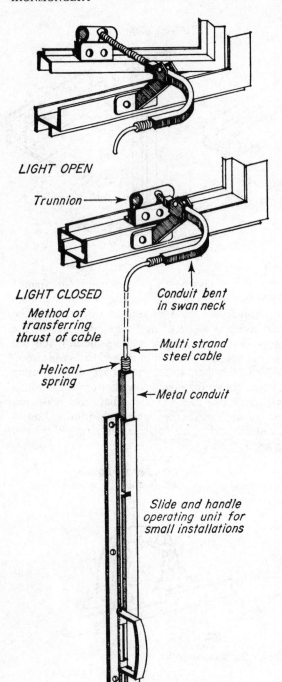

LIGHT OPEN

Trunnion ——

LIGHT CLOSED

Method of
transferring
thrust of cable

Conduit bent
in swan neck

Multi strand
steel cable

Helical
spring

Metal conduit

Slide and handle
operating unit for
small installations

a neat appearance is not essential. Regular maintenance must be organized since the working
parts must be kept clean and well oiled. If they
seize up, the fixings will be wrenched from the wall
by forcing the gearing. Alternative systems in common use comprise a special wire cable sliding in a
metal tube. A system in which the cable is wired
to serve efficiently both in compression and in
tension is shown in figure 218. The wire operates
directly on the window and is in turn worked
either by a slide for small installations or, in the
case of heavier windows, by a geared regulator.
There is a limit to the range of windows which
can be controlled by mechanical means and for
very large installations travelling over long distances electrical or hydraulic systems must be
used. This type of system is, however, uneconomical
for small installations.

Electrical control

For this type of control a motor is installed at the
receiving end which will drive a local installation
of cable gear. The main push-button control can
be situated in a convenient central position and is
coupled to a forward and reverse contactor. The
switching off of the current in both directions is
by micro-switches at the receiving end.

Hydraulic control

This is effected by a small bore copper nylon
tubing filled with oil. A pump, either hand or
electrically operated, delivers the requisite pressure to small hydraulic rams positioned in the
actual opening gear. In this system a single operating position can be used to control a large number
of opening lights remotely situated both from
the operating position and from each other. Because
of their neat appearance both electric and hydraulic
systems are preferable provided that their initial
cost can be justified.

218   Remote control for opening lights

8 Balustrades

FABRICATION OF METAL BALUSTRADES

The making up of metal building components relies on the techniques of forming, fitting and jointing of metal parts and work on finishing to the surface of the metal when the component is complete.

Metals for building work are produced in forms suitable for casting, extruding or rolling. These techniques and various methods of forming and jointing metals are detailed in *MBS: Materials,* chapter 9.

The making of metal components involves one or more of the processes or operations referred to, and the design of the component should take account of these as well as of the physical properties of the metals involved. Bolting and riveting are traditional methods of metal jointing. Ordinary semi-circular headed rivets are used for industrial work, but for decorative work the head is usually cleaned off or a pin is used in place of a rivet. The top of the pin being concealed by the finishing process. Mortice and tenon joints are used in open work such as grilles or balustrading.

Drilling and tapping to receive screws is also used, not only for site jointing but in the metal workshop. Self-tapping screws are used for much commercial sheet metal work as they are quick, cheap, and look presentable from the face side.

Various metalwork details related to a composite metal balustrade are shown in figure 219.

For cladding steel with bronze strips special taper headed screws may be used as shown as 'A'. The screws will be in the same bronze as the strip and the heads left slightly proud to be cleaned off. The buffing up will drag the metal over the joint between the screw head and the strip so that no line is discernible. For specialist work special screws are made in the same metal as the cladding.

Details 'B' and 'D' show the make up of the balusters and rails forming the balustrade infill panel. The half lap joint in the rail is secured by countersunk screws and the baluster is screwed and *riveted* between the rails.

Detail 'C' shows the joint between two sections in a hollow bronze handrail. The rail is plugged by means of a solid steel core which is screwed up from below by say 9 mm countersunk screws.

Detail 'E' shows the junction of the square supporting standard and the lower rail. In effect the upright standard passes through the rail and is screwed in place – the heads of the screws being afterwards removed.

Detail 'F' shows an alternative infill between the standards by using 6 mm toughened glass. The glass is protected and secured at each corner by small steel clips which are screwed to the main uprights. The glass is shown bedded in wash-leather to accommodate movement. This is the traditional way though now glazing compound would probably be used.

BUILDING REGULATIONS

The Building Regulations 1976 stipulate dimensional criteria for handrails and balustrades to stairways, balconies, barriers, and roofs where access is required. The regulations differentiate between *stairways* according to the type of building in which they are located, i.e.

Purpose Groups the requirements for treads, risers, handrails, balustrades, etc being dependent upon whether they are situated in a building which has private use (exclusively one dwelling), communal use (multi-occupancy dwellings), or public uses (places of assembly). The provision of an handrail on one side of a stairway is always necessary: if the stairway is over 1000 mm wide, then handrails must be provided on each side. In addition, any stairway or balcony (and certain other areas above ground level which are likely to be used for other than maintenance) must be provided with a balustrade or *guard*. The dimensional criteria for handrails and balustrades are shown in figure 220 and have been taken from the *Building Regulations 1976,* Part H. Table 3 in CP3, chapter V *Loading:* Part 1: 1967 states that balustrades shall be designed

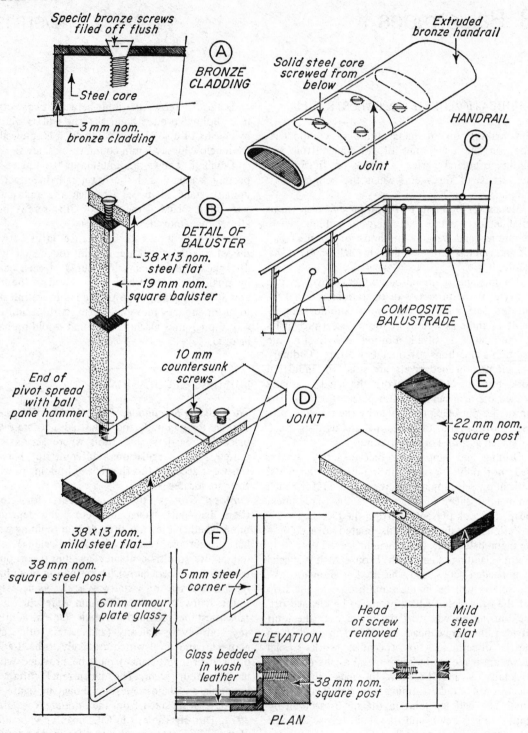

Special bronze screws
filed off flush

(A) BRONZE CLADDING

Steel core

3 mm nom.
bronze cladding

Extruded
bronze handrail

Solid steel core
screwed from
below

HANDRAIL

(C)

Joint

DETAIL OF
BALUSTER

(B)

38 × 13 nom.
steel flat

19 mm nom.
square baluster

End of
pivot spread
with ball
pane hammer

10 mm
countersunk
screws

(D) JOINT

COMPOSITE
BALUSTRADE

(E)

22 mm nom.
square post

38 × 13 nom.
mild steel flat

(F)

38 mm nom.
square steel post

6 mm armour
plate glass

5 mm steel
corner

ELEVATION

Glass bedded
in wash
leather

38 mm nom.
square post

PLAN

Head
of screw
removed

Mild
steel
flat

219 Metalwork joints

WIDTH
OF
STAIRWAYS

Residential	Serving single room not including living room or kitchen	600mm
	Private use	800mm
	Communal use	900mm
Other building types	General use	1000mm
	Other use limited to 50 persons	800mm

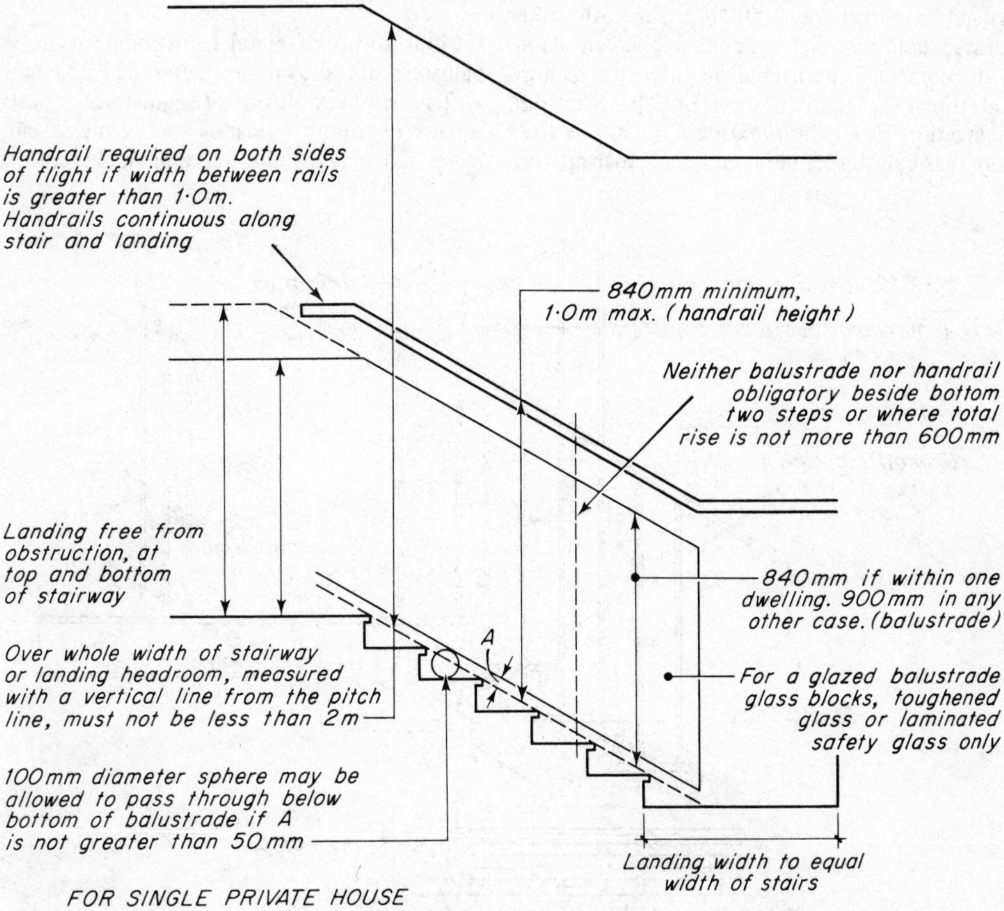

Handrail required on both sides of flight if width between rails is greater than 1·0m. Handrails continuous along stair and landing

840mm minimum, 1·0m max. (handrail height)

Neither balustrade nor handrail obligatory beside bottom two steps or where total rise is not more than 600mm

Landing free from obstruction, at top and bottom of stairway

Over whole width of stairway or landing headroom, measured with a vertical line from the pitch line, must not be less than 2m

840mm if within one dwelling. 900mm in any other case. (balustrade)

For a glazed balustrade glass blocks, toughened glass or laminated safety glass only

100mm diameter sphere may be allowed to pass through below bottom of balustrade if A is not greater than 50mm

Landing width to equal width of stairs

FOR SINGLE PRIVATE HOUSE

Minimum going		220mm
Max. rise 220mm	Min. rise 75mm	
Max. angle of pitch		42°
Risers per flight, max.		16
Risers per flight, min.		2
Sum of going and 2 × rise, min.		550mm
Sum of going and 2 × rise, max.		700mm

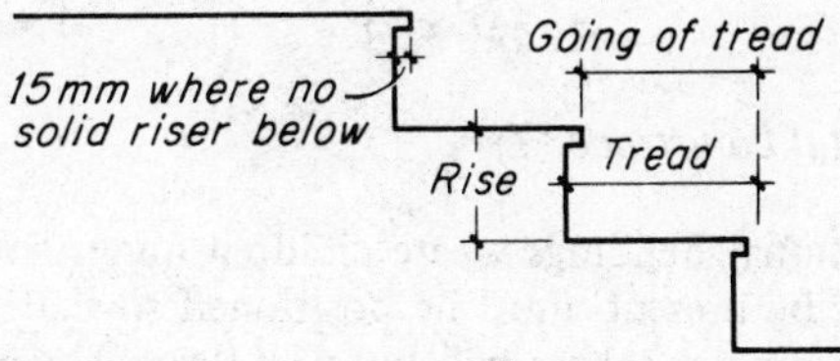

15mm where no solid riser below

Going of tread

Rise

Tread

220 Handrails and balustrades (guards) to stairways

to withstand certain minimum loadings. The code requires that balustrades to light access stairs not more than 600 mm wide are used only for inspection or maintenance shall be designed to withstand a minimum lateral imposed load, ie horizontal thrust at handrail level of 220 N/m run.

Balustrades to light access stairs more than 600 mm wide in connection with domestic and private balconies and landings must be able to withstand a thrust of 360 N/m run. All other stairways, landings and balconies and all handrails to roofs must withstand an intensity of horizontal thrust at handrail level of 740 N/m run.

Regulation H6 of the *Building Regulations 1976* require that balustrades in houses, flats, maisonettes,

see figure 220).

Panic barriers must withstand 3000 N/m run. In view of past experience of dangerous failure this is an important figure, and the reason for these regulations is that poorly designed and constructed stairways have been responsible for a large proportion of accidents.

METAL BALUSTRADES

Various forms of metal balustrading using vertical balusters are shown in figures 221, 222 and 223.

The simplest form of balustrade consists of square or round balusters and a metal rail. This metal rail may be the handrail or the core rail for

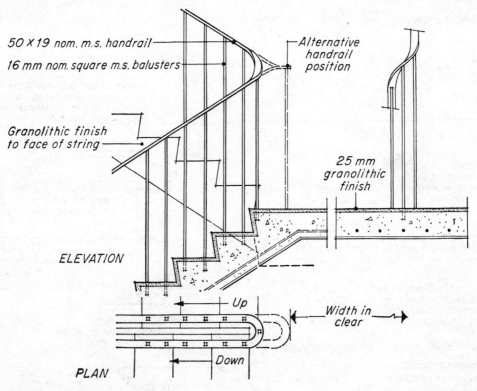

221 *Metal balustrade (1)*

or institutional buildings where children under five years may be present, must be positioned so that a 100 mm diameter sphere will *not* pass through gaps in them, or under them between their bottom edges and the tread and riser (unless gap between bottom edges and nosings is less than 50 mm —

a wood or more elaborate metal handrail. The size of the members depends upon the number and the need for rigidity if stiffening is not provided by other means. In figure 220, 16 mm nom. square balusters are used, two of each tread with a 50 x 19 mm handrail. This is a very close balustrade which may be required for safety and is essential where small children might be tempted to crawl through the gaps. If this could never occur, one 19 mm nom. baluster per tread may be used as in figures 221, 222 and 223. This reduces the number of mortices in the treads and therefore simplifies fixing and the making good of the finish of the treads to the balusters. Using a bottom rail to support intermediate balusters with a standard every third or fourth tread gives an easier fixing detail as shown in figure 222. Standards should be 25 mm nom. square and balusters would be in 13 mm nom. tube, or rod. The bottom and core rail would be 50 x 10 mm

It is very important that ample space be allowed at this part of the staircase. A tight turn not only makes difficulties for the manufacturer of the balustrade and handrail but also makes the neat detailing of the steps difficult to achieve and results in an inconvenient arrangement for the users of the staircase. The most common arrangement for a turn is a half space landing as shown in figure 221 where the faces of risers in both upper and lower flights are opposite or almost opposite each other on plan. The handrail has to drop the equivalent of one risers at the turn so unless the well is wide or the handrail can be extended on to the

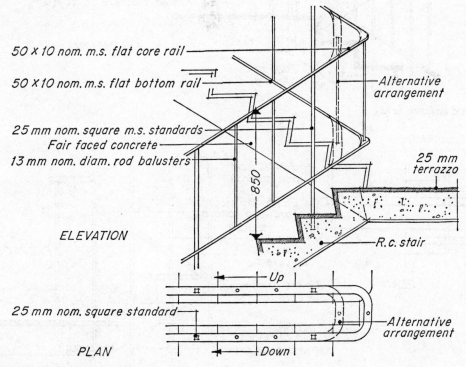

222 *Metal balustrade* (2)

nom. mild steel flat section. Arrangement of the balusters and particularly the handrail will be affected by the planning of the staircase at the turn. There are several arrangements of turn shown in figures 221-223. The alternatives depend upon the size of the stair well and the arrangement of the steps which are themselves governed by the space that can be allocated to the stair at the design stage.

landing, as shown dotted, a very sharp ramp will be needed. There are two points to be borne in mind, a wide well loses space across the staircase but, on the other hand, extending the handrail on to the landing as shown loses space on the width of the landing. These considerations are important, since on staircases used for means of escape in case of fire, the important dimension is the measurement

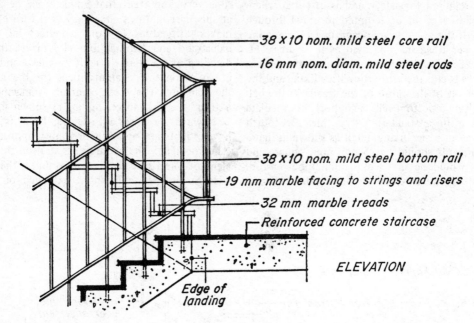

38 × 10 nom. mild steel core rail

16 mm nom. diam. mild steel rods

38 × 10 nom. mild steel bottom rail

19 mm marble facing to strings and risers

32 mm marble treads

Reinforced concrete staircase

ELEVATION

Edge of landing

223   *Metal balustrade (3)*

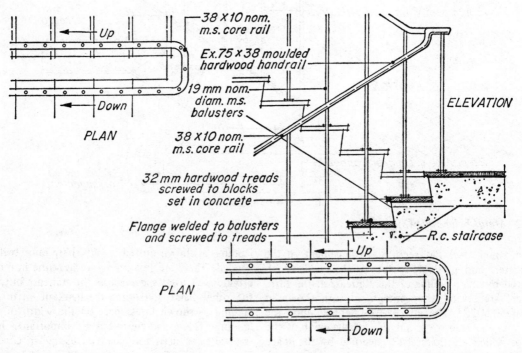

Up

Down

PLAN

38 × 10 nom. m.s. core rail

Ex.75 × 38 moulded hardwood handrail

19 mm nom. diam. m.s. balusters

38 × 10 nom. m.s. core rail

32 mm hardwood treads screwed to blocks set in concrete

Flange welded to balusters and screwed to treads

ELEVATION

R.c. staircase

Up

PLAN

Down

224   *Metal balustrade (4)*

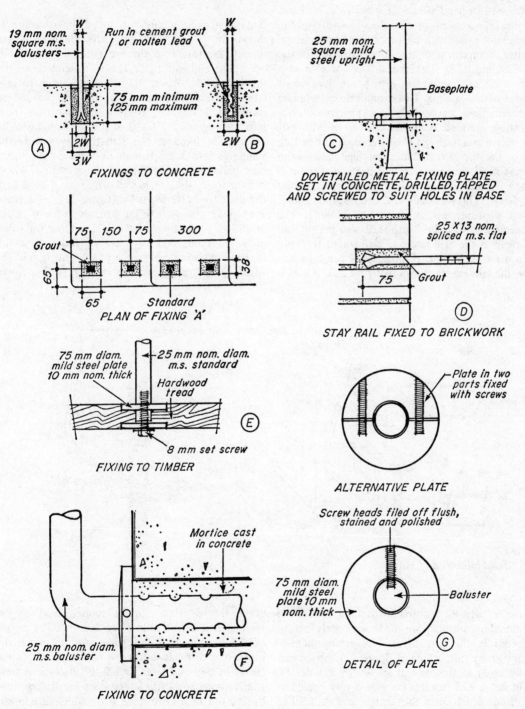

19 mm nom. square m.s. balusters

Run in cement grout or molten lead

75 mm minimum 125 mm maximum

2W

3W

2W

Ⓐ Ⓑ

FIXINGS TO CONCRETE

25 mm nom. square mild steel upright

Baseplate

Ⓒ

DOVETAILED METAL FIXING PLATE SET IN CONCRETE, DRILLED, TAPPED AND SCREWED TO SUIT HOLES IN BASE

Grout

75 150 75 300

65

65

38

Standard

PLAN OF FIXING 'A'

25 x 13 nom. spliced m.s. flat

75

Grout

Ⓓ

STAY RAIL FIXED TO BRICKWORK

75 mm diam. mild steel plate 10 mm nom. thick

25 mm nom. diam. m.s. standard

Hardwood tread

Ⓔ

8 mm set screw

FIXING TO TIMBER

Plate in two parts fixed with screws

ALTERNATIVE PLATE

Mortice cast in concrete

25 mm nom. diam. m.s. baluster

Ⓕ

FIXING TO CONCRETE

Screw heads filed off flush, stained and polished

75 mm diam. mild steel plate 10 mm nom. thick

Baluster

Ⓖ

DETAIL OF PLATE

225 *Metal balustrade fixing*

'in the clear' between the inside of the handrail and the wall or handrail on the other side. In figure 221 the intersections of the sloping soffit of the stairs are not in line with the junction of the landing. A better arrangement of this detail is shown in figures 222 and 223. Here the soffits coincide at a point which can conveniently be made the face of the edge of the landing. This simplifies the detailing of the staircase, particularly if expensive finishes like marble are used as facings both to the string of the staircase and the edge of the landing. The setting back of the top riser in the lower flight makes the staircase much more pleasant to use and it permits a pause in descending before embarking on the next flight. The handrails also intersect at a level to suit a proper height above the landing. The arrangement shown in figure 222 also permits an easy ramp at the turn and one well suited to forming in a metal section. If more space can be taken up on the landing, as shown in figure 223, it is pos-

FIXING DETAILS

General fixing details for metal balustrading is shown in figures 225 and 226. Balustrades are usually fabricated in the workshop in lengths of one flight and one turn. The turn helps to stiffen the balustrade. Where there are no turns to give lateral bracing special stays may be needed as shown in figure 226. These special stays are fixed into the edge of the flight of stairs. The balustrades are usually fixed to the structure by setting the standards into a mortice or by screwing through a base plate set on the face of the structure. Where a standard is split or ragged a mortice should have the dimensions shown as 'A' (figure 225). It is, however, more common to cut indents in the standard as shown alternatively at 'B'. To allow for tolerance in fixing and for ease of fixing generally mortices are preferably wide in the direction of the flight. Mortices are usually run in with cement

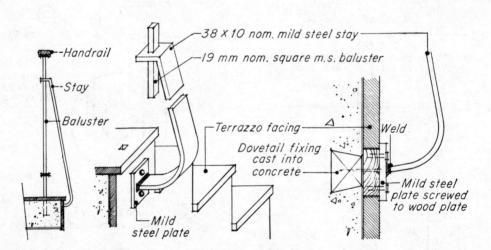

226 *Metal balustrade fixing*

sible to arrange the handrail without a wreath, so that the turns on plan are made separately before the bends to the two slopes. This arrangement is also shown by dotted line in figure 221. Space can also be saved in this way as shown by the dotted line in figure 222 but this involves a very considerable drop which may be dangerous. A further balustrade detail is shown in figure 224.

grout though fixers prefer molten lead as the joint is then rigid within a few minutes. The mouth of the mortice must be made good to match the finish of the treads unless the technique allows the treads to be faced later. Detail 'C' shows a method which permits a little adjustment in all directions by the use of a cover base plate which also covers up any making good. This plate can be drilled and

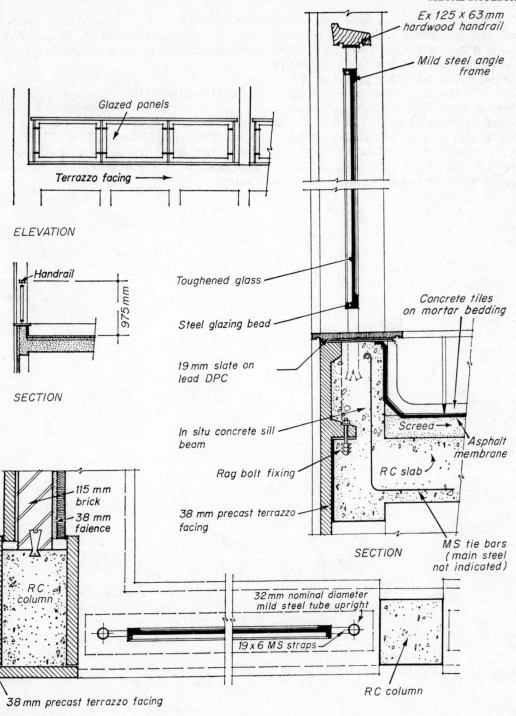

ELEVATION

SECTION

DETAIL PLAN

Ex 125 × 63 mm hardwood handrail

Mild steel angle frame

Glazed panels

Terrazzo facing →

Handrail

975 mm

Toughened glass

Steel glazing bead

19 mm slate on lead DPC

In situ concrete sill beam

Rag bolt fixing

38 mm precast terrazzo facing

Concrete tiles on mortar bedding

Screed

Asphalt membrane

RC slab

MS tie bars (main steel not indicated)

SECTION

115 mm brick

38 mm faience

RC column

38 mm precast terrazzo facing

32 mm nominal diameter mild steel tube upright

19 × 6 MS straps

RC column

227 *External balustrade with glass panels*

tapped in position to suit the base plate of the standard and with power tools this is comparatively easy. A method of fixing a stay rail to brickwork is shown. A short length of rail is grouted in and the flat section rail is then spliced on to it as detailed at 'D'. Fixing to wood is simpler but a large bearing area to resist lateral pressure is necessary. Detail 'E' shows a base plate on the end of a standard let into a hardwood tread and the plate on the underside is held in place and makes the joint rigid, by a set screw, up into the end of the standard. A detail for securing a baluster into concrete is shown at 'F'. Collars or cover plates to cover up the making good of the mortice are shown in two alternative constructions in detail 'G'.

GLAZED BALUSTRADE

A detail of a metal balustrade to a balcony with a glass panel infill is shown in figure 227. Here the glass, which should be toughened, is framed in a small angle frame which is then attached to the uprights.

9 Demountable partitions CI/SfB (22.3)

A partition is a form of construction which is used to divide space within a building in a vertical plane.

This chapter is concerned with 'moveable' or demountable elements which divide the space within the structural envelope of the building. With the ever increasing speed of technological and sociological change, the uses to which spaces within a building are put may change during the life of the building. This is particularly true of Industrail, Commerical and Educational buildings. The advantage of future flexibility must, however, be set against the increased initial cost of demountability.

Dwarf partitions in the form of moveable walls up to say 2.00 m high and used as screens to subdivide office or workshop space, are not included. Demountable partition construction and suspended ceiling design is often inter-related. Both should be based on the same modular frame of construction necessary to provide restraint of the partition at the head may well affect the detail and form of the ceiling construction. Both forms of construction will be 'dry', relying on an interlocking of the parts for stability. In order to meet reasonable cost targets, the number of components must be kept to an economic minimum and the erection techniques should not be too specialized.

The performance of a partition system should be studied in general terms with respect to the following criteria.

METHODS OF CONSTRUCTION

There are numerous proprietary partition systems available, many systems having patented fixing devices. The following notes give a summary of some of the alternative types of construction.

Dimensions: Within a modular framework
It is to be expected that the manufacturer will introduce modular co-ordinated systems, the dimensions of which will follow the recommendations for basic sizes of building components and assemblies set out in BS 4011.

Frame and panel systems

Rolled steel sections or aluminium extruded frame into which panels of a variety of materials are fixed. The panels may be a cellular core of cardboard, or solid core of flaxboard, compressed straw slabs, chipboard, plywood, asbestos wood or foamed plastics and may be faced with hardboard; hardwood veneer; laminated plastic, or metal sheet (see *MBC: Materials,* chapter 3). More complex panel construction may incorporate a single or double skin of pressed steel or aluminium sheet. This type of double skin panel may be filled with glass fibre or mineral wool. Most proprietary systems offer a number of permutations of glazed to solid arrangements and are available as single or double glazed units. The glass is usually secured with a gasket type of fixing. The finishes also vary widely according to considerations of first cost, and maintenance costs. The choice of finish is from an inexpensive material to receive paint, such as hardboard, to self finished decorative laminated plastics or metals which may be stove enamelled or anodized.

Post and panel (Unit) systems

These will have storey height sheets of plasterboard 'egg box' construction, compressed straw slab, wood-wool slab or chipboard. The sheets will be faced with a suitable veneer, and will be secured to timber or metal uprights.

Many systems have special details such as adjustable floor fixing and levelling shoes, telescopic transom rails or removable pilasters to service ducts. Some systems incorporate 'hook on' attachments for cupboards and shelving.

FINISHES

Finishes will be of two categories: 1 *self finish*, such as decorative laminated plastic sheet, which is permanent and requires no maintenance in respect of re-decoration or 2 *base finish*, such as plasterboard, which will be ready to receive a painted finish and will thus require normal maintenance. In choosing the appropriate finish, consideration must be given to initial cost, cost in use, and consistency of surface treatment throughout the building.

PROVISION FOR SERVICES

Provision of space for the normal electric wiring and telephone cables, within a partition is not difficult, but large service ducts for heating and other mains services are not compatible with partition design, and of course, pipework within the partition will seriously inhibit demountability. Wherever possible, the structural envelope should be designed to accommodate major service runs with numerous connection points into the partition (or ceiling) system.

FIRE RESISTANCE

The fire resistance qualities of a partition construction are of primary importance. In particular, since partitions are normally associated with building types having a high occupancy. When a fire occurs, the danger arises both from within the building and in the risk of the spread of fire from one building to the other. The various fire regulations are concerned to limit this spread, the risk of which is related to (a) the use of the building, (b) the resistance of the constructional elements, (c) the resistance of the surface finishes to the spread of flame, (d) the size of the building, and (e) the degree of isolation between the various parts of the building.

The requirements of the Building Regulations (covering England and Wales) are summarized below in respect of the types of partition under consideration.

Notional period of fire resistance

Most systems will give a notional period of fire resistance of ½ to 1 hour. The fire rating and considerations of means of escape from the building will, however, be fundamental to the choice of system and the Building Regulations and other Statutes relevant to particular building types should be studied carefully to determine their particular requirements.

Surface spread of flame

Table 17 is a summary of the requirements from Section E15: Building Regulations (first amendment 1973)

Purpose group	Building type	*Max. floor area of small room m²	Classification		Cir lat spc
			*Small rooms	Other rooms	
I	Small residential	4	3	1	
II	Institutional	4	1	0	
III	Other residential	4	3	1	
IV to VIII	Other building types	30	3	1	

Table 17 Minimum rating for surface spread of flame on wall surfaces

The Building Regulations make no particular reference to demountable partitions, the applicable figures given above being prescribed for structure and permanent finish.

Group I is the normal two storey house (with or without a basement).

Group II — Institutional — is a home, school or hospital which provides sleeping accommodation for small children or people suffering from certain disabilities.

Groups IV to VIII includes offices, shops, factories, places of assembly and storage buildings.

A description of the classifications of rate of spread of flame is also applicable to ceilings and is given on page 237. A 'small room' for the purpose of the Regulations, is a room totally enclosed with an area not exceeding that shown in the table according to the purpose group of the building (or *compartment*). Since the size of a building is a very important factor the Building Regulations put forward the idea of a large building being split up into self-contained units, or compartments where walls and floors will contain the fire without endangering the remainder of the building. Partition systems will normally be used within the structural envelope of the building and so the stringent structural fire precautions contained in the Building Regulations in respect of *compartment* walls (walls which divide a building up into *fire-resistant* units) will not apply. Note that the Building Regulations do not apply in Scotland and in the Inner London area. The regulations in the London area are, however, in essence similar to Section E14 of the Building Regulations, their general objective being to reduce the amount of exposed combustible material in a building. The requirements of the Building Standards (Scotland) Regulations 1963 are summarized below.

No specific mention is made of demountable partitions although regulation 25, which refers to 'separating wall', could be applied. However, the general interpretation by the majority of Scottish authorities is that demountable partitioning is not an element of structure and therefore need only comply with the surface spread of flame standards which are set out in Section 57 of the Regulations. Four grades are specified in the Regulations as follows: Grade A which is equivalent to Class 0, Grade B which is the same as Class 1, and Grade C which is equivalent to Classes 2 or 3. Grade D covers all other classes. Corridor partitions are required to comply with Grade A (Class 0) whilst the internal faces of office walls fall within the requirements of Grade C (Class 2 or 3).

Unlike the Building Regulations for England and Wales, The Scottish standards include a section on *means of escape* and part 5, sections 42 and 46, clearly defines the requirements but once again no mention is made of demountable partition in relation to the division of office areas.

Fire Authorities

In addition to the controls so far mentioned, the Fire Authorities have to be satisfied on the means of escape in case of fire under certain statutes according to the type of building, eg Offices, Shops and Railway Premises Act 1963 which is universally applicable. Section 28 deals with *means of escape* and reads as follows: 'All premises to which this Act applies shall be provided with such means of escape in case of fire for the persons employed to work therein as may reasonably be required in the circumstancesof the case.' This phrasing needs some interpretation but, provided that the necessary *compartment* walls and floors comply with the relevant section of the Building Regulations, most Authorities rule that a demountable partition is a temporary fitting not required to protect escape routes. Nevertheless, some stipulate that certain corridor partitions must have a *half hour* standard of *fire resistance* while others only require this standard if the length of a corridor is more than 18 m from a fire exit or if the partitions are used in a single staircase building. In these instances additional fire doors will often be necessary.

SOUND INSULATION

A demountable partition is an element of construction which by its nature is vulnerable to the passage of sound, and to expect a lightweight site-assembled structure to provide a very high standard of sound insulation is to some extent contradictory as explained below.

The matter of sound control should be considered at the design stage so that 'noise producing' rooms and rooms requiring quiet can be, as far as possible, remote from each other. In order to solve the problem of insulating the occupants of a room against unwanted noise, air and structure borne sound and external noise from whatever source must be considered. Airborne sound is created by fluctuations in air pressure which are perceived by the ear as sound. These sound waves strike the surface of a partition and cause it ot vibrate — in turn vibrating the air in the opposite side. The sound insulation afforded is the degree to which the intensity of the noise is reduced in the process. The heavier and denser a partition, the more difficult it is to vibrate but it is equally important for the materials to have a degree of elasticity — to 'give' with the sound like a loosened drum skin. For example, two 13 mm panels set each side of a 50 mm deep framework will produce a higher standard of insulation than a single panel of equal weight. The sound insulation value is assessed by comparative measurements of sound pressure on opposite sides of a barrier and these noise levels are normally measured on a decibel (dB) scale. This scale is not a measure of sound intensity but is a way of expressing the difference of intensity between one sound and another. The decibel is expressed in terms of familiar sounds in the list below to give a general guide to the relevant levels of sound in respect of partition design.

Quiet conversation	30 dB
Conference room	50 dB
Normal conversation	60 dB
Office machine room	80 dB
(Heavy lorry at 6.000 m)	100 dB
(Sound becomes painful)	140 dB

All sounds differ in pitch and intensity and BS 2750: 1956 has been established for comparative acoustic testing — this test provides the arithmetical average decibel reduction over the range of 100 to 3150 Hz (cycles per second) and all partition systems should be tested to this standard. It is possible to flatter performance figures by testing over a more limited frequency range or by testing single panels in isolation rather than a panel and its framing components, and an apparent gain of 4 to 5 decibels can be incorrectly claimed. Site conditions are very much more difficult than the controlled conditions of the laboratory and, although measured figures are useful for comparison, a poorer acoustic performance on site is almost inevitable. Doors, sliding hatches, ventilators, and every junction with the structure are all potentially points of serious sound leaks. It is also important that ceiling voids, continuous lighting troughs and heating ducts are adequately baffled.

In some systems, sophisticated constructions, such as resilient air seals at abutments to walls and ceilings, are incorporated to assist in sound reduction and to take up possible dimensional inaccuracies in the enveloping structure and, in general terms, acoustics are improved with refined detailing.

The standard of insulation against external noise is governed by the size and position of the windows. With single glazed windows of 'average' size, the net reduction of noise would be say 10 dB, and with sealed double windows — designed for acoustic and not thermal insulation — the reduction could be as high as 45 dB, so that it is between these two ranges that sound reduction would be required, in the partition system. Since the awareness of noise is to some extent a subjective matter the question of acceptable background noise is important. An intruding noise will not be a nuisance unless it approaches the general loudness of the background.

One irritating source of noise, that of door slamming can easily be prevented by the fitting of automatic door closers, and rubber seals.

Rooms which require good sound insulation such as directors' offices, interview rooms, libraries, sick rooms and rest rooms will require partitions which give a sound reduction of 45 dB between them and other rooms. On the other hand, rooms in which background noise is acceptable such as general offices will be satisfactory if a 30 dB reduction factor is obtained through the partitions. In general terms, provided that the cost of more sophisticated detailing is acceptable, partitions giving a 45 dB insulation level can be obtained. The 'average' solid, full height partition will give 30 dB whilst a half glazed partition with single glazing will not give more than a 25 dB reduction.

DEMOUNTABILITY

Changing demands over the life span of a building may require the reorganization of the internal space and so far as this factor is applicable, it is advantageous to be able to take down (demount) and re-erect a partition system. In these circumstances the enveloping structure of external wall, structural floor and ceiling are considered to be permanent and fixed construction, with the elements which divide the space within the building being capable of re-arrangement to provide variable layout.

The option of demountability is a most significant factor in respect of initial cost and the effect it will have on the fulfilment of the other requirements of the performance specification. Taking down a partition and re-erecting in a new position may involve adaptation to the lighting and heating systems, and will almost certainly necessitate redecoration and possible repairs to flooring and wall surfaces.

The greater the degree of demountability required the more difficult it is to provide adequate sound insulation and satisfactory provision for services within the partition. A demountable partition system which provides a high degree of sound insulation will be expensive, both in first cost and cost of re-assembly, since the jointing technique will be complex. A system which gives demountability only at junction points such as doors, abutments and intersections will, however, be less expensive than a partition which by reason of more sophisticated jointing techniques can be demounted at each panel on the planning module.

Figure 228 shows examples of two alternative methods of obtaining flexibility.

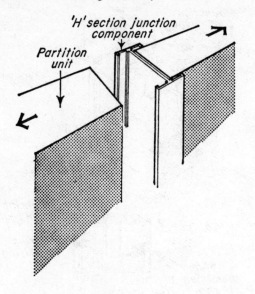

(a) '*H' sections at abutments and intersections*

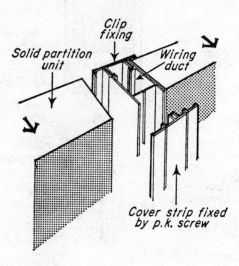

(b)   *Breakdown post at each module width*

228   Two methods of obtaining demountability

(a) by the use of an H section vertical member into which the partition panel fits. The sequence of erection with this type of partition is to fix the wall channel at the abutment and then continue — panel — post — panel, the panels being fitted from the side. The demountability is therefore at junction points only.

(b) by the use of a 'breakdown' post. The post is in 3 sections so that the panels can be fitted from the front or rear and that demountability is at each module. Note also the opportunity to use the column as a vertical duct for wiring.

CONSTRUCTION

Frame and panel systems

Figure 229 shows an example of a simple concealed fixing frame and panel system.

The frame is of anodized aluminium alloy to BS 1615, the panels can be designed to fit any module using standard sheets. The infill panels are sandwich construction with a core of polystyrene, or flax board or similar material according to the required performance specification faced with hardboard and finished with decorative PVC sheet, decorative laminated plastic or hardwood veneers. The total thickness of the panel is nom. 50 mm. As with most partition systems the doors are pre-hung, in this case on nylon washered, aluminium built hinges and have a rubber strip air seal around the perimeter of the frame. Note the use of PVC glazing beads which fit neatly into the I section frame and the 'clip on' cornice and skirting trim.

The junction at floor and ceiling is most important, particularly in respect of partitions which must have a high sound reduction factor. Here a foam rubber sealing strip is used.

A more sophisticated system is shown in figure 230. This is a modular ceiling and partitioning system with integrated storage and accessories. The ceiling grid has a dimensional relationship with the partitioning providing complete flexibility within the dicipline of a modular layout. The framework to the ceiling is of extruded aluminium alloy channels suspended from the structure by rod or strap hangers attached to the main span members of the ceiling.

Notched and turned aluminium connecting members are fixed to the spine framework at mod-

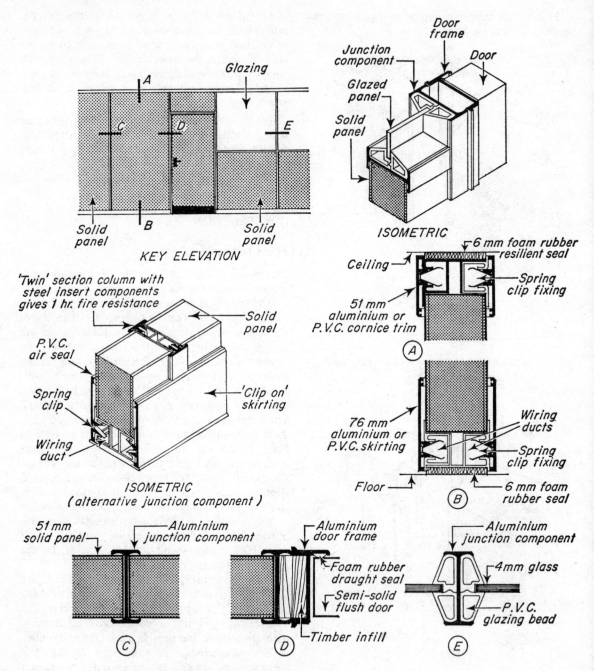

KEY ELEVATION

Glazing

A

C · D · E

Solid panel · Solid panel

B

Door frame

Junction component

Door

Glazed panel

Solid panel

ISOMETRIC

'Twin' section column with steel insert components gives 1 hr. fire resistance

Solid panel

P.V.C. air seal

Spring clip

'Clip on' skirting

Wiring duct

ISOMETRIC
(alternative junction component)

6 mm foam rubber resilient seal

Ceiling

Spring clip fixing

51 mm aluminium or P.V.C. cornice trim

Ⓐ

76 mm aluminium or P.V.C. skirting

Wiring ducts

Spring clip fixing

Floor

Ⓑ

6 mm foam rubber seal

51 mm solid panel

Aluminium junction component

Ⓒ

Aluminium door frame

Foam rubber draught seal

Semi-solid flush door

Timber infill

Ⓓ

Aluminium junction component

4mm glass

P.V.C. glazing bead

Ⓔ

229   A simple concealed fixing frame and panel system

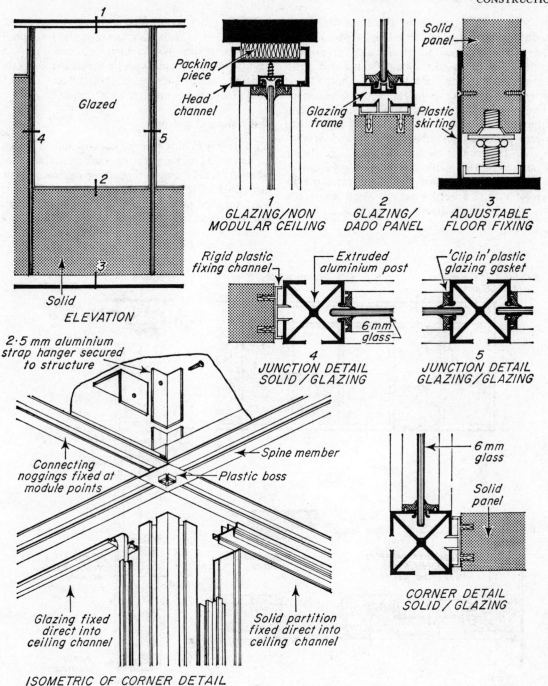

ELEVATION

1 Glazed

4 5

2

3

Solid

1 GLAZING/NON MODULAR CEILING

Packing piece

Head channel

2 GLAZING/ DADO PANEL

Glazing frame

3 ADJUSTABLE FLOOR FIXING

Solid panel

Plastic skirting

4 JUNCTION DETAIL SOLID/GLAZING

Rigid plastic fixing channel

Extruded aluminium post

6 mm glass

5 JUNCTION DETAIL GLAZING/GLAZING

'Clip in' plastic glazing gasket

ISOMETRIC OF CORNER DETAIL

2·5 mm aluminium strap hanger secured to structure

Spine member

Plastic boss

Connecting noggings fixed at module points

Glazing fixed direct into ceiling channel

Solid partition fixed direct into ceiling channel

CORNER DETAIL SOLID/GLAZING

6 mm glass

Solid panel

230   A more sophisticated system than 229

ule points. The junction of the spine and intermediate members is concealed by a plastic boss. The grid is designed to receive any proprietary acoustic boards or tile ceiling. Ceiling and partition modules are standard 1.220 m. The partition system has a maximum height of 3.050 m with a 51 mm overall thickness. Panel cores are flax, chipboard or expanded polystyrene faced with 3 mm hardboard or asbestos board and finished in PVC, laminate or hardwood veneer. The glazing is into extruded plastic beads with glass up to 6 mm thick. One feature of this system is the design of various special brackets which screw clip into the cruciform framing to provide anchorage

for such items as shelves, coathooks, pinboards, and chalkboard. Storage cabinets can also be clipped and hung from the framing, provided that the rigidity of the supports to the ceiling is checked.

Storey height (or normal height) doors are supplied prehung and complete with furniture.

Post and panel system

An example of this form of construction is shown in figure 231. This partition uses a hardboard or asbestos faced timber lipped compressed straw slab panel of total thickness 58 mm nom. There is a dry tongued joint between the edges of the panels and posts and the units are housed at floor and

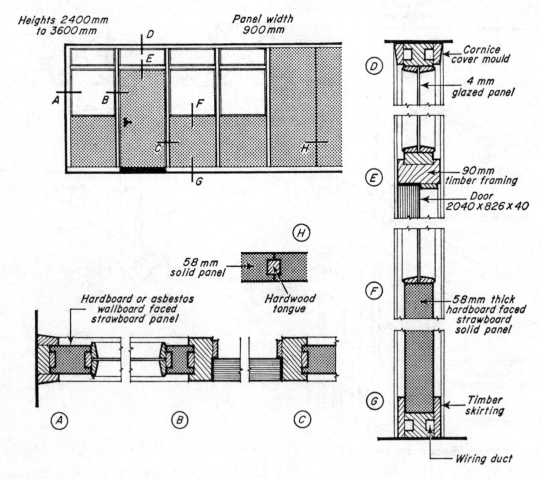

231 *Post and panel system*

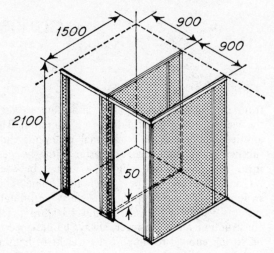

ceiling positions by means of timber plates. The partition uses a standard 900 mm wide panel and a 100 mm post, and can be built to a height of 2400 mm and 3600 mm. The asbestos faced panel gives a Class I spread of flame rating, the hardboard faced a Class III with half hour fire resistance.

WC partitions

This used to be a much neglected field of design, but there are now many proprietary systems on the market providing not only standard WC cubicles but also prefabricated compartments, showers, clothes lockers, and changing cubicles. Figure 232 shows an example of a surfaced paper laminate covered plywood cubicle.

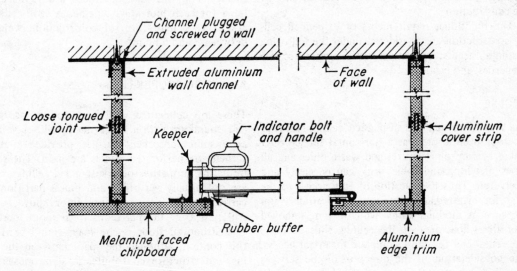

232 *Prefabricated WC compartment*

10 Suspended ceilings Cl/SfB (35)

A suspended ceiling is defined in BS 3589: 1963: *Glossary of General Building Terms* as 'a ceiling hung at a distance from the floor or roof above and not bearing on the walls.'

The method of construction may vary widely, from a jointless ceiling constructed on a foundation of expanded metal, or a PVC sheet stretched between bearers, to a ceiling of small infill panels of suitable building board supported on a lightweight metal frame. The ceiling may incorporate lighting, heating or ventilation services as part of the construction.

The functional requirements of suspended ceiling construction are considered under the following headings: access; weight; acoustic properties; fire properties; and cost.

ACCESS

The space between the suspended ceiling and roof or floor over is used as a horizontal service duct where heating pipes, water and waste pipes and all types of wiring and cable work can be easily and freely run. Thus the question of easy access to the duct for maintenance pruposes, is of primary importance. A modular panel, which can be removed over the whole area of the ceiling, thus becomes the easiest and the most complete means of access. The consideration of the direction of the services and the amount of access required will help to determine the tupe of suspended ceiling most suitable. Narrow strips which can be removed over certain areas will give access to parallel service runs, whilst jointless ceilings will be satisfactory where one or two pre-determined access points are acceptable.

A ceiling system which gives full access may lead to an uneconomic design of the service runs. There is also the risk that the ceiling may be damaged if too many panels are removed.

WEIGHT

Because, by definition, the ceiling is suspended from the main structure, it is important to keep the weight of the construction to a minimum. The jointless ceilings using traditional techniques and finished by a skim coat of plaster is the heaviest form of suspended ceiling, weighing between 20 and 50 kg/m^2. The 'panel and frame' construction will be much lighter, most proprietary systems weighing between 5 and 15 kg/m^2. The construction must, however, always be designed to be strong enough to support the weight of lighting fittings, and this loading should always be calculated for each individual scheme. A strip ceiling is also a very light form of construction, weighing between 3 and 5 kg/m^2.

ACOUSTIC PROPERTIES

These are concerned with both sound absorption and sound insulation. Suspended ceilings will act as a sound absorbent surface provided that absorbent or perforated panels are used. The sound insulating properties of a suspended ceiling system are not usually very high and unless partitions are carried up to the structural floor above, sound will pass over the partitions from room to room. The structural floor is the main sound barrier in this context, although the space between the ceiling and structure contributes in some measure to the sound insulation of the whole construction.

There is a wide range of sheet material available which are suitable for use as infill to the frame as panel ceilings. Usually the sheets are textured, perforated or embossed to increase sound absorbency, but re-decoration by painting will reduce the acoustic properties of such a material over a period of time (see *MBS: Materials,* chapter 1 and chapter 6 of *MBS: Finishes.*

FIRE PROPERTIES

The surface of the ceiling can constitute a considerable fire hazard in respect of the spread of flame. The Building Regulation (E15) controls the surface of a ceiling according to its location (and the particular purpose group of the building) in respect of the ease with which the surface may allow flame to spread over its surface.

The classifications in respect of rate of 'spread of flame' are as follows:

Class 1 a surface of very low flame spread.
Class 2 a surface of low flame spread.
Class 3 a surface of medium flame spread.
Class 4 a surface of rapid flame spread.

These four classifications are those given in BS 476. The four British Standard classifications were, however, not considered adequate in all cases and the Building Regulations introduce a further class designated '0' which is defined as follows:

(i) non-combustible throughout.
(ii) The surface (or if bonded to a substrate) the surface and substrate have an index of Performance (I) not exceeding 12 and a sub-index (i$_i$) not exceeding 6 when tested in accordance with BS 476 Part 6 1968. If however the face is of a plastic material with a softening point below 120°C (when tested in accordance with tests laid down in BS 2782: 1970) it must either:

(a) be bonded to a substrate which is not a plastic material and the material in conjunction with the substrate satisfies the test in (ii) above

or

(b) must satisfy the test in (ii) and be so used that

if the lining were not present, the exposed surface satisfies the test criteria and the exposed surface would not be a plastics material with a softening point below 120°C.

Pur-pose groups		* Small rooms	Other rooms	Circu-lation spaces	* Max. floor area of small rooms m²
I	Small residential	3	3	3	4
II	Institutional	1	1	0	4
III	Other residential	3	1	0	4
IV to VIII	Office, shop. factory, place of assembly, place for storage of goods and all other buildings	3	1	0	30

Table 19 *Minimum class of surface spread of flame designation for ceilings*

The terms used in the above table are defined on p. 228.

For the purposes of fire risk, the Building Regulations divide the space inside a building into three categories, namely: small rooms; other rooms; and circulation spaces. Table 19 is a summary of

Height of building	Type of floor	Fire resistance of floor	Description of suspended ceilings and class of surface spread of flame
Less than 15 m	Non-compartment	1 hour or less	Surface of ceiling exposed *within* the cavity not lower than *Class 1*
	Compartment	Less than 1 hour	
	Compartment	1 hour	As above but *Class 0*, and with supports and fixings not combustible
15 m or more	Any	1 hour or less	Surface of ceiling exposed *within* the cavity, not lower than *Class 0* and *jointless*. Supports and fixings not combustible
Any	Any	More than 1 hour	Ceiling of non-combustible construction and *jointless*; supports and fixings not combustible

Table 20 **The contribution to fire resistance by suspended ceilings**

the regulations in respect of spread of flame to ceilings in the purpose groups of buildings indicated.

If it is intended that a suspended ceiling shall contribute to the overall fire resistance of the floor construction of which it may be said to form a part, the suspended ceiling construction must fulfil the criteria set down in the table to Regulation E6 of the *Building Regulations 1976*. These include the height of the building, and whether or not the floor is a compartment floor and the total period of fire resistance required. Table 20 gives details of the contribution to fire resistance of various suspended ceilings.

The inference from the table is that the type of suspended ceiling relying on separate tiles within a framework of metal angles or Ts is not allowed as a factor contributing to the fire resistance of the total floor construction in buildings more than 15.24 m high where the period required is 1 hour, or in buildings of any type where the period required is more than 1 hour. In the latter circumstances the ceiling construction must be jointless. However, it must be borne in mind that the Regulation is concerned only with the contribution made by suspended ceilings to the fire resistance of the total floor construction. The question of the protection afforded by suspended ceilings to structural steelwork is a separate consideration.

COST

The comparative installation costs, costs in use and subsequent maintenance costs for the systems under examination must be considered at the design stage of a project.

METHODS OF CONSTRUCTION

1 Jointless

(a) Lath and plaster supported and suspended on metal framework and hangers.
(b) PVC membrane stretched over a frame.
(c) Plasterboard and skim, or suitable building board with cover strips supported on timber framework and suspended from the floor above, by timber (or more usually) by metal or wire hangers. See chapter 13.

Jointless ceilings, with the exception of the PVC membrane type, are usually non-proprietary and rely on traditional materials and methods. They are relatively low cost and give a good fire resistance. The slowness of the wet construction where plastering is used, is, however, a disadvantage.

2 Frame and panel

Infil panels of fibre building board tiles; asbestos tiles; mineral wool tiles; metal trays or plastic tiles dropped to a suspended framework of metal angles and tees. There are various methods of securing the panels and framing.

The erection of a frame and panel ceiling is speedy and clean, and this type of ceiling is usually easily demountable.

3 Strip ceiling

(a) Profiled aluminium strips.
(b) PVC strips on metal cores.

4 Service ceiling

Suspended ceilings in which the services form an integral part of the construction fall into the following categories:

(a) Fully illuminated ceilings, having infill panels of translucent plastic which form the diffusers for the light fittings suspended above them. The diffusers may be plain face, three dimensional, corrugated, embossed or 'egg box' construction.

This type of ceiling should not be confused with the use of modular light fittings, which fit into the grid spacing of the panel, and frame type of ceiling discussed previously.

(b) Ceiling panels which incorporate low temperature heating elements, or small bore hot water circuits, usually in conjunction with sound absorbing panels.

(c) Ceilings in which the whole of the space above is used as a plenum chamber for the cirulation and direction of hot or cold air.

(d) A fully 'service' integrated ceiling which gives an element of construction providing heat, light and sound absorption. This arrangement, though expensive, permits the ultimate in flexibility of use of the space below.

The detailed consideration of the technical aspects of the 'service' ceilings is a specialist matter outside the scope of this volume.

CONSTRUCTIONAL DETAILS

There are many proprietary suspended ceiling systems available and some typical details are indicated in figures 233, 234 and 235.

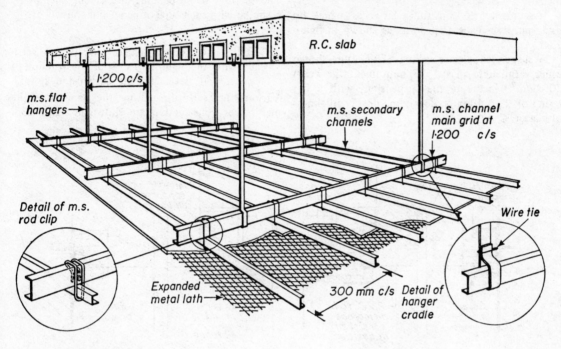

233 Suspended plastered ceiling

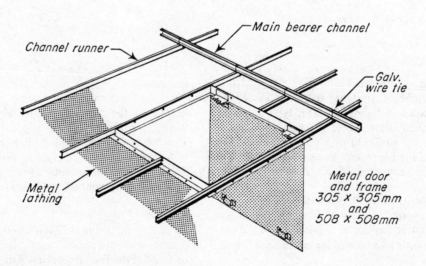

234 Prefabricated access door to suspended ceiling

239

Jointless plaster

The ceiling shown in figure 233 is a suspended plaster ceiling on metal lathing.

Two methods of securing the hangers to support the lath are shown.

It is possible to construct neat access panels by using purpose made trap doors as shown in figure 234.

A suspended plaster ceiling of the type shown using vermiculite plaster 15 mm thick will weigh 20 kg/m², including the suspension, with a fire rating of 2 to 4 hours, depending on the thickness of plaster.

cate. These Certificates, which relate to a particular product, are valid for three years.

Frame and panel ceilings

The method of suspending the ceiling membrane is similar with each type of panel and consists of:

1 *Hangers*
   Metal straps, rods or angles which hang vertically from the main floor or roof construction to support and 'level up' the suspension system.

Various methods of securing the hangers to the main floor construction are shown in figure 235.

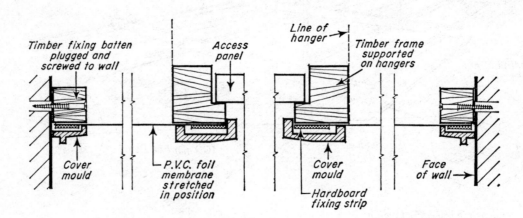

MEMBRANE CEILING

235 Jointless PVC membrane ceiling

Jointless PVC

An example of the application of the use of a PVC foil membrane, stretched to form a suspended ceiling is shown in figure 235. This type of ceiling can be installed in one sheet 0.2 mm thick, forming a panel up to 7.500 m x 6.000 m nom. The method is adaptable to any shape of room and will accommodate any size of access panel or light fitting.

The finish of the PVC foil is semi-matt, and does not require decoration. Where a higher degree of sound absorption is required, a special perforated foil with a loose backing of absorbent quilt is used.

This construction received an Agrément Certifi-

2 *Bearers*
   These are the main supporting sections connected to the hangers and to which the subsidiary horizontal runner supports are fixed. The use of bearers enables the hangers to be at wider centres than the basic ceiling module. There are many ingenious proprietary methods of attaching the runners and hangers.

3 *Runners*
   These are the supporting members which are in contact with the ceiling panels. They are usually of aluminium T or Z sections. The runners span in the opposite direction to the bearers.

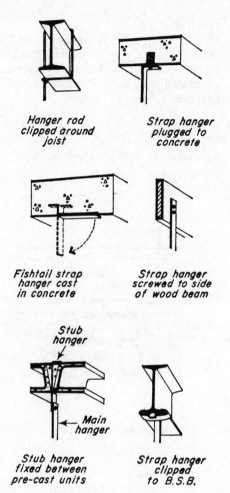

Hanger rod clipped around joist

Strap hanger plugged to concrete

Fishtail strap hanger cast in concrete

Strap hanger screwed to side of wood beam

Stub hanger

Main hanger

Stub hanger fixed between pre-cast units

Strap hanger clipped to B.S.B.

236 *Hangers for suspended ceilings*

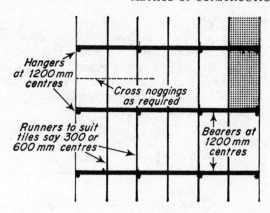

Hangers at 1200 mm centres

Cross noggings as required

Runners to suit tiles say 300 or 600 mm centres

Bearers at 1200 mm centres

237 *Plan layout of suspended ceiling*

minium T section. Unless there is a risk of the panels being lifted by wind pressure (say in an entrance hall) they can be left loose and are thus very easy to remove where the void above is used as a duct. Where they require to be held down, a wire or spring metal clip is slotted into the web of the T to hold the panel down from above.

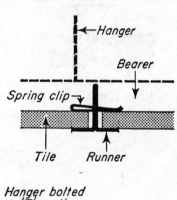

Hanger

Bearer

Spring clip

Tile   *Runner*

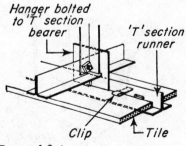

Hanger bolted to 'T' section bearer

'T' section runner

Clip   *Tile*

(*a*)   *Exposed fixing*

4 *Noggings*

These are subsidiary cross members which span in the same direction as the bearers but in the same plane as the runners in order to complete the framework. Runners and noggings can be concealed or exposed. A typical layout is shown in figure 237.

Fixings

Typical methods of securing the ceiling panel into the suspension system are shown in figure 238 as follows:

(a) *Exposed fixing*

Here the ceiling panel or tile drops into the suspended framework formed by the extruded alu-

(b) *Concealed fixing*

This is a concealed type of fixing since the method of support is not visible from below. The diagram shows the grooved tiles slotted into the Z section runner. An alternative form of concealed fixing using a tongued and grooved tile is shown in figure 239.

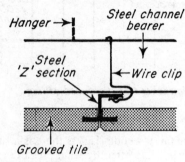

(*b*) *Concealed fixing*

(c) *Clip fixing*

In this detail a special runner is used which holds the metal tray in position. The tray will be perforated and will probably have an infill of mineral wool or similar inert, sound absorbent material.

(d) *Screw fixing*

This detail shows two alternative forms of securing the ceiling panels by direct screw fixing.

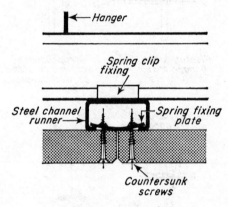

METHOD OF FIXING

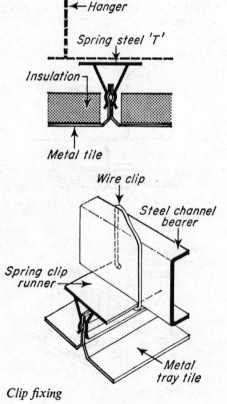

(*c*) *Clip fixing*

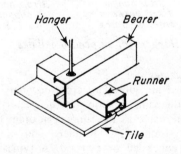

(*d*) *Screw fixing*

238 Typical methods of fixing ceiling panels

A large range of building boards are suitable for infill panels as follows:

Asbestos insulation board
Corkboard
Expanded plastics

Metal tiles
Mineral fibre boards
Plasterboard, cut sheets or tiles
Plasterboard faced with PVC sheet
Fibrous plaster tiles
Plywood
Resin bonded glass fibre tiles

Vermiculite slabs
Wood fibre boards

For details of the sizes and physical properties of these materials see *MBS: Materials* and *MBS: Finishes*. Details of a concealed suspension system with fibre board tiles are shown in figure 239.

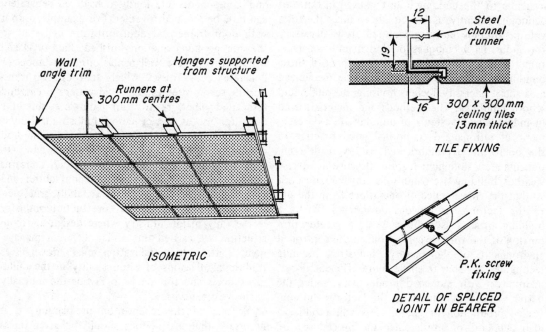

ISOMETRIC

TILE FIXING

DETAIL OF SPLICED JOINT IN BEARER

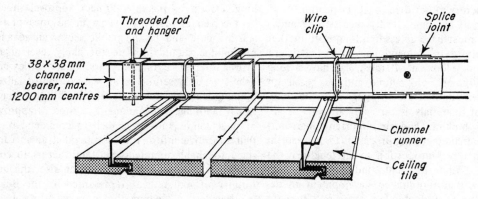

SUSPENSION SYSTEM

239 Concealed fixing of suspended ceiling tiles

11 Industrialized system building

The industrialization of the building process is the increasing utilization of factory techniques of production in relation to the total process of building. The number of skilled and semi-skilled workers available to the building industry, even in times of economic stability, is inadequate to meet the total volume of new building required. It is necessary for industrial techniques of design and construction to be applied, particularly in respect of those building types which have come to be recognized as a social necessity such as housing, hospitals, and school buildings. The methods and materials used in industrialized systems of building are a development of rationalized traditional good practice to the point where prefabricated factory made components are a dominant feature. Because of adverse weather, building site conditions are generally poor so that the transference of operations from the site to the factory has obvious advantages. Where a building process is industrialized, a greater proportion of the work is carried out in the controlled environment of the factory. Industrial building techniques are able to make more efficient use of manpower with increased productivity under the better working conditions in the factory, and controlled production of components will produce a high standard of finish since the procedures are linked to factory rather than to site inspection.

In order to be commercially successful, a building system must have an assured long term market with continuity of demand backed by sufficient capital for development. It must also have a long term development programme and be based on sensible cost limits. Pre-ordering and the bulk purchase of materials is an integral part of industrialized building and an important characteristic of the manufacturing process is an increase in economy in direct proportion to the length of the production run. Efficient industrialization is achieved by the co-ordinated development of design procedures, production processes and erection techniques. Examples of the early industrialization of building were the introduction of standard parts for fixing, such as the nail and the screw, and then the development of standard parts for cladding, such as the standard window and door. With advanced technology, production processes, and handling equipment larger units can now be made and components previously considered separately can now be grouped together. For example, a door with door frame and door furniture delivered to the site pre-hung and pre-finished; factory glazed windows; complete wall panels either in timber or concrete; roof trusses which fold up for transporting to the site; hot and cold water systems and associated pipework to form complete plumbing units for use as service cores. Industrialization is not exclusively concerned with changes of method on site or in the factory but it involves a new attitude to design and construction which concerns client, architect, administrator, manufacturer and contractor. Traditionally, it is generally true, perhaps surprisingly, that the construction industry is the only major industry where design and construction are carried out under different management control. Industrialization breaks down these traditional divisions of responsibility in the building process and this tends to favour the mutually exclusive organization.

Because of the reliance on pre-planning it is necessary that instructions should be given on as long a term as possible. Project approval should be received at least two years in advance of the starting date and in the public sector an advance programme should indicate the likely level of approval for periods of five years. Uncertainties and delays are very serious in the case of industrialized building since the system is less flexible than traditional methods. The Agrément method of approval of new components has much to commend it, in that objective information is provided at an early stage to enable architects and contractors to consider new products. In this respect also, the uniformity of requirement represented by the Building Regulations favours the more widespread use of industrialized techniques. It is interesting to not that, in this respect, Part F (Thermal) and Part E (Fire Regulations) are in the form of a performance specification giving more freedom of choice to the designer providing the conditions are met.

Industrialized systems require large investment in building research with specialist knowledge of the techniques of factory production, site organization and mechanization. Research into the optimum economic levels for the production of building components is required to give a sound basis on which to plan the proper scale for building programmes. New ways of assessing user requirements and the development of drawings, specifications and contractual procedures, particularly applicable to industrialized building are also necessary.

A common factor running through the design process is the size or dimension of the component. Following from this the key to industrialization in building is a rational approach to the co-ordination of dimensions. There isnow a new opportunity for progress on an international scale with the introduction of metrication. Handling equipment for components assumes special importance, particularly in respect of heavy units both within the factory, factory to site and on the site. The limits of road and rail transport assume growing importance as the use of factory made components increases and the problems of off-site assembly and packaging are of paramount importance.

'OPEN' AND 'CLOSED' SYSTEMS

In connection with industrialized building the terms *open system* and *closed system* are used. Sometimes the term *method building* is used and this is a technique in which inter-related factory proceduced components are used in a manner which combines freedom of design for each individual building, with the maximum use of standard components. In a *closed* system of building the components are not inter-changeable with any other system or method and thus the building is formed from components specifically designed for and applicable to the particular building type in question, for example schools or housing.

The designer's choice is governed by the variations allowed within the system but the system is developed to meet precisely the requirements of its users. The idea of client participation at the design stage and close co-operation with the component manufacturers should produce a *closed* system

building which fulfils its function within exacting economic limits. An *open* system of building is where components are inter-changeable with other systems, and the aim of an open system of building is to produce a complete range of standard components which are inter-changeable over a wide range of building types. This inter-changeability could well be the result of the acceptance of dimensional co-ordination (see chapter 1). The *open* system being one for which components are chosen within the agreed range of dimensions from components available on the open market. Thus the designer's choice is wide and limited only by his experience and knowledge of the market. Both *open* and *closed* systems can incorporate traditional forms of construction such as brickwork but this tends to detract from the efficiency of the system as such. Since site works take up a large proportion of construction time and effort, these operations should be rationalized as far as possible. Many systems of building which started as *closed* systems are likely to become *open* systems mainly through the application of dimensional co-ordination, where it is obviously an advantage to be able to combine various systems in respect of the supply of components and fittings.

CLIENT SPONSORED AND CONTRACTOR SPONSORED SYSTEMS

Systems of building have been developed and sponsored by both client organizations and contractors' organizations. In the case of client sponsored systems, because of the necessity for a large and continuing building programme, and in order to make a particular system viable, various local authorities (which may include new towns and government departments) have created between themselves associations for the development of a particular system of building. An association of this kind is called a consortium and its members are able to exchange information on building problems, engage in bulk purchase of materials and support the joint use of a particular building technique. Examples of client sponsored systems are those of the various consortia of local authorities for schools and similar buildings such as CLASP, SEAC and SCOLA. In the case of the contractor sponsored or proprietary system the contractor will provide a specialist erection service. In the case of a client sponsored system the contract is put out to competitive tender in accordance with normal procedure. Systems are sub-divided into light systems using steel and timber or heavy systems using storey height concrete panels and classified *high* or *low* according to the number of storeys that can be constructed.

Many proprietary low rise (1 to 3 storeys) housing systems are currently in use. Because of the importance of providing sufficient good housing the National Building Agency has been formed. This is an independent advisory body whose main function is to promote the use of improved techniques of design, management and site operation in both public and private house building. The Agency is managed by a board of directors appointed by the Government and represents a wide rande of professional, industrial and administrative experience. The National Building Agency provides an advisory service to local authorities, contractors or architects on such subjects as work-study, project planning, plant utilization, production control and management accounting. The Agency also investigates system building for housing and issues an appraisal certificate to the selected systems. The National Building Agency's appraisal certificates are subject to review periodically and systems are added and occasionally withdrawn. Low rise housing systems generally, are based on a basic construction of either precast or in-situ concrete, steel framing, or timber framing or a combination of these materials. In each case the system attempts to make the maximum use of dry construction, sometimes in conjunction with traditional materials such as in-situ concrete or brickwork, but in rationalization of traditional building methods aims at reducing site labour and at the same time increasing the speed of erection. It is claimed for one system that 6 men can erect a house completely in fourteen days. The systems use as much off-site fabrication of components as possible but in different ways depending on the particular skills or facilities of the manufacturers. Some examples of the pre-fabrication of various component parts from a selection of the systems is given below:

1 Pre-cast, pre-finished, storey height concrete external wall units.
2 Long-span, pre-stressed concrete floor unit panels.
3 Pre-cast storey height flank and cross wall panels.
4 Pre-cast concrete internal patition wall panels ready to receive decoration.
5 Non-loadbearing in-fill panels of timber framing complete with pre-hung and glazed windows, pre-hung doors and with flashings in place.
6 Pre-formed plumbing units for warm iar heating and hot water supply.
7 Pre-formed first floor sections with timber joists and chipboard finish.
8 Double storey height timber framing with plywood sheathing, with a selection of external cladding materials such as tile hanging, metal panels, weather boarding or glass fibre panels.
9 Pre-formed service units incorporating hot and cold water storage, electric service duct, soil and waste stack and the heating unit.
10 Prefabricated internal timber frames partitions with engineering and plumbing service ducts and pre-hung doors and frames.

Most of the systems incorporate in-situ solid concrete ground floor slabs, sometimes in modified raft form with edge beams. Framed construction has the usual concrete pad foundations. Most roof forms are still traditional pitch with some form of tiling and prefabricated timber trusses. Some of the more flexible systems, although designed principally for housing have been used for other building types.

Many proprietary systems have also bee developed for medium rise (3 to 5 storeys) and high rise housing. High rise systems can of course be conveniently adapted to low rise dwellings particularly in mixed development. Most systems are based on pre-cast concrete units and use storey height wall panels, floor panels, and even room sized elements, which require specialist plant and equipment. Some of these types of heavy prefabrication were originally used and developed on the continent in France and in Denmark and Sweden. The construction of high rise buildings is a complex technical problem and where large units are used the question of site jointing is of paramount importance.

In addition to building systems for housing there are a wide range of proprietary contractor sponsored systems which have been developed for schools, commercial buildings and industrial buildings. Some form of concrete, steel or timber frame or frame and panel construction is used. The systems are based on a structural grid and the recommendations of BS 4330 for the co-ordination of controlling dimensions in building are now relevant to these systems.

CONSORTIA SYSTEMS

There are several client sponsored local authority consortium systems currently in use at this time. Most of the systems were developed from the need to build schools quickly and of course they can be, and are, modified for other types of local authority building such as training centres, old peoples homes, libraries, fire and police stations and office building. The main consortia are briefly described below:

Consortium of Local Authorities Special Programme (CLASP)

This system was originally established in 1956 to develop and control a prefabricated system of building aimed at reducing the amount of labour used on site. The use of prefabricated techniques in particular for school buildings was pioneered immediately after the end of the war in 1945. In particular, the CLASP system was required to solve a specific problem, namely the design of school buildings for sites which were liable to mining subsidence. It should be noted that CLASP like the other Consortia has no formal legal organization, and it does not therefore enter into contracts. Individual members or sponsoring authorities negotiate tenders for components on behalf of the Consortia from contractors and suppliers. The various components are then included in the Bill of Quantities as prime cost (PC) items. The actual orders for the components are placed through the general contractor for each separate contract. CLASP utilizes a light steel frame with steel lattice floor and roof beams. The roof deck is of prefabricated timber, and the floors are also of timber construction either prefabricated or in-situ. The cladding materials are chosen from pre-cast concrete slabs with exposed aggregate facing or tile hanging, protected metal sheeting or timber boarding on timber cladding frames. The window frames are factory glazed with gasket glazing. Opening lights are in metal

frames. The CLASP construction described can be used up to 4 storeys in height. The system has a development group and a contracts group for component supply contracts and programming. The system is extremely well documented, being illustrated in a series of excellent handbooks. A *Planning Handbook* illustrates the design disciplines, and a *Technical Handbook* gives detailed information for working drawings. An *Administration Handbook* is provided for use of architects and consultants in pre-contract procedure and an *Assembly Handbook* is used as a guide to the erection process and on site. CLASP has been used on the continent and in South Africa.

Second Consortium of Local Authorities (SCOLA)

This Consortium was established in 1961, and has developed the SCOLA mark I, II and metric mark III systems. The following notes refer to the SCOLA mark II system. This has a pin jointed light steel frame with square section steel columns supported on a modified form of raft foundation for single storey buildings or reinforced concrete strip foundations for multi-storey buildings. The system is designed to be built up to 4 storeys. The roof construction is steel channel edge reinforced woodwool slab with a felt or asphalt finish. Suspended floors are pre-cast concrete panels on steel lattice beams. Various lightweight dry cladding can be used such as tile hanging, protected metal sheeting or timber boarding. Brickwork can be used as an alternative cladding. The window walling is of metal frame with various types of opening light incorporated. The internal partitioning is of dry plasterboard units and ceilings are of asbestos or mineral board slabs. The Consortium obtains quotations for the supply, and fix and supply only items which are then included in the Bills of Quantities as PC items. The Consortium has developed the use of computers and automatic data processing in the preparation of Bills of Quantities and a computer is also used in the design and manufacturing documentation of the steel window walling, see page 252.

Consortium for Method Building

This Consortium is concerned with a whole range of local authority building types. The headquarters are in Somerset.

247

The Organization of North West Authorities for Rationalized Design (ONWARD)

This is a recent formation concerned with a wide range of building types but excluding housing.

South Eastern Architects Collaboration (SEAC)

This Consortium is based in Hertfordshire and is concerned with a wide range of buildings to the cost levels dictated by local authority programmes. It was established in 1963 and is based on the use of modular principles to incorporate proprietary commercial components. The Consortium has developed the use of computers and automatic data processing for Bills of Quantities.

INNOVATIONS

The above list is not exhaustive, and in addition to the main consortia there are also consortia concerned with bulk purchasing, in particular of kitchen equipment and science equipment and furniture for schools. The type of consortia mentioned have been instrumental in bringing about many innovations in system building which are now accepted as commonplace. For example, the use of dry construction wherever possible above foundations; the use of suspended ceiling acting as a fire barrier and the use of the space above for services; storey height window wall assembly and an agreement on dimensional co-ordination within the system. This pre-dates by several years the current dimensional co-ordination in respect of the change to metric.

The following points are given for general consideration in respect of industrialized system building:

1 The user has a finished product carefully developed as a result of widely based studies and proto-type testing.
2 Production drawings are simplified. The content of the drawing becoming more diagrammatic and less pictorial.
3 The known production run will permit early cost planning and encourage experiment with contractual methods to reduce costs.
4 Orders for components can be placed well in advance so that effective control of production and delivery can be maintained.

5 Assembly on site can be rationalized so that more economic use is made of mechanical plant and manpower.
6 Use of components encourages performance testing so that modifications can be fed back to designers and manufacturers.

The aim of standardization is not to produce standard buildings in the architectural sense but to create a standardized system of construction made from interchangeable parts of good design and high quality which can be used to fabricate a great variety of building.

A point to note is that following the change to metric all building which is Government controlled through the various consortia will have the same metric dimensional basis. This will follow the recommendations in respect of dimensional co-ordination discussed in chapter 1.

DOCUMENTATION

The consortia systems are very well documented providing a comprehensive manual of data sheets in various forms. To illustrate the method of working of a consortia system in respect of job drawing procedure the following information is based on the SCOLA mark II system of building. The documentation being divided into five main sections which can be grouped or bound separately. If required the sheets can be intermixed, eg component drawings and specifications.

The sections are:

Design data

A series of information sheets to illustrate the principles, limitations and range of the system. These do not include detail component assembly information but do include composite axonometrics and isometrics. The design data sheets give information under the following headings:

Job drawing production
Site investigation and foundations
Steel frame
External walls
Partitions
Suspended floors

Stairs
Ceilings and blindboxes
Flat roof
Deck, finish, rooflights, tank rooms, fans, flues
Ironmongery
Doors, internal
Floor finishes
Services: Heating
Services: Electrical
Fixtures and equipment
Sanitary equipment

Assembly details

Standard drawings of combinations of components or units, fully annotated and coded. These cross reference to the design data sheet ranges and component sheets.

Component drawings

A series of information sheets to illustrate consortium components, used for tendering or prepared from specialist shop drawings, or components provided by the general contractor.

Specification sheets

Component specifications state the standards which have to be met set out in regularized format so that individual items can be pinpointed, eg material, quality, dimensions, tolerances, finish. General specification items are also included in this section.

Schedule of rates

Unit prices for all consortium components set out in standard format.

Procedure sheets

A series of information sheets to illustrate SCOLA job drawing procedure and job procedure from brief to completion, advance schedule procedure and coding procedure.

Job drawings

In addition to the relevant standard drawings and details appropriate to all projects the following drawings are required, particular to each contract:

Design drawings

These are prepared in order to obtain committee, planning, ministry, regulation and other statutory approvals.

To obtain approval to steel layout by specialist manufacturer and to establish the cost plan.

Basic layout drawings

Ground floor layout plan
Upper floor layout plan(s)
Elevations

Site layout drawings

Block plan
Site layout plan
Site works + drainage adjacent to building
Site landscaping layout

Subsidiary layout drawings

Foundation plan
Ground floor slab plan
Roof steel layout
Upper floor steel layout(s)
Upper floor slab plan(s)
Partition plan(s)
Ceiling plan(s)
Heating + Mechanical ventilation plan(s)
Gas + cold water services
Electrical layout

Schedules

Elevations
Internal door schedule
External door schedule
Ironmongery schedule – internal doors
Ironmongery schedule – external doors
Sanitary fittings schedule
Room fittings: furniture schedule
Finishes schedule
Internal decoration schedule
External decoration schedule

Examples of a selection from the above list of drawings is shown in figures 240 to 250 prepared for a particular school project in Shropshire.

It should be noted that the drawings take the form of coded charts which relate to standard detail

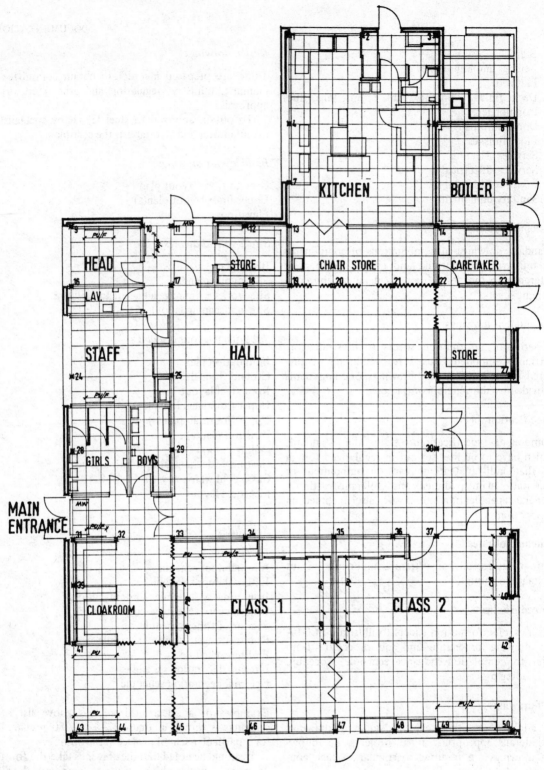

240   *Ground floor layout plan*

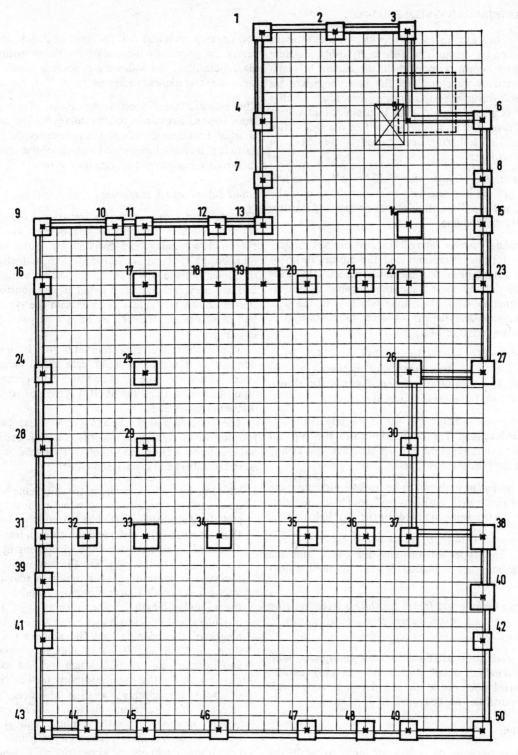

241 *Foundation plan*

sheets and assemblies upon which the contractor develops his erection procedure. By using a system of *copy negatives* upon which subsequent information can be superimposed the basic negatives are re-used throughout the drawing procedure so that the completed layout plan is produced in stages. This saves a considerable amount of drawing office time. The following information is contained on the drawings:

Ground floor layout plan – figure 240 shows the plans of the building with reference to the modular grid, and the disposition of the fittings and fixtures within the building.

Foundation plan – figure 241 shows the pad foundations for the stanchions and the ground beam or strip foundations for the infill panels. The stanchions are numbered and the drawing is read in conjunction with a schedule which gives the plan dimensions and depths of each foundation pad, as shown in figure 242.

Roof steel layout – figures 243 and 244. These drawings show the coded roof steelwork at two levels. The position of the roof lights is also shown and the roof bracing is indicated.

Ceiling plan – figure 245 shows the grid of the suspended ceiling. The coding indicates the type of construction required for the recess in the ceiling to receive the window blind.

The roof plan is shown in figure 246, indicating the rainwater outlet positions and roof falls, together with the trimming required for the roof lights.

The coded elevations are shown on figure 247 and 248. The types of opening are coded and the dimensions are indicated by stating the number of modules.

A typical door and frame schedule is given in figure 249, and an *ironmongery schedule* is shown in figure 250.

For each project, the contractor is supplied with the standard detail sheets and assembly details, standard documentation and drawings and schedules particular to the contract.

Coding

Various systems of coding are used to relate the components required to the manufacturing processes. In respect of the coding for the elevational glazed cladding, the following procedure based on computer techniques is adopted:

The manufacturers receive the coded elevations from the architect and quantity surveyor. The code is an alpha numeric code which is designed to give sufficient manufacturing details to allow the manufacturer to produce an accurate quotation.

Input data sheet for computer

The architect indicates on the elevational drawing the bay number, the modular size of each part of the window walling, and specifies by initial or a number the types of glass or infill and the method of opening of the windows. This is shown in figure 251 for a typical bay. The detail of the construction is shown in figure 252 to explain the system, but of course this drawing would not be produced in practice.

The quantity surveyor translates this information on to a computer input data sheet using a code devised by the manufacturer. A specimen input data sheet using the SCOLA system of coding is given in figure 253.

The construction is 'separated' into three parts for purpose of coding, so that the coding is carried out in three sections as follows: 1 unit; 2 horizontal members and 3 vertical members.

1 Unit section, which includes the top hung window unit, the projecting top hung window unit and the dado infill panel. The bay number location reference (4) is given and the column headed 1 is used to indicate the type of opening light; top hung (T) in this case. The (T) also indicates the type of opening control unless a standard alternative is coded later. Columns 2 and 3 give the modular length of the opening light (12 modules), and columns 4 and 5 give the modular height of the opening light (04 modules). Columns 6, 7, 8 and 9 are to indicate optional variations of construction which may be associated with the top hung ventilator such as type of bead for glazing; weather stripping, fly screens, or a variation on the standard cam opener. In the example the top hung light is required to be weather stripped (W). Column 10 codes the thickness of glass (or infill panel),

STANCHION NO.	PLAN DIMENSION 'A'	DEPTH DIMENSION 'B'	STANCHION NO.	PLAN DIMENSION 'A'	DEPTH DIMENSION 'B'
1	750	225	26	975	675
2	750	225	27	975	675
3	750	225	28	750	225
4	750	225	29	750	225
5	SPECIAL	SPECIAL	30	750	225
6	750	525	31	750	225
7	750	225	32	750	225
8	750	525	33	1125	675
9	750	525	34	1125	675
10	750	525	35	750	225
11	750	225	36	750	225
12	750	225	37	750	225
13	750	525	38	1125	675
14	1050	675	39	750	525
15	750	225	40	1125	675
16	750	225	41	750	525
17	975	675	42	750	225
18	1275	675	43	750	525
19	1275	675	44	750	525
20	750	225	45	750	225
21	750	225	46	750	225
22	1050	675	47	750	225
23	750	225	48	750	225
24	750	225	49	750	525
25	975	675	50	750	525

242 *Schedule*

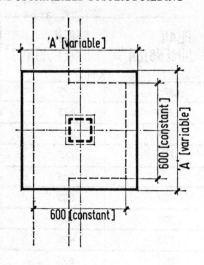

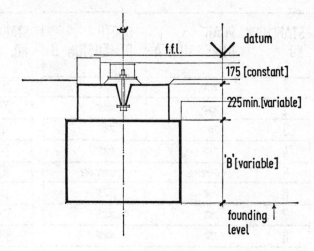

PLAN   SECTION

242 – continued

3 mm coded (1) in this example. Column codes the type of glass, clear sheet (0) in this case. The procedure is repeated for each of the other 'units' in the bay: (F) for the fixed lights, (P) for the projecting top hung window and (F) for the 'fixed light' with infill forming the dado construction.

2 Horizontal members. This coding indicates the horizontal components associated with the bay in addition to the units already coded, such as flashings, transom and sill. The bay which forms part of the full elevation is located by code (0108) and the columns headed 1 and 2 are used to code the component, in this case a particular type of flashing (AF). Columns 3, 4 and 5 are used to give the modular length of the component part. The remaining component parts indicated on the example are head member (HCH), the transom above the projecting top hung window (TR) and the sill member (GC).

3 Vertical members. This coding shows the vertical component types required, in this case a mullion. The bay is forst located (4) and the columns headed 1 and 2 are used to indicate the mullion and its width (M3), the columns headed 3, 4 and 5 give the modular height of the mullion (024).

There are very many more alternative components available, each with a separate code or

initial and it will be seen from the example that it is possible, by a simple coding, to translate a drawing to provide numerical rather than dimensional information, so that the information can be processed by *mechanical* means — in this case, a computer. The coding having been set down on the input data sheet, the computer programme is punched on tape from this after certain other coded information has been included by the manufacturer. The manufacturer in this instance checks the architect's drawings against the data sheets since errors in coding can be costly to put right.

The computer produces a priced print-out giving the following information:

1 For each unit section (ie fixed or opening light) the computer prints out a repeat of the data sheet with the addition of a particular coding relevant to the manufacturer's processing.

2 The computer checks the total area in modules against the sum of the units in modules and accepts the data if the end figure is zero.

3 The computer also costs the infill materials which may be glazed or sheet materials and prints in words the specification of the infill.

4 The computer gives the cost of each item as *supply only* or *supply and fix* as required.

254

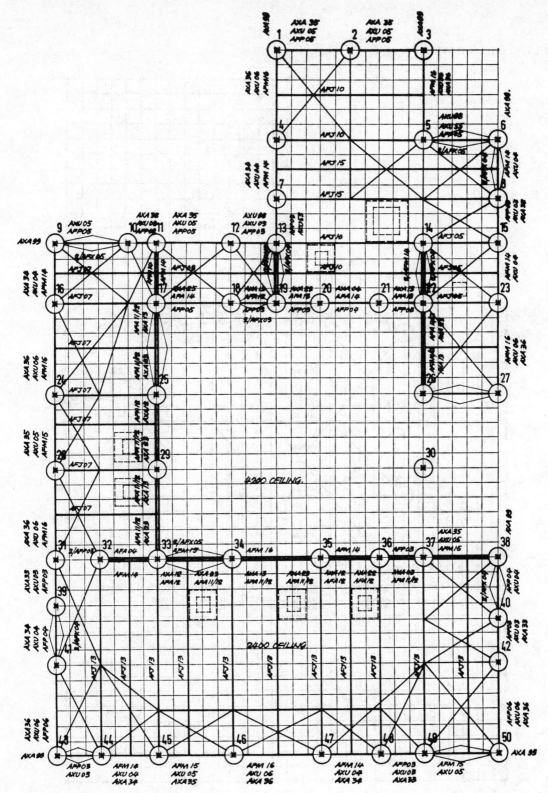

243 *Roof steel layout*

255

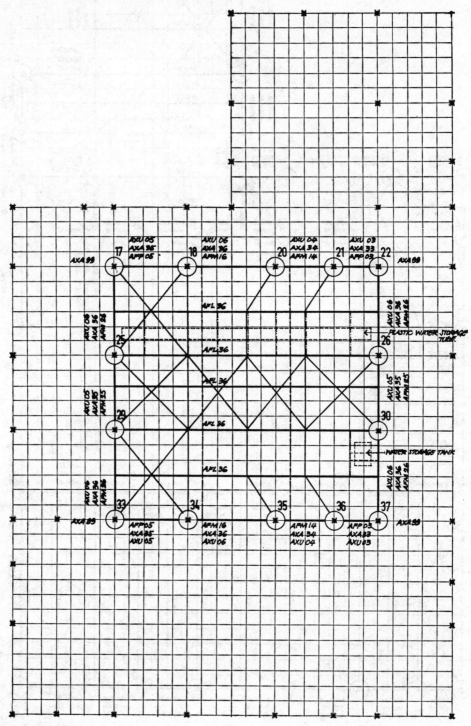

244 *Roof steel layout*

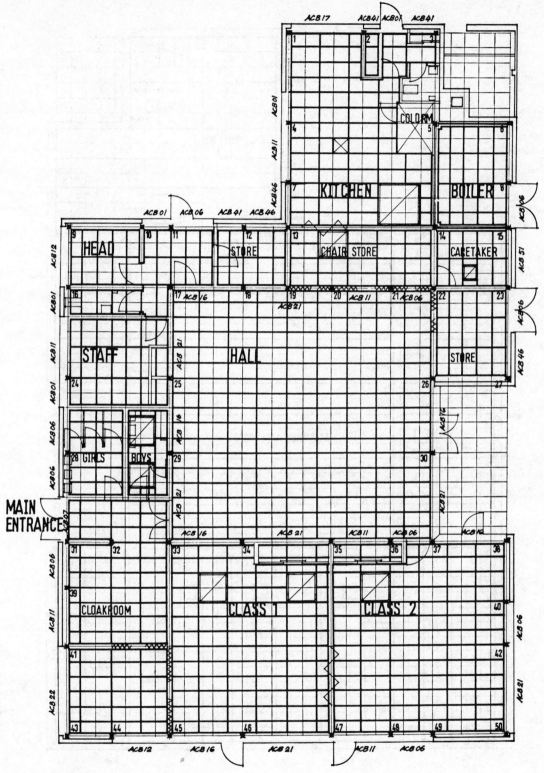

245　*Ceiling plan*

257

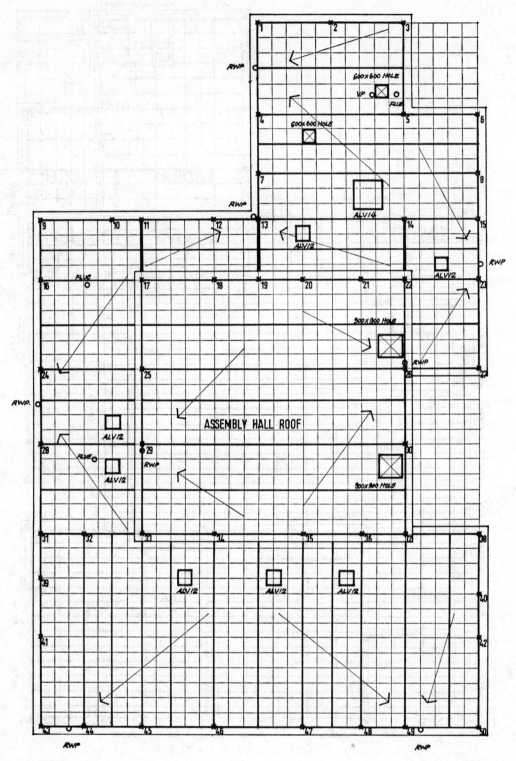

246 *Roof plan*

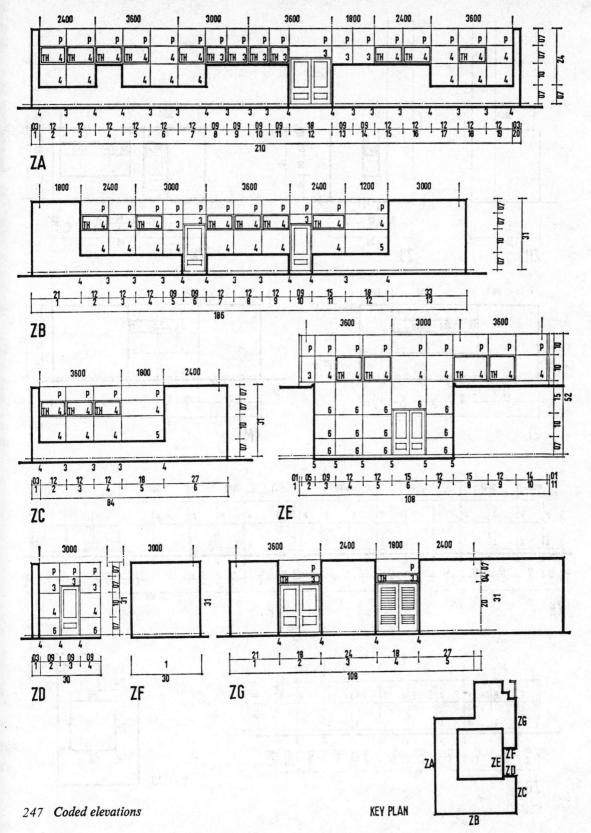

ZA

ZB

ZC

ZE

ZD ZF ZG

KEY PLAN

247 *Coded elevations*

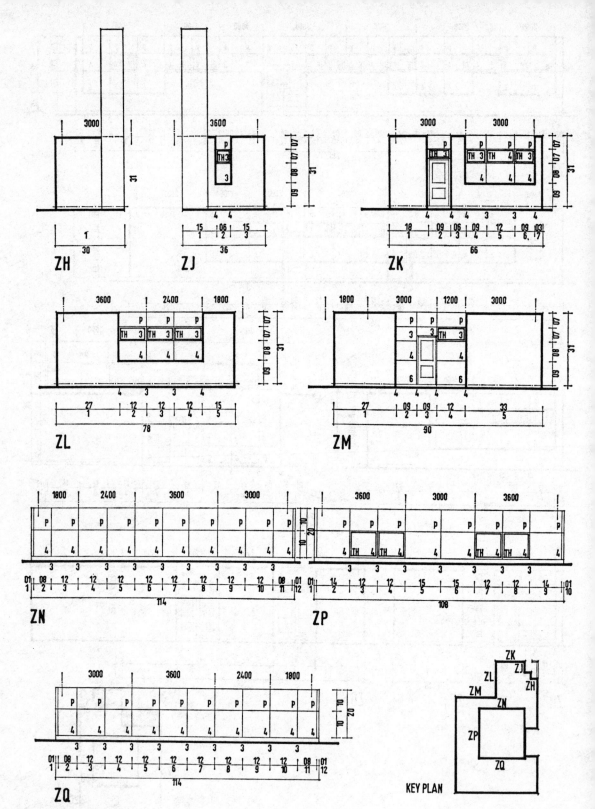

248　*Coded elevations*

DOOR GROUP	DOOR NO.	JOB SPECIAL	DOOR-FRAME SET	DOOR PANEL	FRAME PANEL	DOOR FINISH	FRAME FINISH
	1		ADC 274		LOUVRES TO DETAIL DRG. E-535	POLYURETHENE	WHITE GLOSS
	2		ADC 278		4mm CLEAR GLASS	POLYURETHENE	WHITE GLOSS
	3		ADC 262	6mm 'ARMOURPLATE'	6mm 'ARMOURPLATE'	WHITE GLOSS	WHITE GLOSS
	4		ADC 244		4mm CLEAR GLASS	POLYURETHENE	WHITE GLOSS
	5		ADC 264		4mm CLEAR GLASS	POLYURETHENE	WHITE GLOSS
	6		ADC 244		4mm CLEAR GLASS	POLYURETHENE	WHITE GLOSS
	7		ADC 254		4mm CLEAR GLASS	POLYURETHENE	WHITE GLOSS
DOUBLE	8		ADR 242	6mm 'ARMOURPLATE'	6mm 'ARMOURPLATE'	WHITE GLOSS	WHITE GLOSS
	9			6mm 'ARMOURPLATE'		WHITE GLOSS	WHITE GLOSS
	10		ADC 272	6mm 'ARMOURPLATE'	6mm 'ARMOURPLATE'	WHITE GLOSS	WHITE GLOSS
	11		ADC 244		4mm CLEAR GLASS	POLYURETHENE	WHITE GLOSS
	12		ADC 260	6mm 'ARMOURPLATE'	4mm CLEAR GLASS	WHITE GLOSS	WHITE GLOSS
	13		ADC 234		VENEERED PLY. PANEL	POLYURETHENE	WHITE GLOSS

249 *Typical door and frame schedule (part)*

DOOR GROUP PREFIX LETTERS — INTERNAL DOORS — EXTERNAL DOORS coded XD

DOOR NUMBERS: Internal 1–13 (8, 9 = DOUBLE); External 1–13 (1 double, 5 double, 7 double, 9 double)

6mm min SUITING MASTER KEYING.

Group	Reference	AZA	I1	I2	I3	I4	I5	I6	I7	I8	I9	I10	I11	I12	I13	E1	E2	E3	E4	E5	E6	E7	E8	E9	E10	E11	E12	E13
UPRIGHT LOCKS	WITH ONE KEY	100																										
	LOCKS TO PASS	101	1	1	1		1				1	1	1															
	WITH TWO KEYS	102																										
	REBATED COMPONENTS	103																										
	ROLLER BOLT, ONE KEY	104																										
	ROLLER BOLT, LOCKS TO PASS	105																										
	ROLLER BOLT, TWO KEYS	106																										
	ROLLER BOLT REBATED COMP'S	107																										
UPRIGHT DEADLOCK	WITH ONE KEY	112																										
	LOCKS TO PASS	113								1						1		1	1	1			1		1		1	1	1
	WITH TWO KEYS	114																										
	REBATED COMPONENTS	115														1		1	1	1			1		1		1	1	1
LEVER HANDLES	PAIR ON ROSE	130																										
	PAIR ON BACKPLATE, KEYHOLE	131	1	1	1		1				1	1	1															
	PAIR ON BACKPLATE, NO KEYHOLE	132																										
	ESCUTCHEONS	133								2						2		2	2	2			2		2		2	2	2
PULL HANDLES	150 mm CENTRES FIXING	134																										
	225 mm CENTRES	135				1	1	1	1						1	1	1	1	1	1	1	1	1	1	1	1	1	1
	300 mm CENTRES	136																										
FINGER PLATES	300 x 75	140				1	1	1	1	1					1	1	1	1	1	1	1	1	1	1	1	1	1	1
KICKING PLATES	625 mm WIDE	141													1.													
	725 mm	142				1	1	1	1	2	2		1															
	775 mm	143	1	1	2						2		2							1	1					1	1	
	825 mm	144													1	1	1	1		1	1	1	1					1
	875 mm	145																										
FLUSH AND BARREL BOLTS	PAIR FLUSH BOLTS	150								1						1				1		1						
	SOCKET FOR WOOD	151																										
	SOCKET FOR CONCRETE	152																										
	PAIR BARREL BOLTS	153																										
OVERHEAD CLOSERS	FOR EXTERNAL DOORS OPEN OUT	160																										
	FOR INTERNAL DOORS	161				1		1	1				1	1														
	DOOR SELECTOR	162																										
	OVERHEAD LIMITING STAY	163													1	1	1	1	1	1	1	1	1	1	1	1	1	1
DOOR STOPS	FOR TIMBER	170																										
	FOR CONCRETE	171				1					1	1	1	1														
	POST MOUNTED DOOR HOLDER	172																										
	CABIN HOOK	173																										
LETTER BOX	LETTER BOX.	174																								1		
HAT AND COAT HOOKS	ALUMINIUM	180																										
	NYLON COATED SECRET FIX.	181																										
	PAIR NYLON COATED SECRET FIX	182																										
	NYLON COATED SCREW FIX.	183																										

250 *Ironmongery schedule (part)*

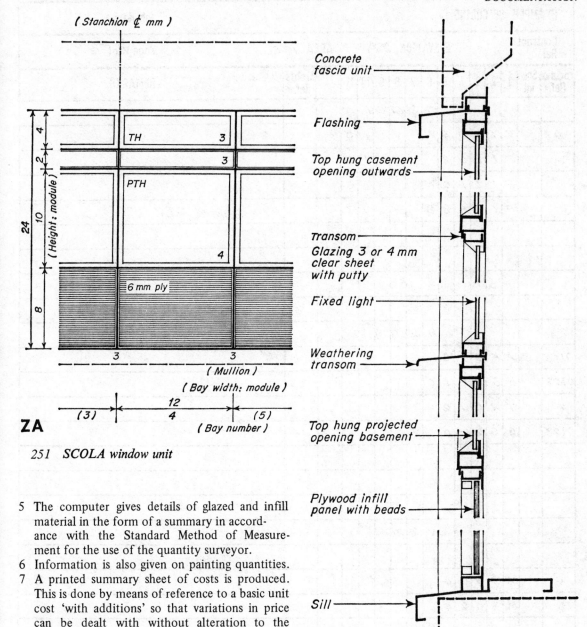

251 *SCOLA window unit*

252 *Detail of the construction*

Concrete fascia unit

Flashing

Top hung casement opening outwards

Transom

Glazing 3 or 4 mm clear sheet with putty

Fixed light

Weathering transom

Top hung projected opening basement

Plywood infill panel with beads

Sill

Concrete plinth

5 The computer gives details of glazed and infill material in the form of a summary in accordance with the Standard Method of Measurement for the use of the quantity surveyor.

6 Information is also given on painting quantities.

7 A printed summary sheet of costs is produced. This is done by means of reference to a basic unit cost 'with additions' so that variations in price can be dealt with without alteration to the punched tape.

8 The cost per square metre of the elevation is given which allows comparisons to cost relevant to the type of construction.

Minor alternations to design, such as the reduction of the number of window opening lights can be accommodated after the computer *print out* has been done, but this is documented by means of

| EXAMPLE OF CODING | | | | | | | | | | | | | | Job No. |

| Contract Ref. | | | ELEVATION **ZA** | | | AREA *1096* | | | | | | | | Page *2* of *12* |

Location Ref.	Spec ial	1	2	3	4	5	6	7	8	9	10	11	Archts Ref.	REMARKS
						U SECTION								
4	T	1	2	0	4	W					1	0		
	F	1	2	0	2						1	0		
	P	1	2	1	0	W					2	0		
	F	1	2	0	8	B					4	7		7 = *plywood infill*
	?													
						H SECTION								
0108	A	F	2	1	2									
0108	H	C	H	2	1	0								
4	T	R	0	1	2									
0108	G	C	2	1	0									
						V SECTION								
4	M	3	0	2	4									
5	M	3	0	2	4									

253 Specimen input data sheet

handwritten variation sheets. Major variations necessitate reprogramming and since this is expensive, it is an *on cost* charge to the client. Thus, the principle of preplanning in this context makes obvious economic good sense. After the computer print out, no further work is done by the manufacturers until a letter of intention to proceed (from the client) or a contractor's order is received. The computer is then required to translate the print out into manufacturing documents. These manufacturing documents are in the form of coded sheets and are used in the works for manufacture.

In respect of manufacturing procedure all frames for the window unit are *bars* in the form of rolled steel sections until they reach the end of the main processing. They are then ready to be welded together to form the various completed frame units.

The documents produced by the computer for manufacturing are as follows:

1 Coding of the maching document: this gives detailed information with regard to the drilling required on each length of bar.
2 Welding document: this gives details of quantities and references to the elevational coding.
3 *After galvanizing* and despatch document: this gives instructions in respect of assembling the various components for each job.

The above manufacturing documents are in respect of fixed lights and similar documentation is produced for opening lights, plus additional information on hinges and fixings. There is also a *parts list* for each job based on numbers of units per elevation, which is used for despatch purposes, and, in addition, a bay location document for the site fixers, which gives all the details of the openings required to complete each elevation. There are no *working drawings* in the traditional sense, either for manufacturing details or for fixing on site.

CI/SfB

The following information from the *Construction Indexing Manual 1976* is reproduced by courtesy of RIBA Publications Ltd.

Used sensibly and in appropriate detail, as explained in the manual, the CI/SfB system of classification facilitates filing and retrieval of information. It is useful in technical libraries, in specifications and on working drawings. *The National Building Specification* is based on the system, and BRE Digest 172 describes its use for working drawings.

The CI/SfB system comprises tables 0 to 4, tables 1 and 2/3 being the codes in most common use. For libraries, classifications are built up from:

Table 0	Table 1	Tables 2/3	Table 4
-a number code	-a number code in brackets	-upper and lower case letter codes	-upper case letter code in brackets
eg 6	eg (6)	eg Fg	eg (F)

An example for clay brickwork in walls is: (21) Fg2, which for trade literature, would be shown in a reference box as:

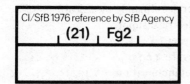

CI/SfB 1976 reference by SfB Agency
(21) Fg2

The lower space is intended for UDC (Universal decimal classification) codes – see BS 1000A 1961. Advice in classification can be obtained from the SfB Agency UK Ltd at 66 Portland Place, London, W1N 4AD.

In the following summaries of the five tables, references are made to the six related volumes and chapters 11, 12 *Mitchell's Building Series* in which aspects of the classifications are dealt with. The following abbreviations are used:

Environment and Services	*ES*
Materials	*M*
Structure and Fabric, Part 1	*SF (1)*
Structure and Fabric, Part 2	*SF (2)*
Components	*C **
Finishes	*F †*

Table 0 **Physical Environment**
(main headings only)

Scope: End results of the construction process

0	Planning areas
1	Utilities, civil engineering facilities
2	Industrial facilities
3	Administrative, commerical, protective service facilities
4	Health, welfare facilities
5	Recreational facilities
6	Religious facilities
7	Educational, scientific, information facilities
8	Residential facilities
9	Common facilities, other facilities

---

*Previously Chapters 1-11 in *CF – Components and Finishes*
†Previously chapters 12-18 in *CF*

CF	F
12	1
13	2
14	3
15	4
16	5
17	6
18	7

TABLE 1

Table 1 **Elements**

Scope: Parts with particular functions which combine to make the facilities in table 0

(0-) Sites, projects
  Building plus external works
  Building systems *C 11*
(1-) Ground, substructure
(11) Ground
(12) Vacant
(13) Floor beds *SF (1)* 4, 8; *SF (2)* 3
(14), (15) Vacant
(16) Retaining walls, foundations *SF (1)* 4;
  SF (2) 3. 4
(17) Pile foundations *SF (1)* 4; *SF(2)* 3, 11
(18) Other substructure elements
(19) Parts, accessories, cost summary, etc

(2-) Structure, primary elements, carcass
(21) Walls, external walls *SF (1)* 1, 5;
  SF (2) 4, 5, 10
(22) Internal walls, partitions *SF (1)* 5;
  SF (2) 4, 10; *C 9*
(23) Floors, galleries *SF (1)* 8; *SF (2)* 6, 10
(24) Stairs, ramps *SF (1)* 10; *SF (2)* 8, 10
(25), (26) Vacant
(27) Roofs *SF (1)* 1, 7; *SF (2)* 9, 10
(28) Building frames, other primary elements
  SF (1) 1, 6; *SF (2)* 5, 10
  Chimneys *SF (1)* 9
(29) Parts, accessories, cost summary, etc

(3-) Secondary elements, completion of structure
(31) Secondary elements to external walls, including
  windows, doors *SF (1)* 5; *SF (2)* 10;
  C 3, 4, 5, 7
(32) Secondary elements to internal walls, partitions including borrowed lights and doors *SF (2)* 10; *C* 3, 7
(33) Secondary elements to floors *SF (2)* 10
(34) Secondary elements to stairs including
  balustrades *C 8*
(35) Suspended ceilings *C 10*
(36) Vacant

(37) Secondary elements to roofs, including roof
  lights, dormers *SF (2)* 10; *C 6*
(38) Other secondary elements
(39) Parts, accessories, cost summary, etc

(4-) Finishes to structure
(41) Wall finishes, external *SF (2)* 4, 10;
  F 3, 4, 5
(42) Wall finishes, internal *F* 2, 4, 5
(43) Floor finishes *F 1*
(44) Stair finishes *F* 1
(45) Ceiling finishes *F* 2
(46) Vacant
(47) Roof finishes *SF (2); F* 7
(48) Other finishes
(49) Parts, accessories, cost summary, etc

(5-) Services (mainly piped and ducted)
(51) Vacant
(52) Waste disposal, drainage *ES* 13 /*ES* 11, 12
(53) Liquids supply *ES* 9, 10; *SF (1)* 9;
  SF (2) 6, 10
(54) Gases supply
(55) Space cooling
(56) Space heating *ES* 7; *SF (1)* 9; *SF (2)* 6, 10
(57) Air conditioning, ventilation *ES* 7; *SF (2)* 10
(58) Other piped, ducted services,
(59) Parts, accessories, cost summary, etc
  Chimney, shafts, flues, ducts independent
  SF (2) 7.

(6-) Services (mainly electrical)
(61) Electrical supply
(62) Power *ES* 14
(63) Lighting *ES* 8
(64) Communications *ES* 14
(65) Vacant
(66) Transport *ES* 15
(67) Vacant
(68) Security, control, other services
(69) Parts, accessories, cost summary, etc

(7-) Fittings with subdivisions (71) to (79)
(74) Sanitary, hygiene fittings *ES* 10

TABLE 2

(8-) Loose furniture, equipment with subdivisions (81) to (89)

Used where the distinction between loose and fixed fittings, furniture and equipment is important

(9-) External elements, other elements

(90) External works, with subdivisions (90.1) to (90.8)

(98) Other elements

(99) Parts, accessories etc. common to two or more main element divisions (1 -) to (7 -)

Cost summary

Note: The SfB Agency UK do not use table 1 in classifying manufacturers' literature

---

Table 2 Constructions, Forms

Scope: Parts of particular forms which combine to make the elements in table 1. Each is characterized by the main product of which it is made.

A   Constructions, forms – used in specification applications for Preliminaries and General conditions

B   Vacant –   used in specification applications For Demolition, underpinning and shoring work

C   Excavation and loose fill work

D   Vacant

E   Cast in situ work *M* 8; *SF (1)* 4, 7, 8; *SF (2)* 3, 4, 5, 6, 9

Blocks

F   Blockwork, brickwork
     Blocks, bricks *M* 6, 12; *SF (1)* 5, 9
     SF (2) 4, 6, 7

G   Large block, panel work
     Large blocks, panels *SF (2)* 4

Sections

H   Section work
     Sections *M* 9; *SF (1)* 5, 6, 7, 8; *SF (2)* 6

I   Pipework
     Pipes *SF (1)* 9; *SF (2)* 7

J   Wire work, mesh work
     Wires, meshes

K   Quilt work
     Quilts

L   Flexible sheet work (proofing)
     Flexible sheets (proofing) *M* 9, 11

M   Malleable sheet work
     Malleable sheets *M* 9

N   Rigid sheet overlap work
     Rigid sheets for overlappings *SF (2)* 4; *F* 7

P   Thick coating work *M* 10, 11; *SF (2)* 4;
     F 1, 2, 3, 7

Q   Vacant

R   Rigid sheet work
     Rigid sheets *M* 3, 12, 13; *SF (2)* 4; *C* 5

S   Rigid tile work
     Rigid tiles *M* 4, 12, 13; *F* 1, 4

T   Flexible sheet and tile work
     Flexible sheets eg carpets, veneers, papers, tiles cut from them *M* 3, 9; *F* 1, 6

U   Vacant

V   Film coating and impregnation work *F* 6;
     M 2

W   Planting work
     Plants

X   Work with components
     Components *SF (1)* 5, 6, 7, 8, 10; *SF (2)* 4;
     C 2, 3, 4, 5, 6, 7, 8

Y   Formless work
     Products

Z   Joints, where described separately

Table 3 Materials

Scope: Materials which combine to form the products in table 2

---

a   **Materials**
b, c, d, Vacant

Formed materials e to o

e   **Natural stone** *M* 4; *SF (1)* 5, 10; *SF (2)* 4

e1   Granite, basalt, other igneous

e2   Marble

e3   Limestone (other than marble)

TABLE 3

e4	Sandstone, gritstone
e5	Siate
e9	Other natural stone

f   **Precast with binder** *M* 8: *SF (1)* 5, 7, 8, 9, 10
SF(2) 4 to 9; *F* 1

f1   Sandlime concrete (precast)
Glass fibre reinforced calcium silicate (gres)

f2   All-in aggregate concrete (precast) *M* 8
Heavy concrete (precast) *M* 8
Glass fibre reinforced cement (gre) *M* 10

f3   Terrazzo (precast) *F* 1
Granolithic (precast)
Cast/artificial/reconstructed stone

f4   Lightweight cellular concrete (precast) *M* 8

f5   Lightweight aggregate concrete (precast) *M* 8

f6   Asbestos based materials (preformed) *M* 10

f7   Gypsum (preformed) *C* 2
Glass fibre reinforced gypsum *M* 10

f8   Magnesia materials (preformed)

f9   Other materials precast with binder

g   **Clay (Dried, Fired)** *M* 5; *SF (1)* 5, 9, 10;
SF (2) 4, 6, 7

g1   Dried clay eg pisé de terre

g2   Fired clay, vitrified clay, ceramics
Unglazed fired clay eg terra cotta

g3   Glazed fired clay eg vitreous china

g6   Refractory materials eg fireclay

g9   Other dried or fired clays

h   **Metal** *M* 9; *SF (1)* 6, 7, *SF (2)* 4, 5, 7

h1   Cast iron
Wrought iron, malleable iron

h2   Steel, mild steel

h3   Steel alloys eg stainless steel

h4   Aluminium, aluminium alloys

h5   Copper

h6   Copper alloys

h7   Zinc

h8   Lead, white metal

h9   Chromium, nickel, gold, other metals, metal alloys

i   **Wood** including wood laminates **M** 2, 3;
SG (1) 5 to 8, 10 *SF (2)* 4, 9; *C* 2

i1   timber (unwrot)

i2   Softwood (in general, and wrot)

i3   Hardwood (in general, and wrot)

i4   Wood laminates eg plywood

i5   Wood veneers

i9   Other wood materials, except wood fibre boards, chipboards and wood-wool cement

j   **Vegetable and aminal materials** − including fibres and particles and materials made from these

j1   Wood fibres eg building board *M* 3

j2   Paper *M* 9, 13

j3   Vegetable fibres other than wood eg flaxboard *M* 3

j5   Bark, cork

j6   Animal fibres eg hair

j7   Wood particles eg chipboard *M* 3

j8   Wood-wool cement *M* 3

j9   Other vegetable and animal materials

k, 1   Vacant

m   **Inorganic fibres**

m1   Mineral wool fibres *M* 10; *SF (2)* 4, 7
Glass wool fibres *M* 10, 12
Ceramic wool fibres

m2   Asbestos wool fibres *M* 10

m9   Other inorganic fibrous materials eg carbon fibres *M* 10

n   **Rubber, plastics, etc**

n1   Asphalt (preformed) *M* 11; *F* 1

n2   Impregnated fibre and felt eg bituminous felt *M* 11, *F* 7

n4   Linoleum *F* 1

Synthetic resins n5, n6

n5   Rubbers (elastomers) *M* 13

n6   Plastics, including sythetic fibres *M* 13
Thermoplastics
Thermosets

n7   Cellular plastics

n8   Reinforced plastics eg grp, plastics laminates

TABLE 3

n9   Other rubber, plastics materials eg mixed natural/synthetic fibres

o   **Glass** *M* 12 *SF (1)* 5;*C* 5
o1   Clear, transparent, plain glass
o2   Translucent glass
o3   Opaque, opal glass
04   Wired glass
o5   Multiple glazing
o6   Heat absorbing/rejecting glass
     X-ray absorbing/rejecting glass
     Solar control glass
o7   Mirrored glass, 'one-way' glass
     Anti-glare glass
o8   Safety glass, toughened glass
     Laminated glass, security glass, alarm glass
o9   Other glass, including, cellular glass

Formless materials p to s
p   **Aggregates, loose fills** *M* 8
p1   Natural fills, aggregates
p2   Artificial aggregates in general
p3   Artificial granular aggregates (light) eg foamed blast furnace slag
p4   Ash eg pulverized fuel ash
p5   Shavings
p6   Powder
p7   Fibres
p9   Other aggregates, loose fills

q   **Lime and cement binders, mortars, concretes**
q1   Lime (calcined limestones), hydrated lime, lime putty, *M* 7
     Lime-sand mix (coarse stuff)
q2   Cement, hydraulic cement eg Portland cement *M* 7
q3   Lime-cement binders *M* 15
q4   Lime-cement-aggregate mixes
     Mortars (ie with fine aggregates) *M* 15; *SF (2)* 4
     Concretes (ie with fine and /or coarse aggregates) *M* 8
q5   Terrazzo mixes and in general *F* 1
     Granolithic mixes and in general *F* 1
q6   Lightweight, cellular, concrete mixes and in general *M* 8

q7   Lightweight aggregate concrete mixes and in general *M* 8
q9   Other lime-cement-aggregate mixes eg asbestos cement mixes *M* 10

r   **Clay, gypsum, magnesia and plastics binders, mortars**
r1   Clay mortar mixes, refractory mortar
r2   Gypsum, gypsum plaster mixes *SF* 2
r3   Magnesia, magnesia mixes *F* 1
r4   Plastics binders
     Plastics mortar mixes
r9   Other binders and mortar mixes

s   **Bituminous materials** *M* 11; *SF (2)* 4
s1   Bitumen including natural and petroleum bitumens, tar, pitch, asphalt, lake asphalt
s4   Mastic asphalt (fine or no aggregate), pitch mastic
s5   Clay-bitumen mixes, stone bitumen mixes (coarse aggregate)
     Rolled asphalt, macadams
s9   Other bituminous materials

Functional materials t to w
t   **Fixing and jointing materials**
t1   Welding materials *M* 9; *SF(1)* 5
t2   Soldering materials *M* 9
t3   Adhesives, bonding materials *M* 14
t4   Joint fillers eg mastics, gaskets *M* 16
t6   Fasteners, 'builders ironmongery'
     Anchoring devices eg plugs
     Attachment devices eg connectors *SF (1)* 6, 7
     Fixing devices eg bolts, *SF (1)* 5
t7   'Architectural ironmongery' *C* 7
t9   Other fixing and jointing agents

u   **Protective and Process/property modifying materials**
u1   Anti-corrosive materials, treatments *F* 6
     Metallic coatings applied by eg electroplating *M* 9
     Non-metallic coatings applied by eg chemical conversion

TABLE 4

u2 Modifying agents, admixtures eg curing agents *M* 8
Workability aids *M* 8

u3 Materials resisting specials forms of attack such as fungus, insects, condensation *M* 2

u4 Flame retardants if described separately *M* 1

u5 Polishes, seals, surface hardners *F* 1: *M* 8

u6 Water repellants, if described separately

u9 Other protective and process/property modifying agents, eg ultra-violet absorbers

v **Paints** *F* 6

v1 Stopping, fillers, knotting, paint preparation materials including primers

v2 Pigments, dyes, stains

v3 Binders, media eg drying oils

v4 Varnishes, lacquers eg resins
Enamels, glazes

v5 Oil paints, oil-resin paints
Synthetic resin paints
Complete systems including primers

v6 Emulsion paints, where described separately
Synthetic resin-based emulsions
Complete systems including primers

v8 Water paints eg cement paints

v9 Other paints eg metallic paints, paints with aggregates

W **Ancillary materials**

w1 Rust removing agents

w3 Fuels

w4 Water

w5 Acids, alkalis

w6 Fertilisers

w7 Cleaning materials *F* 1
Abrasives

w8 Explosives

w9 Other ancillary materials eg fungicides

x **Vacant**

y **Composite materials**
Composite materials generally *M* 11
See p. 63 *Construction Indexing Manual*

z **Substances**

z1 By state eg fluids

z2 By chemical composition eg organic

z3 By origin eg naturally occurring or manufactured materials

z9 Other substances

Table 4   **Activities, Requirements**
(main headings only)

Scope: Table 4 identifies objects which assist or affect construction but are not incorporated in it, and factors such as activities, requirements, properties, and processes.

Activities, aids

(A) Administration and management activities, aids *C* 11; *M* Introduction

(B) Construction plant, tools *SF (1)* 2; *SF (2)* 2, 11

(C) Vacant

(D) Construction operations *SF (1)* 11; *SF (2)* 2, 11

Requirements, properties, building science, construction technology
Factors describing buildings, elements, materials, etc

(E) Composition, etc

(F) Shape, size, etc

(G) Appearance, etc *M* 1; *F* 6

Factors relating to surroundings, occupancy

(H) Context, environment

Performance factors

(J) Mechanics *M* 9; *SF (1)* 3; *SF (2)* 4

(K) Fire, explosion *M* 1; *SF (2)* 10

(L) Matter

(M) Heat, cold *ES* 1

(N) Light, dark *ES* 1

(O) Sound, quiet *ES* 1

(Q) Electricity, magnetism, radiation *ES* 14

(R) Energy, other physical factors *ES* 7

(T) Application

TABLE 4

Other factors

(U) Users, resources
(V) Working factors
(W) Operation, maintenance factors
(X) Change, movement, stability factors
(Y) Economic, commerical factors *M* Introduction; *SF (1)* 2; *(SF (2)* 3, 4, 5, 6, 9

(Z) Peripheral subjects, form of presentation, time, place — may be used for subjects taken from the UDC (*Universal decimal classification*), see BS 1000A 1961

Subdivision: All table 4 codes are subdivided mainly by numbers

Index

Index